# TOURISM: GROWTH, MANAGEMENT AND INCENTIVES

# TOURISM: GROWTH, MANAGEMENT AND INCENTIVES

Dr. M. Sajnani
Dr. V.K. Goswami

PUBLICATIONS
KALPAZ PUBLICATIONS
DELHI - 110052

TOURISM: GROWTH, MANAGEMENT AND INCENTIVES
[*Management, Tourism*]

Rs. 890

ISBN: 81-7835-104-8



Published in 2002 in India by
Kalpaz Publications
C-30, Satyawati Nagar
Delhi-110052
e-mail: kalpaz@hotmail.com

*Laser Typeset at:* ALPHABET, Delhi
*Printed at:* Mehra Offset Press, New Delhi

# Contents

## PART IV: TRIBES OF INDIA: A RICH TOURISM RESOURCE

# Foreword

India is known for its ancient civilisation and rich culture. Nature has also been kind to it and the country can boast of its rich wild life, long range of mountains housing beautiful hill stations, long coastal line offering numerous beaches, Thar desert of Rajasthan rich in heritage tourism, many world famous historical monuments and lush green chain of islands in Arabian Sea and Bay of Bengal. It gave birth to three religions and is full of diversity. In India you can see the primitive villages and the most cosmopolitan cities. A nuclear power and member of space club it has recently acquired leadership in IT. Indians are known for their beauty and hospitability. In short, India in its diversity could be a heaven for tourists.

Recognising its potential, tourism has been given the status of industry. In spite of these strengths and strong support of both central and state governments, India has not been able to derive full benefits. This is primarily due to the fact that many players deny value for money to their customers.

Here, I will like to narrate an incident that took place at Indira Gandhi International Airport few years back. Department of Tourism had made elaborate arrangement at IGI Airport to receive the two millionth tourist in the country. On arrival he was garlanded and even a *tilak* was planted on his forehead followed by welcome *aarti* in the traditional style. He was happy to receive the VIP status. Soon after the reception he came out of the arrival hall and found the area filled with Government cars. There was a scramble and all officials who had come for the function were hurrying to go back. The garlanded tourist was running from pillar to post to locate his contact/car. What to talk of the VIP who has received him, even the petty officials did not bother to help him in locating his car as it was parked in the remote area. His happiness vanished in no time. To him the whole affair looked artificial and in no time he got frustrated and threw away the garland on the airline official muttering why the hell he was the two millionth tourist. I have heard many such stories from tourism officials, tour operators, travel agencies, airline officials and others. I am yet to see these players particularly the small operators making serious efforts to satisfy their customers. Many experts say that the country has excellent tourism potential but the industry lacks professionalism and ethics and to plant these values among the small operators to name a few; taxi drivers, souvenir shops, two-three star hotels is a big challenge.

As per forecast of World Tourism Organsation and World Travel and Tourism Council, the tourism industry will become world's largest export industry by 2010. Tourism with its multiplier effect can foster the economic growth. Communities who could recognise its potential have derived rich benefits. If India wishes to take advantage of that growth then it should create awareness among the players that they should learn to market tourism in preference to selling it. Therefore larger emphasis should be on creating this awareness among its players. Ideally tourism should be people's movement.

In this regard, I see another useful work of Prof. Manohar Sajnani. To make his work effective and useful he has divided the book in four parts. I hope his work will be useful not only in research but also for the government officials responsible for promoting tourism. Tourism consultants and other members of tourism industry will also be benefitted.

**Dated : 03.07.2002**

**(Gurcharan Bhatura)**
Executive Director,
National Institute of Aviation Management & Research

# Preface

Tourism is neither a theme nor a situation. There are no longer two distinct classes of people, one mobile and another static. We are all tourist to some extent or otherwise. In the world of today, few of us stay but all the time and most of us have had the experience of being visitors in other people's towns, cities, regions, villages or countries other people, in turn, come as tourist to our areas. There is nothing new in this. Afloating population of explorers, pilgrims and traders have been moving about the earth since ancient times. What is new is the rapidly increasing speed of travel and growing volume of travellers.

Today, travel and tourism industry is the largest individual industry in the world and the biggest contribute to global economic development. Annually 696 million tourists travel across the world making purchases worth US $ 4.3 trillion, i.e., approximately 10.96 per cent of GDP. Tourism also provides or creates jobs worldwide at a faster rate than manufacturing, i.e., every 2.54 seconds a new job is created by tourism, to put it another way 25 jobs a minute or 1500 jobs an hour or 36000 new jobs a day.

It is due to this immense importance and potential of this industry that a growing number of colleges and universities have started offering courses at undergraduate, Postgraduate and doctoral level in preparing professionals to manage this growth well. With this in view the author has opted for a subject that would interest a cross section of readership, viz., teachers and students of tourism management, commerce, economics, social sciences as well a practitioners in tourism trade.

There is not much literature available on this subject combining practical occupational skills with essential academic qualities. Therefore, the author has attempted in his way to provide a text book as well as a guide. Collection of articles may serve as a treasure to those who want to improve their skills and go about their jobs taking the proper direction and approach.

I am grateful to Kalpaz Publications for publishing my work in such a short time and helping me in my mission of spreading the awareness of the importance of tourism in today's times.

**Dr. M. Sajnani**
**Dr. V.K. Goswami**

# Acknowledgements

*Acknowledgements are many,*
*but lines are few,*
*A gratitude so deep,*
*that words would not do.*

This is to acknowledge some of the people, for their help, efforts and guidance.

First of all, I would like to express my immense gratitude to Prof. (Dr.) V.K. Goswami, Director General, Institute of Management Studies, Ghaziabad, who as a co-author of this text has contributed significantly in the completion of this book. Besides as the Director General of the Institute he has always inspired me in hours of distress and goaded me to achieve my long cherished goal.

I am also extremely grateful to my research guide Prof. S.C. Bagri, Head Department of Tourism and Hoteliering Management, HNB Garhwal University, Srinagar, Garhwal for sparing his valuable time and expert advise to enable me to give final shape to this text.

I wish to thank my parents, my wife Madhu and son Ishan, who have inspired and stood with me always without any grudge.

I am indebted to Prof. Kapil Kumar, Director, School of Social Sciences, Indira Gandhi National Open University, New Delhi, for his expert guidance in completing this work.

A lot of credit also goes to Mr. Shekhar Ghose, Director, HRD, Indian Airlines Ltd., who helped me in completing papers related to HRD and personnel management. A very special debt of gratitude is also due to Dr. Neena Rao, Head of the Department, Tourism, College of Vocational Studies, University of Delhi; Prof. Natasha Raina Kanwar, Head of the Department, History, College of Vocational Studies, University of Delhi; Prof. Ravindra Kumar, Professor of History, School of Social Sciences, Indira Gandhi National Open University, New Delhi, are a few among those who also deserve my heartfelt thanks for their help at various stages of the preparation of this text.

I also express my gratitute to the editors, authors and compilers from whose works I culled some materials to be used in the present study.

# Introduction

This book aims to serve the knowledge needs of all new entrants in to this field. Be it students, teachers, research scholars, entrepreneurs or even parliamentarians. Only objectives of this book is to familiarize the reader with basic fundamentals which are not only its principles but has become important dimensions of Tourism management in recent times of globalization and competitiveness. In the result the author has made an attempt to discuss all Applied Tourism dimension, i.e., all directions with which Tourism is integrated today.

**Tourism: Concepts and Forms**

The word "Tourism" has its origin in a Latin word *Tornos* meaning a tool for describing a circle or turners wheel. This refers to a pin at the end of a stretched string used to describe a circle. From the same Latin word, terms like "round-tour" or a "package-tour" have emerged to give essence to tourism. However, this term has evolved from an ancient Greek word referring to a circular arrangement (*Webster New International Dictionary, The Oxford English Dictionary*). But this etymology does not explain how "tour" came to mean particular types of trips among various trips where itineraries are circular. A possible explanation is given that "tour" meaning a trip evolved from "tower" meaning castle and referred as to leisurely relaxing and sight-seeing while going around the parapets of tower. It was only by early eighteenth century that tour in modern sense of a temporary trip away from home for some pleasurable purpose had become well established. Defoe's "A tour through the whole Island of Britain" provides the best example to testify this fact.

It was in late eighteenth century that one Scottish Professor,

But these different perspectives give rise to three important dimensions in the form of: Tourism Market; Tourism Industry; and Tourism System.

*Tourism Markets*

The range of tourism market is huge as well as distinct. In both cases market can be defined as identifiable collection of persons who are willing and able to buy, consume, use or experience some category of goods or services offered for exchange. Therefore, within broader of tourism markets, marketeers identify tourists whom they wish to cater.

In certain cases an individual tourist who may be a targeted market to a business organisation by the same individual tourist may be an incidental market to the departmental store of the city where this business organisation is located.

*Tourism Industry*

Since tourism is an amalgamation of various sectors, thereby tourism industry assumes a complex structure comprising of a wide variety of business and other organisations, touching virtually all spheres of our economy. But some scholars like Kaiser, Helber (1978), and Kaul (1981) are in the opinion that there exists nothing of sort like Tourism industry, what really lies under that appellation is collection of separate industries with different kinds of links with tourists, for instance, with some perceived and aimed and with others incidental.

However, an alternative and balance approach is proposed by Leiper (1979). According to him, it is true that some of the identifiable sets of tourists are catered by segments like travel agents, tour operators, airlines and hotel in a non-fragmented manner but other components like restaurant and general stores, though do nothing in this manner, but they may be important and perhaps vital, to the region, as a tourist destination to provide complete satisfaction and to give value to tourist for the money they spend here. This alternative approach helps in understanding the notion that tourism tends to be partially industrialised and partially not.

*Tourism System*

Tourism, due to its being trans-disciplinary subject, has been accepted as a complex subject.

Fifty research scholars like Jafari (1989) and Leiper (1990) have adopted a comprehensive approach. A system can be defined as a set of elements interacting with one another; whereas in an open system elements and system as a whole are also interacting with the environment. This is truly applicable for the study in this field as that of Leiper (1990) who has suggested a model to study tourism system as a very open system with different elements.

*Environments: Human, Socio-Cultural, Physical, etc.*

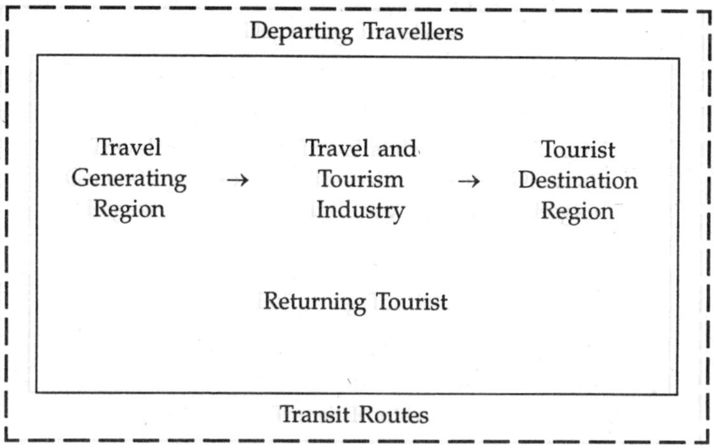


(a) Travel Generating Region—where travel begins and ends, i.e., one per trip, location where motivation forces are tried, resources to be spent on trip are accumulated and where pre-trip arrangements are made.

(b) Transit Routes—are paths along which a traveller must go to reach his destination.

(c) Touristic Destination—which may be one or more in one trip itself where normally these visitors are connected as tourist.

(d) Departing traveller—once they have enjoyed their holidays at the destination, travellers return to region of their origin.

(e) Travel and Tourism Industry—is most vital element of the model which comprises of organizations in the business of tourism located all along the itinerary of tourist. In the place of origin this may include travel agents and tour operators. Along transit routes it may include airlines, other modes of carriers as well as transit from a accommodation. At destination it includes accommodation, local tour operators restaurants, specialist retailers, and entertainment elements of tourist market.

**Indian Tourism: A Quantitative and Qualitative Glance**

Tourism industry is a limitless industry with immense growth potential. It ranks number two, next to oil industry and third in India next to Gems and Garments. It has tremendous positive impacts on the economic and social aspects in developing countries. This is why every country is trying with each other to woo more domestic and international tourist and India is not an exception though her achievements are not astonishing. If we see the figures available we can see that tourists arrivals have increased manifold between 1960 and 2000, i.e., from a meagre figure of 16829 to 2641157.

A detailed analysis of immense importance as available statistics reveal that during 1997, 2152926 foreign tourists were of other than the nationals of Pakistan and Bangladesh. This figure of foreign tourist arrival in India during this period constitute to be only 0.38 per cent of global tourist arrivals, which stood at 698.8 million during the year under consideration. Tourism industry earned foreign exchange to the tune of Rs. 14238 crore (US $ 3168 million). At the point of time when economies of several developing and developed nations are banking on the contribution of tourism industry. India is able to receive only 0.67 per cent of world tourism receipts. US$ Billion 475.8 (excluding fare receipts).

Foreign tourists arrivals in the country (including the nationals of Pakistan and Bangladesh) registered a growth rate of 6.5 per cent from 2481928 in 1999 to 2641157 in 2000. The arrival (excluding the nationals of Pakistan and Bangladesh) increased from 2025031 in 1999 to 8154926 in 2000, registering a growth of about 6.3 per cent. A summary of international tourist traffic to India has been given in Table 1.

**TABLE 1**
**SUMMARY OF INTERNATIONAL TOURIST TRAFFIC TO INDIA**

| *Year* | *Including Nationals of Pakistan and Bangladesh* | |
|---|---|---|
| | *Number* | *% Change* |
| 1981 | 1279210 | |
| 1982 | 1288162 | 0.7 |
| 1983 | 1304976 | 1.3 |
| 1984 | 1193952 | -8.5 |
| 1985 | 1259384 | 5.5 |
| 1986 | 1451076 | 15.2 |
| 1987 | 1484290 | 2.3 |
| 1988 | 1590661 | 7.2 |
| 1989 | 1736093 | 9.1 |
| 1990 | 1707158 | -1.7 |
| 1991 | 1677508 | -1.7 |
| 1992 | 1867651 | 11.3 |
| 1993 | 1764830 | -5.5 |
| 1994 | 1886433 | 6.9 |
| 1995 | 2123683 | 12.6 |
| 1996 | 2287860 | 7.7 |
| 1997 | 2374094 | 3.8 |
| 1998 | 2358629 | 0.7 |
| 1999 | 2481928 | 5.2 |
| 2000 | 2641157 | 6.4 |

Nationals of the United Kingdom with an arrival figure of 354217 continued to occupy the first position in the tourist arrival to India during 2000 and accounted for 16.5 per cent of total tourist traffic as against an arrival figure of 345085 (17.1 per cent) during 1999. The United Kingdom was followed by the USA with 309309 tourist arrivals during 2000 accounting 14.4 per cent as compared to 251926 (12.5 per cent) arrivals in 1999. The other major Countries whose relative shares in total tourist traffic were significant, include Sri Lanka (128444 or 6.0 per cent), Canada (98259 or 4.6 per cent) and Australia (90456 or 4.2 per cent). Tourists from France, Germany, Japan, Malaysia, Italy and Netherlands each constituted between 4.5 per cent and 2.1 per cent of total traffic during 2000. The top fifteen market generating tourist arrivals to India are summarised in Table 2.

**TABLE 2**

**SUMMARY OF TOP TEN MARKETS GENERATING ARRIVALS TO INDIA**

| *Nationality* | *Number* | | *% change 2000/99* | *% of the Total* | |
|---|---|---|---|---|---|
| | *1999* | *2000* | | *1999* | *2000* |
| UK | 345085 | 354217 | 206.0 | 17.1 | 16.5 |
| USA | 251926 | 309309 | 22.8 | 12.5 | 14.4 |
| Sri Lanka | 120072 | 128444 | 7.0 | 5.9 | 6.0 |
| Canada | 82892 | 98259 | 18.5 | 4.1 | 4.6 |
| Australia | 73041 | 90456 | 23.8 | 3.6 | 4.2 |
| France | 85891 | 89565 | 4.3 | 4.2 | 4.2 |
| Germany | 85033 | 84989 | -0.1 | 4.2 | 4.0 |
| Japan | 79373 | 79167 | -0.3 | 3.9 | 3.7 |
| Malaysia | 52613 | 57927 | 10.1 | 2.6 | 2.7 |
| Italy | 50677 | 52529 | 3.7 | 2.5 | 2.5 |
| Singapore | 53310 | 49198 | -7.7 | 2.6 | 2.3 |
| Netherlands | 48820 | 45398 | -7.0 | 2.4 | 2.1 |
| Switzerland | 34824 | 31402 | -9.8 | 1.7 | 1.5 |
| South Africa | 23909 | 26502 | 10.8 | 1.2 | 1.3 |
| Israel | 23417 | 25005 | 6.8 | 1.2 | 1.2 |
| Others | 614148 | 620559 | 1.0 | 30.3 | 28.8 |
| Total | 2025031 | 2152926 | 6.3 | 100.0 | 100.0 |

**Note:** The analysis given in the above paragraphs excludes the arrival figures from Pakistan and Bangladesh.

*Source:* Tourist Statistic 2000, Market Research Division, Ministry of Tourism and Culture, New Delhi.

During 2000 arrivals from ten out of top fifteen tourist generating countries registered positive growth. Maximum increase was registered in case of Australia (23.8 per cent) followed by USA (22.8 per cent), Canada 18.5 per cent), South Africa (10.8 per cent), Malaysia (10.1 per cent), Sri Lanka (7.01 per cent), Israel (6.8 per cent), France (4.3 per cent), Italy (3.7 per cent), and UK (2.6 per cent). However, negative growth was registered in case of Switzerland (-9.8 per cent), Singapore (–7.7 per cent), Netherlands (–7.0 per cent), Japan (–0.3 per cent) and Germany (–0.1 per cent).

Tourist arrivals were highest during the month of December while lowest number of arrivals were recorded in May. Over the years the tourist arrivals tend to establish increasing trends. However, the factors like global economic situation, political instability, tourism facilities, touristic image, etc., introduce distorting trend and produce short-term variations. There are also seasonal variations, which produce identical patterns during corresponding months of successive years. A month-wise variations in tourists arrivals in India are given in Table 3.

*Variations in Tourists Arrivals in India*

**TABLE 3**

**QUARTERLY BREAK-UP OF TOURIST ARRIVALS DURING 1999-2000**

| *Period* | *Tourist Arrivals* | | *Tourist Arrivals* | | *% Change 2000/99* |
|---|---|---|---|---|---|
| | *1999* | *% Share* | *2000* | *% Share* | |
| January-March | 722157 | 29.1 | 757019 | 28.7 | 4.8 |
| April-June | 459020 | 18.5 | 507479 | 19.2 | 10.6 |
| July-September | 543053 | 21.9 | 576163 | 21.8 | 6.1 |
| October-December | 757698 | 30.5 | 800496 | 30.3 | 5.6 |
| Total | 2481928 | 100.0 | 2641157 | 100.0 | 6.4 |

*Source:* "Tourist Statistics", Market Research Division, Ministry of Tourism and Culture, Government of India, New Delhi.

**TABLE 4**
**SEASON OF TOURIST ARRIVAL QUARTERLY**

| Year | January-March | April-June | July-September | October-December |
|---|---|---|---|---|
| 1994 | 29.3% | 19.7% | 24.5% | 26.5% |
| 1993 | 25.7% | 18.2% | 23.2% | 32.9% |
| 1992 | 26.5% | 19.2% | 24.0% | 30.3% |
| 1991 | 23.8% | 19.0% | 24.1% | 33.1% |
| 1990 | 28.9% | 19.1% | 22.8% | 29.2% |

*Source:* DoT, Government of India.

**TABLE 5**
**PEAK AND LEAN MONTHS OF ARRIVALS DURING 2000**

| Nationality | Lean Month | Peak Month |
|---|---|---|
| UK | May | December |
| USA | September | December |
| Sri Lanka | June | August |
| Canada | May | November |
| Australia | May | November |
| France | May | February |
| Germany | June | January |
| Japan | June | January |
| Malaysia | July | November |
| Italy | June | January |

*Source:* "Tourist Statistics", Market Research Division, Ministry of Tourism and Culture, Government of India, New Delhi.

Table 3 gives the percentages of foreign tourist arrivals during the year 1999-2000. It indicates that growth during first quarter was 4.8 per cent, quarter ending June recorded increase of 10.6 per cent, third quarter ending September witnessed an increase of 6.1 per cent and the last quarter saw an increase of 5.6 per cent over the corresponding period of previous year. Winter months first and fourth quarter and summer months second and third quarters recorded arrivals of 59.0 per cent and 41.0 per cent respectively.

The chapterisation of book is done in order to categorise papers related to Tourism Management; Tourism Technology; Community Approach; Economies of Tourism; Sociology of Tourism.

In the first section focus is on management and its integration with tourism. Whether it is Human Resources, Marketing Management, Management Information System or Research in Leisure, every sphere of management is applied in tourism to take it on the path of growth that it has became world's largest and fastest growing economic activity.

Second section is devoted to technological advancements and their application in tourism. In fact it would not be an exaggeration to say that if any economic activity has received maximum impetus from these developments it is travel and tourism. It is true through internet a large number of websites are available to provide every type of information which a tourist would require before reaching his/her destination.

Section three focusses upon community approach of tourism growth and management. From earliest time state has always provided incentives or support to people who desire to travel but couldn't afford so, government provided them financial assistance. With the passage of time this assistance also came for provider of services, i.e., different components of the industry. More and more entrepreneur started their own tourism or transport enterprises and this is how tourism trade could the status of an industry as well as its related incentives.

Fourth section of this book is deveted to characteristics of various tribes of India, with the objective of highlighting rich tribal heritage of India. This would enable the entrepreneur to develop their knowledge of sociology and anthropology in context with these tourism products.

**Dr. M. Sajnani**
**Dr. V.K. Goswami**

*Part One*

# Tourism Management

# One

# Tourism Management and Role of Human Resource Management

Tourism industry is limitless industry with immense growth potential. It ranks number two, next only to oil industry and third in India being gems and garments. It has tremendous positive impacts on the economic and social aspects in developing countries. This is why every country is competing with each other to woo more domestic and international tourists and India is also not an exception, though her achievements are not astonishing. If we analyze facts and figures of last few years we see that road ahead for travel professionals is very promising.

An analytical glance at international tourism would also reveal that tourism is world's largest industry accounting for 11.6 per cent of world GDP. This reflects that disposable income of people living across the world has tremendously gone up. According to statistical figures provided by World Travel and Tourism Council, Tourism Industry generates 9.4 per cent of the labour force, i.e., out of every ten jobs, one job is directly or indirectly provided by tourism industry. In other words, every investment of one million dollars creates sixty new jobs. Considering this in Indian context if Ministry of Tourism is demanding Rs. 35,000 crores for development of tourism infrastructure, it would generate massive employment opportunities.

World Tourism Organization has projected that annual arrival growth would be around 4.5 per cent by 2020 and international tourist arrivals would go up from 613 million to 1.6 million, as well as spending during the same period would touch a figure of US $2 trillion from present figure of US $ 447 million.

Geographic distribution analysis of tourist arrivals reveal that France stands at top with 62 million tourists followed by United States (45 million), Spain (41 mn), Italy (36 mn), China (26 mn), United Kingdom (26 mn), Mexico (22 mn), Hungary (21 mn), Poland (19 mn), Canada (17 mn) and India (2.2 million). This data is sufficient enough to convince that India is still to go a long way and as the Industry would grow so will its employees. It means tourism industry in the new millennium would be full of opportunities and challenges for its employees.

Tourism in modern times forms the primary basis of large number of national economies. In terms of foreign exchange earnings it ranks on top in Thailand and Australia and Number 2 in case of Hong Kong and Malaysia and Number 3 in case of Singapore and Indonesia. Not only does it provide foreign exchange to countries but also generates employment. For instance, 12 per cent of total employment in Hong Kong and 14 per cent of employment in Singapore comes from tourism. In other words tourism is a large income multiplier, for every dollar of tourist expenditure involves so many hands and same number of benefits are delivered.

According to World Tourism Organization, in 1980, India received 1.25 million tourists (0.44 per cent of global share) which have marginally declined to 0.30 per cent in 1998 when India received 2.3 million tourists. This declined in share both in terms of receipts and arrivals is largely due to condition of political uncertainty. Yet, tourism is able to make significant impact on economy. This industry employs more than 10 million people directly and 10 million indirectly. In other words, this is the only industry which generates such a high employment opportunity, i.e., every investment of Rs. 10 lakhs creates 47.5 jobs in tourism as against only 12.6 in manufacturing and a comparable 44.7 in agriculture. Therefore, Indian tourism, despite negligible presence in the world market, provides significant gains for the economy.

A study of consumption patterns in United States reveals that almost 67 per cent of population prefer to go on vacation and prefers eating out. Fifty per cent of population love to watch or participate in sports, and it is only 20 per cent people who love to spend money on shopping or social events. Thus, it is crystal clear from the available data that a greater percentage of population prefers to spend on holidaying.

It was in 1988 that for the first time the Ministry of Tourism projected a figure of 2.5 million as annual tourist arrival but after more than a decade we have failed to accomplish this achievement.

On the infrastructural front we are not able to meet the requirements. According to one of the estimates forwarded by Union Minister for Tourism. To develop infrastructural amenities the ministry requires an amount of Rs. 35,000 crores.

If we put a glance on transport sector we see that Air Shortages are compounded by aviation policy of "principle of reciprocity". Against an annual international demand of 10 million seats we are able to supply only 5.3 million seats and against annual domestic demand of 19 million seats we are able to supply only 9.75 million seats. Similarly, Railway is also suffering from deficiencies, so much so, that even the most visited track of Agra-Jaipur is still to be established. Currently it is only a meter gauge link but off late decision has been taken to upgrade it to broad gauge.

In one of recent report on Indian infrastructure submitted by Dr. Rakesh Mohan Committee to meet the Road Shortages investment need is assessed at Rs. 320 billion for new roads and Rs. 90 billion for maintenance of existing roads. Our neighbouring countries like Singapore, Hong Kong, Malaysia, Mauritious, etc. have super and express Highways or Mass Rapid Transport System. As a result movement of tourists, within countries is very smooth and comfortable. Our country has planned all such activities but due to the lack of investment, execution of these would be a challenge in this new millennium.

Why only infrastructure, even in the sphere of accommodation there is a huge gap between demand and supply. At present we have a supply of only 65,000 rooms against a demand of 1,30,000 rooms. In comparison the city of Los Angles or Vagas has supply of more than 2.5 lakh rooms, against annual demand of 1.95 lakh rooms. Of course, this huge gap is due to difference in pattern of government spending and capital investment in India and other countries. Whereas in India it is only 1 per cent of public spending in comparison with 6.8 per cent of world, and 6.4 per cent capital investment in India against 11.8 per cent of world's capital investment. This, therefore, would be another challenge to be faced by our planners that there should be substantial increase in both public spending and capital investment. Which in consequence would increase the face of tourism related development activities.

Tourism Industry in India a largely unorganized which means it is more or less a family business. To add to it there are only handful of international players. Although segmentation of tourists market is according to specialization like inbound/outbound tour operation, i.e., of a tour operator and corporate travel, i.e., of a travel agent. But with the increasing pressure of global players this family business is facing a challenge to develop themselves to international standards, failing which, they would be acquired by or merged with these big brothers.

Role of Information Technology as a greatest challenge is unquestionable. Impact of technology on Tourism Industry is so apparent seeing the use of internet by maximum number of people for travel. Results of a survey on the Internet's impact on business productivity and individual work habits reveal that 94 per cent of the sample group access internet for online maps, 89 per cent of respondents get flight information through internet, 82 per cent of respondents access net to conduct competitive intelligence, 67 per cent of respondents make hotel reservations, 58 per cent purchase online tickets. Last two segments are likely to increase by 20 per cent in next 2-3 years. This illustration is sufficient to prove that human resource in travel trade needs to upkeep themselves with latest changes in technology to work effectively and efficiently. Not only this, but this technology revolution has also made the customer aware of the vast choices available. This has made the customer the 'self declared king'. Needs, wants, likes and dislikes of customers are changing as fast as their moods. Consequently it is extremely discern to meet the challenge of bridging the supply gap.

All these developments are the indicators of a changing role of travel professionals in this new millennium. They are not mere "ticket-cutters" but their role will be that of travel counsellor. Travel houses would more or less be like "one stop shop", offering entire range of services under same roof. In other words, customization would be the need of the time with "perceived value addition" and a higher quality and degree of interaction with customers.

To convert these challenges into opportunities, successful travel professionals must possess required qualities. They must have passion for job with high level of energy and contagious enthusiasm. Besides, they must also have missionary zeal to arrange for "holiday of a life time" every time. Last but not the least these travel professional of new millennium should be technology savvy. In short, we must remember that positive attitude creates positive results. Before people buy anything being offered, they buy attitude to travel professional no matter what he or she is selling.

To conclude, tourism industry offers a whole range of challenges and opportunities in this new millennium. In developing countries like India where tourism is all set of develop, if these challenges are successfully converted into opportunities, results are imminent and sky would be the limit. It is required to be ensured that proper input is supplied to reap the dividends, which are enjoyed by all developed countries.

# Two

# Tourism Training: Emerging Challenges

Business environment is changing rapidly in the new millennium, this has created certain compulsive and motivational forces for tourism business to adapt itself to change and this is going to be a continuous process. As a result, the techniques of tourism management are to be reoriented to cope with emerging pressures.

**Tourism a Social Activity: People Oriented**

Tourism is essentially about people and places, the places that one group of people leave, visit and pass through, the other group who make their trip possible and those they encounter along the way. It is an important social activity of human beings from time immemorial in India. It has been an integral part of Indian tradition and culture *Atithi Devo Bhavo* and *Vasudhaiva Kutumbakam* (World is one family) have always been the bywords of Indian social behaviour.

**Global Tourism Development: Its Multiplier Face**

Travel and tourism, where we work for a living and help develop, generates an economic value of US $ 3 trillion. It is today larger than the oil and automobile industry. Services are the fastest growing sector accounting almost 60 per cent of GDP (In India represents 48.6 per cent of GDP). Tourism being one of the major service sector contributes 5.6 per cent in India's GDP against 11.7 per cent world wide. It employs over 145 million people and has grown globally at an average of 4 per cent each year for last ten years. Expected to grow at the same rate up to 2010. In India it employs 9.3 million directly and nearly 17.4 million indirectly. According to WTTC by 2010 this is expected to rise to 12.9 million direct jobs and 25.0 million jobs indirectly (6.8 per cent total employment).

**Tourism Developments in India**

If we look at the hard facts it comes into light that India has slipped down to 43rd rank on world list with 2.4 million tourist arrivals, i.e., less than 0.5 per cent of world tourism traffic. In our own region India has slipped from fourth place in 1985 to seventh in 1997.

**SATELLITE ACCOUNT OF TOURISM IN INDIA**

| | *1999 US$ Million* | *% of Total* | *Real growth 1998-1999* | *2010 US$ Million* | *% of Total Growth* | *Real Growth 1999-2010* |
|---|---|---|---|---|---|---|
| Personal Travel and Tourism | 13100.0 | 5.1 | 11.2 | 40020.0 | 5.6 | 7.4 |
| Business Travel | 1850.0 | - | 5.7 | 5550.0 | - | 7.3 |
| Government Expenditure | 340.0 | 0.9 | -17.6 | 1800.0 | 2.2 | 12.9 |
| Capital Investment | 5610.0 | 6.5 | 11.5 | 18790.0 | 7.6 | 8.2 |
| Visitor Exports | 4760.0 | 9.1 | 17.5 | 18060.0 | 8.5 | 10.4 |
| Other Exports | 1120.0 | 2.1 | 17.5 | 5300.0 | 2.5 | 10.4 |
| T & T Demand | 26780.0 | - | 11.6 | 89520.0 | - | 8.3 |
| T & T Industry GDP | 10200.0 | 2.7 | 12.0 | 33280.0 | 3.2 | 8.1 |
| T & T Economy GDP | 21000.0 | 5.6 | 11.6 | 70160.0 | 6.8 | 8.2 |
| T & T Industry Employment | 8760.0 | 2.9 | 5.1 | 11840.0 | 3.2 | 2.9 |
| T & T Economy Employment | 18030.0 | 5.9 | 4.8 | 24960.0 | 6.8 | 3.1 |

**Note:** T & T stands for Travel and Tourism

Why we have failed to achieve our targets. According to Tourism Task Force (constituted by Ministry of Tourism in 1997) among other factors which have impeded the growth of sector is

Poor Human Resource Development which should be a cutting edge in service sector.

According to Dr. R. Venkataraman, President of India (1988), "Even though a country may possess abundant physical resources it can not make rapid economic and social advancements unless there are people who are enterprising and have developed necessary skills, and attitudes. Human goods are required to mobilize, organize and use these resources effectively and efficiently towards the production of required goods and service".

**Unleash Potential: Meaning and Impact**

The biggest challenge in this new millennium is to unleash tourism potential in a planned manner. Educators must make budding professionals realise the impact of one extra daily international flight in to India. At micro level

It means : 400 passengers per flight (assume)
200 foreign visitors per flight (assume)
minimum stay of 7 days.
average expenditure of Rs. 2,000 per day.

Its impact : Earning per flight Rs. 28 lakhs
Earning 365 flights Rs. 100 crores
20000 jobs per year

At micro level, we assume that if India's Travel and Tourism sector grows to equal average performance in countries like Singapore, Malaysia, Thailand, Romania and China.

Its Impact : A total GDP contribution of over Rs. 8,50,000 crores against less than Rs. 100,000 crores today.
33 million jobs against 17 millions today
Rs. 180,000 crores in export earnings against Rs. 20,000 crores today.
More equal distribution of employment and wealth.

This forecast obviously necessitates to create professionals. It is another important challenge before tourism educators to produce professionals rather than profit creators. We must make our students feel the relevance of what Pt. Nehru said, "Welcome a Stranger and Send Back a Friend". If we fail to achieve this, we will keep on lagging behind. Even China, who has opened doors a decade ago today receives 53 million tourists a year. If we practice relationship marketing or participatory tourism we will not be required to maintain overseas offices.

**Integrating Communication and Information Technology**

Technology in the form of computers and NET has had and shall continue to have effect on tourism industry. The competitive market place with tourist orientation will demand a shift in service delivery system. Educators have to prepare students and meet unanticipated environment. New technologies will not only impact new product development, but also will greatly change the way, in which, the product is delivered to the customer. Computer based interactive information and product buying system will enable the customers to see destinations and facilities on CD ROM or video and make direct purchases. Already the Worldwide Internet and the US based compu serve and America Online are providing individual subscribers, information and travel product and online facilities for buying. Virtual reality travel and robotics will offer new products and experiences to visitors. Therefore, it becomes all the more important for educational institutions to integrate WEB as an overall strategy so as to use it as a database for information and educate their students than just teaching them about ticketing, tour packaging, tour planning, cruises, etc.

**Mergers and Acquisitions**

The travel industry in India is currently witnessing a shakeout in form of mergers and acquisitions. In this process big companies are taking over small ones. For instance, Kuoni's take over of SITA's travel division. It conveys that India is slowly merging with global trends. It is true that Kuoni will inject professionalism but as a result of their capital strength these bigwigs will push smaller companies in the corner. So, these agents will have to find alternate travel related sources of income and must improve retention.

Consequently, we as educators must train our budding

managers as travel consultants and not as travel agents/assistant. These consultants will not live upon the commission but their main source of income will be management fee. As of now, a very large share of clientele in India for airfare and hotels have direct access to NET and are prepared to pay a service charge. They do not leave room for profit and bargaining to the agents. This in turn means complete transparency in all transactions which at the same time makes business for intermediaries very insecure.

**Emergence of New Products and Destinations**

With the emergence of new demand segments in the market, new products will need to be developed. Since most will demand more and more active holidays as against the resort holidays of the past, more animations will be needed in packaging with quality and value. The major products will need to be differentiated adding value at all stages. Therefore, students and budding managers will need to be equipped to handle wider information needs than they do now as education will form an integral part of travel experience of new visitors of future.

**Interdependence Integration in Destination Development**

During present times more and more destinations are building up on each other's complementary and combined strengths. This development includes introduction of growth triangles for instance: Singapore, Malaysia and Indonesia—Malaysia and Thailand and Malaysia Brunei and Philippines are good examples of growth triangles in our own region. There will also be new competition to the established destinations countries and new developments will need to be developed within established destinations. Therefore, as educators we will face a challenge to train our students in such a manner so that they can cope with all developments in destination planning and development more effectively and efficiently.

Therefore, amidst all these new developments, education, training, retraining, multi-skilling and career path development will need to be given top priority in travel and tourism industry, it is a people industry dependent entirely on people who run it. The good health of our industry depends on how we manage our environment and people. Not to forget there should be right technology-human interface service with a human touch, is a key ingredient to the success of our industry. Technology used in its right form will assist us to be more efficient and be cost effective in delivery of service. Therefore, we must consider technology as a tool and not an end in itself. Hence, the challenge for us is to pick and choose the right mix of the technology/service interface that will suit our industry.

# Planned Tourism Growth through Trained Manpower

Tourism Industry is a limitless industry with immense growth potential. It is considered as the world's largest industry with 613 million people travelling every year and the industry accounting for an earning of US $ 447 million excluding air fares. Tourism accounts for 11.6 per cent of world GDP. Tourism industry creates employment for 262 million people or 10.5 per cent of global workforce. This employment generation is expected to be 383 million by year 2007. A gain of 121 million jobs or one new job every 2.4 seconds. Over the same period international tourist arrivals would go up by 4.5 per cent, i.e., it would be 1.6 billion and their spending would touch a figure of US $ 2 Trillion from present figure of US $ 4.5 billion.

In India, despite its proven economic potential tourism is a neglected subject. Even the Government of India's Economic Survey presented to Parliament before budget every year does not give more than a line's mention to tourism. Tourism is the only sector which in return to small incentives can provide big gains. But whether this negative attitude of Government of India to tourism has adversely affected employment opportunities in India is a burning question.

Therefore, we need to analyze the manpower planning and training components of Indian Tourism Plan which represents the recognized approach to provide the trained personnel for effective operations and efficient management of tourism sector. At the same time it aims at taking into consideration the particular constraints that exist in India.

As stated earlier according to Shri R. Venkataraman (1988), "Even though a country may possess abundant physical resources it cann't make rapid economic and social advancements unless there are people who are enterprising and have developed necessary skills and attitudes. Human efforts is required to mobilise, organise and use these resources effectively and efficiently towards the production of the required goods and services. We have examples of countries who have hardly natural physical resources, yet they have achieved tremendous economic growth. Japan is perhaps the most notable example. On the other hand, we have countries and states which have large natural resources but have not been able to exploit them effectively and they continue to lag behind in economic development".

In most of the developing countries the development of human resources has been regarded as one amongst many objectives of long term economic growth. As a result priorities shift away from purely growth oriented development strategies to those that recognize and partly remedy the past neglect of such social sectors like population planning, health planning and education, housing, social security and other social services.

Indian Tourism Plan, uptill 1988, was only an integrated part of total planning exercise. This planning exercise, with the objective of planned development, has appeared since 1951, in form of five year plans. Past independence plans, atleast first few, could only focus their attention on providing basic infrastructural facilities. Primarily these facilities were meant for local population but could also be used by tourists. However, it was only during Fourth Five Year Plan that specific tourism development programmes were taken up.

A careful study of development of tourism in India through plans reveals that it is of late when our plans have realised the significance of tourism as the only solution available to cyclical financial recession in most of developed and underdeveloping countries.

Government of India made its first serious attempt by setting up a National Committee on Tourism in 1988. This Committee was constituted to assess and analyze the then prevailing situation of tourism and its development in India. In its recommendation the committee acknowledged the significant role of trained manpower in following words.

"Employees are the musicians of the orchestra that members of the audience — the guests — have come to watch perform. If the employees are not skilled at their jobs, then the performance they give will get bad reviews. Just as an orchestra can have a fine musical score from a great composer and still perform poorly because of incompetent musicians. So, a hotel or restaurant can have the finest cuisines, service procedures and quality standards and still have dissatisfied guests; because of poor employee performance". This Committee, therefore, can be considered as a milestone attempt in the direction of not only highlighting the shortcomings in existing system but also in providing guidelines with regard to plan tourism growth through trained manpower.

Recommendation forwarded by National Committee on Tourism proved eye opening facts for Government of India. In the result, the Government's Industrial Policy Statement of July 1991, declared hotels and tourism related businesses a high priority industry for the purpose of foreign investment and foreign collaboration. In the subsequent year (1992) National Action Plan for tourism envisaged an increase in India's share of world tourist arrival from 0.4 per cent to 1 per cent in 5 years. In terms of actual arrivals target worked out to be 5 million tourist. But the expected results would have been possible only if our government would have given a thought to most vital component of total plan layout, i.e., Manpower.

**Trained Manpower Requirements: Hospitality Industry**

An insight into hospitality industry in the direction of trained manpower requirement reveals that approximately 8.2 million people are employed in hospitality industry. Of them, nearly 30 per cent work in hotels. Of these, only 4200 of hotel employees are trained either at government or privately run training institutes. Hostels alone employ 65 per cent of trained staff and employment has been growing, at an average rate of 5 per cent per annum for last three years. Thus, even though the growth of industry is about 5 per cent, the requirement is growing at the rate of about 10 to 11 per cent per annum.

*Projected Requirements*

Since hotels and restaurants are even now faced with a shortage of trained manpower, the estimated additional requirement for the future can be arrived at only after taking the present shortage in consideration. By 1999-2000 AD, an estimate based on compounding gap between demand and supply reveals industry will require (1) 10,000 additional trained people against present capacity of producing only 1600 diploma holders produced by 21 Institutes of Hotel Management, Catering Technology and Applied Nutrition under National Council. (2) 18 food Craft Institutes under state government producing approximately 3000 certified craft holders. (3) In addition there are numerous private institutions which have mushroomed all over the country either being patronised by some leading hotel chain or are operating at their own, but reports reveal that only a handful of these have the required infrastructural facilities and trained faculty. But these are in a position to add another 1000 trained manpower. After taking into account all these there still exist an estimated gap between demand and supply of 4400 by year 1999 against a figure of 3097 in the year 1994.

According to one of the survey conducted by one of the associations related with hospitality and catering, the compounding gap between required trained manpower and supplied trained manpower can be illustrated as :

| *Segment* | *1990 -91* | *1991 -92* | *1992 -93* | *1994 -95* | *1995 -96* | *1996 -97* | *1997 -98* | *1998 -99* | *1999- 2000* |
|---|---|---|---|---|---|---|---|---|---|
| Hotels | 18079 | 18770 | 19909 | 33867 | 37253 | 40979 | 45077 | 51066 | 5999 |
| Restaurants | 3143 | 3184 | 3430 | 11987 | 12497 | 13028 | 13582 | 14222 | 15800 |
| Others | 6836 | 7323 | 7654 | 8686 | 13993 | 9763 | 10338 | 13600 | 14200 |
| Total | 28058 | 29277 | 30993 | 54540 | 58937 | 63743 | 68997 | 78888 | 89999 |

To make the situation of trained manpower in India worse when by 2000 AD the hospitality industry is all set to grow by 20 per cent per annum Indians would be aging. According to 1991 census, 45 per cent of Indian population is under 29, by 2000 AD those 45 per cent will be 40. In these statistics there is a good news as well as a bad news. The good news is that the middle aged workers are usually more experienced and dependable than their counterparts. The bad is that there will be lack of experience and scarcity of young workforce.

**Suggestions**

The need for trained personnel in the hospitality industry can therefore, hardly be exaggerated. A concerted effort is needed to get enough trained hands in future. Government of India, along with private sector must take concrete steps in the improvement and development of this most vital asset, i.e., Human Resource. Uptil now not much of careful thought has gone in to the proper planning of this asset. Exercises have been performed in tits and bits. What we require is a precise and specific master plan to assess the actual demand of trained manpower on the lines given in this study as well as to devise ways to bridge the ever increasing gap between demand and supply of trained manpower. It is also suggested that :

A. New Institutes be set up under the National Council and functioning of these institutes be carefully and properly monitored;

B. Intake capacity of the existing Institutes under National Council and Food Craft Institutes under state government shall be substantially increased;

C. The mushrooming of so called private institutes be stopped or an attempt must be made to regularise them through a centralised agency, preferably by National Council;

D. There should be a clear uniform curriculum in all institutes imparting training in Hotel Management, Catering Technology and Applied Nutrition;

E. Efforts must be directed towards screening the quality of teaching staff;

F. A strict surveillance of training system for hotel personnel be instituted to ensure that youngsters are not duped;

G. Last but not the least, planners must focus on developing some more Manpower Development Centres like that of India Tourism Development Centre. At present the only existing centre conducts about 300 programmes a year to train approximately 4000 employees of ITDC belonging to diverse disciplines of hospitality industry. The success of the training centres would only be able to reap the harvest if the gates of these training centres are also opened to outsiders to produce additional trained manpower for the industry.

To conclude, we can say that a target of 5 million tourist arrival by 2005 is not an exaggeration if our Government is all set to take up the challenge of bridging the gap between demand and supply of this most vital resource. Besides, planners focus should also be on improving the image of the country abroad. It is only then that we can attract tourists to India and give an opportunity to this trained manpower resource to prove their worth. As a reward, we can ensure repeat business and more foreign exchange for our economy.

*Four*

# Role of Public and Private Sectors in Tourism

Tourism has come to be recognized as one of the most significant factors in the economy of many nations. In some cases, it has ever become the most important factor. Tourism is the biggest foreign exchange earner for countries like Nepal, Thailand Spain and New Zealand, and ranks second among the export earnings of India.

Without question, tourism effects the economy of the host nations. An increase in expenditure by foreign tourists in a country raises the level of national income. On the reverse side, an increase in expenditure on tourism abroad by the nationals of a country lowers the national income. Thus, the net income generated in a country by tourism will vary directly with the expenditure of visitors in the host country and inversely with the expenditure abroad by their own nationals.

However, for rich and developed nations like the USA and Japan, an unfavourable balance in tourism is an investment. It provides greater economic stability in the world to boost trade and investment. Japan, which used to discourage its people to travel overseas, changed its mind to boost overseas tourism in the mid eighties. It had piled up huge trade surplus from exports of its manufactured goods and products. It took a decision to offset the surplus through aggressive promotion of overseas tourism from Japan. A target of 10 million overseas travellers by the close of 1990 was set but the target was achieved even earlier. The number of Japanese overseas travellers now is over 20 million (1999).

In the Indian context, tourism has an advantage in bridging the gap of India's balance of payments. According to

Dr. N.K. Sengupta, a former Secretary of the Planning Commission of India, "Tourism has the capacity to generate valuable foreign exchange with almost 100 per cent value added, thus making it the most readily available source for resolving the balance of payment crunch."

Private/Public National Organization of Tourism. (Responsible for overall programme development, advice and cooperation).

(1) (A) Private Investors and Leading Institutions.

(B) Self-liquidating facilities.

(C) Tourists pay all costs:

Examples :

(i) Hotels

(ii) Supplementary accommodation

(iii) Restaurants

(iv) Night Clubs

(v) International and Domestic Transportation.

(D) Projects financed by charging Admission fees :-

(i) Roads

(ii) Bridges

(iii) Tunnels

(iv) Aquariums

(v) Zoo

(vi) Museums

(vii) National Monuments

(viii) Shrines

(ix) Special Events.

2. (A) Private Carriers.

(B) Partly self liquifying facilities.

(C) Tourists and government share costs :

(i) Water, Electricity (e.g., hotel lighting)

(ii) Roads (Paid in partly by ticket sale)

(iii) Rail-roads (Paid in partly by ticket sale)

(iv) Air Strips (Paid in part by income from concessions)

(v) International Transportation

(vi) Domestic Transportation

(vii) Welcoming Programmes (Paid in part by carriers, etc.).

3. (A) Other Tourism Groups : Private/Public
   (i) Hoteliers
   (ii) Restauranteurs
   (iii) Guide Association
   (iv) Travel Agents
   (v) Publicity Organization
   (vi) Local Cultural and Historical Groups
   (vii) Tour Operators (facilities used by Tourists).
4. (A) Government Agencies
   (i) Finance Department
   (ii) Office of the Prime Minister
   (iii) Immigration Department
   (iv) Civil Aviation Department
   (v) Department of Industry and Commerce
   (vi) Foreign Affairs
   (vii) Public Works Department
   (viii) Reserve Bank
   (ix) Development Bank
   (x) Government Carriers
   (xi) Ministry of Culture and Information
   (xii) Ministry of Tourism.

   (B) Non Self liquidating facilities : Government pays all costs:

   Examples :
   (i) Water, Electricity (street light, etc.)
   (ii) Roads, Airstrips (minus charges to carriers)
   (iii) Air terminals (minus revenues obtained from leasing)
   (iv) Sewage
   (v) Projects paid by Government
   (vi) Bridges
   (vii) Tunnels
   (viii) Aquariums
   (ix) Museums
   (x) National Monuments
   (xi) Shrines
   (xii) Scenic Areas
   (xiii) Subsidized Special Events (festival, pageant, etc.)
   (xiv) Welcoming programmes.

How does the State benefits from tourism revenue ?
The following chart explains—

Revenue from Tourism

| Property Tax | Import Duty | Sales Tax | Income Tax | Hotel Tax | Transport Tax | Entertainment Tax |
|---|---|---|---|---|---|---|

The economic benefits of tourism are reflected in Balance of Payment, Higher Employment, Rising Incomes and from new entrepreneurial activities in a country.

The most noticeable economic argument in favour of tourism is its Multiplier Effect. All industries have multiplier effect but in tourism it is much higher. States benefit the most from tourism through taxes. It is estimated that 6-10 cents of out of every dollar earned through tourism go to governments in the form of taxes in the USA. Indian States too have similar advantages. It is estimated that 15 paise out of every rupee spent by tourists go to the government coffers.

Among the disadvantages of developing tourism are leakages from the economies of developing countries through imports, high inflation, land speculation, low investments return due to seasonal nature of tourism, etc. An important disadvantage of small countries with rich tourist assets is that they tend to depend too much on tourism which is vulnerable to local and regional conflicts as well a national catastrophes.

The following chart explains the relationship between tourism investment and revenue derived from it once it is developed.

| *Expenditure* | | *Revenue* | |
|---|---|---|---|
| *Public Sector* | *Private Sector* | *Public Sector* | *Private Sector* |
| - Master Planning<br>- Land Acquisition<br>- Development of markets<br>- Infrastructure Development<br>- Monitoring Private Sector development<br>- Maintenance | - Feasibility analysis<br>- Planning<br>- Construction<br>- Operation | - Property tax<br>- Import duty<br>- Sales Tax<br>- Income Tax | - Hotel Revenue<br>- Shops<br>- Transport<br>- Entertainment |

India has tremendous potential for domestic tourism. The economic contribution of domestic tourism is estimated at Rs. 33,000 crores compared to Rs. 3300 crores of the International tourism. So, from an economic point of view domestic tourism is more significant than international tourism, especially for a country like India and for that the role of public and private sector in the development of economy should be complementary.

**Role of Tourism in Economic Development**

Tourism development has been advanced as a policy alternative, particularly for developing countries, to aid economic growth. This trend comes owing to the fact that :

(i) the demand for international travel continues to grow in developed countries;

(ii) as incomes in the developed countries increase, the income elasticity of demand for international travel will increase at a faster rate;

(iii) developing nations need foreign exchange earnings to aid their own economic development to satisfy the rising expectations of their growing populations.

The Organization for Economic Cooperation and Development (OECD) has concluded, in fact, that tourism provides a major opportunity for growth of countries that find themselves at the intermediate stage of Economic Development and are experiencing rather fast economic growth and increasingly require more foreign exchange earnings. They also caution that "there are few if any developing countries which could or perhaps even should rely principally on tourism for their economic salvation."

**Economic Impacts of Tourism**

*Increasing Foreign Exchange Earnings*

Because of economic benefits many countries have embraced tourism as a way to increase foreign exchange earnings to produce the investment necessary to finance economic growth. This certainly can and does occur. Some countries even require tourists to bring in a certain amount of foreign currency for each day of their stay and do not allow them to take it out of the country at the end of their vacation.

However, the foreign exchange earnings generated by tourism can be overstated unless the import factor is known. The value of goods and services that must be imported to service the needs of tourism are referred to as leakage. The money spent leaks from the host economy and must be subtracted from foreign exchange earnings to determine the true impact.

*Increasing Income*

*The Multiplier Effect:* The tourism industry obviously generates income within a destination country. The amount of income generated, however, is difficult to determine. The difficulty arises from the fact that tourism is comprised of many different sectors of the economy. Additionally, many small businesses are involved, which leads to great difficulty in getting precise data.

Probably the most common method for estimating the income generated from tourism is by determining the multiplier for a destination. The multiplier effect is illustrated in figure below:

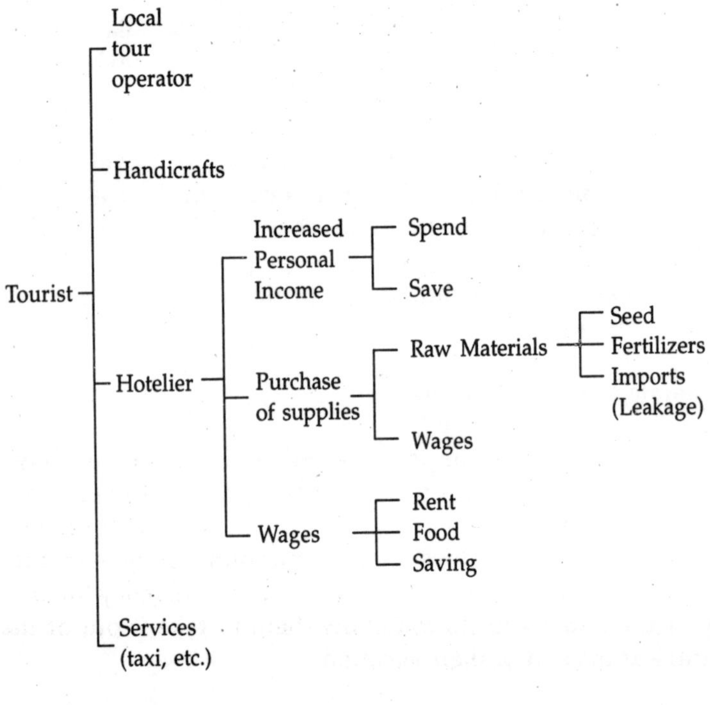

As per the multiplier effect a tourist makes an initial expenditure into the community. This expenditure is received as income by local tour operators, handicrafts store owners, hoteliers and taxicab drivers. In the first round of transactions, a hotelier may use some money received to buy some supplies, pay some wages, and retain some profits. The income in the second round may be spent or saved, while the employee who has received payment for services rendered may spend some of that on rent and some on food and may put some into savings. The money spent on supplies in the third round of spending, goes for things such as seed, fertilizers, and imported raw materials. Any income spent on imports has leaked out of the local economy. This process goes on until the additional income generated by a new round of spending essentially becomes zero.

*Increasing Employment*

A principal argument made for encouraging the development of tourism is that it produces many jobs. Tourism creates primary or direct employment in such areas as lodging, restaurants, and sight seeing operations. Indirect employment can also be created in the construction, agriculture, banks, insurance, support services and manufacturing industries. The amount of indirect or secondary employment generated depends upon the extent to which the tourism sector is integrated with the rest of the local economy. The more integration and diversification that occurs, the more indirect employment is generated.

*Multinational Control*

As tourism has developed among nations, the opportunity has arisen for international expansion of businesses in four areas — hotels, airlines, restaurants and tour operations. Much criticism has been leveled at the multinational businesses (multinational) charging that they operate to benefit their own operation at the expense of the destination region.

Overwhelmingly, multinationals have their offices in developed countries. Approximately, 80 per cent of the hotels abroad are accounted for by companies headquartered in the United States, France, and the United Kingdom, and there is a trend toward more ownership by Japanese and Hong Kong interests. Most problems for the destination corporations have had no financial investment in the hotels. Most overseas properties are operated without any foreign equity involvement trend that is increasing. Control is exercised through management controls or as to a far lesser extent through franchise agreements.

It appears that foreign ownership of hotels is of greatest benefit to the host country in the early stages of tourism development. At this point, the destination can really benefit from the foreign know-how. Maximization of benefits comes from direct financial involvement of the transnational business in the development of local managerial and supervisory talent.

Most countries have a national airline, although the airline may be owned and operated by a foreign company. Tourists will generally prefer to travel by the airline of their country of origin rather than by the airline of the destination country. This is particularly true, because of the perception of quality and safety in the event of travel to a lesser developed country.

Tour operators can yield a great deal of influence over destinations. Operators have the ability to guide large numbers of tourists to particular destinations. If a country has decided to develop tourism for the masses, and if it has consequently built the infrastructure and facilities to service these tourists, it must attract sufficient numbers of visitors to utilize and pay for the facilities.

To conclude we can say that tourism development or rather sustainable development of tourism is due to increasing cooperative attitude of private and public sector. Gone are the days when private sector was hesitant in initiating efforts towards development of tourism. Authorities responsible for planning and promotion of tourism at local, regional and national level have started involving private sector in decision making process. The overall objective of both the sectors is to create a positive image of our country as a destination of this mellennium.

# Five

# Role of Public Relations in Tourism

Public relations perhaps the most misunderstood part of marketing communications, can be the most effective tool in promoting products and services. Public relations is the process of management function or in management function that evaluates public attitudes, identifies the policies and procedures of an individual or an organization as they effect the public interest, and executes a programme, of action to acceptance, earn public understanding. Public relations is an important marketing tool which until recently was treated as a marketing stepchild. PR is moving in to explosive growth stage. Most of companies are realizing that mass marketing is no longer the answer to some of their communication needs. Advertising costs continue to rise, while audience reach continues to decline. Advertising clutter reduces the impact of each ad. Sales and promotion costs have also increased as channel intermediaries demand lower price and better commissions and deals. In this environment, public relations hold the promise of a cost-effective promotional tool. The creative use of new events, publications, social events, community relations, and other public relations techniques offers companies a way to distinguish themselves and get products from their competitors.

## Integration of Marketing and Public Relations

In the past it was common for the marketing function of PR function to be handled by two different departments within the firm. Today, these two functions are increasingly integrated. There are several reasons for this integration.

Firstly, companies are calling for more market oriented PR. They want their PR departments to manage PR activities that contribute towards marketing the company and improving the bottom line.

Secondly, companies are establishing marketing PR groups to directly support corporate product promotion and image making. These marketing PR, like financial PR and community PR, serve a special constituency — the marketing department.

**Public Relations in Tourism**

In the field of tourism, the public relations assumes special significance because of the peculiar nature of the tourism product. Here the need for making complete information and facts available to both potential and actual tourist assumes importance. It involves measures designed to create and improve the image for the tourist product, create a more favourable climate for advertising and sales support activities, especially in regard to travel trade intermediaries and news media. Favourable acceptance of any tourist destination by the public is of utmost importance. In fact, no business is more concerned with human relations than the business of tourism. Public relations in tourism is used to create and maintain a positive image for a country. A tourist destination in the minds of people who are in a position to influence public opinion (journalists, editors, travelwriters, etc.) or in the minds of sales intermediaries (travel agents, tour operators, hoteliers, airlines, etc.) PR is oriented towards creating and maintaining an atmosphere whereby the travelling public at large is convinced of the advantages of visiting the country concerned.

**Implementing PR Strategies in Tourism Industry**

Public relations can never be some kind of special sugar that can be sprinkled or coated on a sour or difficult situation to make its task sweet or comparatively functionally easy. Public relations, as a marketing communication function, aims to supplement the total communications/promotional effort by helping to create and enhance a favourable image of the hotel organization, and by communicating and adverse influence that may exist from time to time, as also by creating a proper goodwill for the hotel organization. Public relations ought to be a sustained ongoing affair and should be harmoniously integrated into the total promotional effort.

When it comes to operational level, public relations must be distinguished in terms of variety of public. Public may differ like guests, media professionals, governmental agencies, community and employees, which are of interest to the Hotel as a unit or the organization and therefore strategies are evolved to exercise healthy relations with all such publics.

**Public Relations in Hotels**

The public relations department of a hotel has a big responsibility in building awareness, credibility, stimulating the sales force and channel intermediaries and hold down promotion costs of the hotels.

To bring about an effective public relations activities into play, the PR managers use different sets of PR tools, so that the hotel's image and its product, publicity are done in an effective manner.

**Press Relations**

Through press relations, hotel's place news worthy information into the news media to attract attention to a person, product or service. A favourable write-up of a hotel in the local newspaper by the travel writer has more impact than an advertisement written by the hotel's management.

**Product Publicity**

Publicity is a task of securing editorial space in print and broadcast media to promote a product or service. Hotels, to make product publicity, employ various methods to publicize their specific product. New product, special events, such as food, festivals, newly renovated Hotel and products that have become popular and are of current trends such as non-fat desserts, are made public through publicity.

**Familiarization Trips**

This is a very effective PR tool for the PR manager in a Hotel. These familiarization trips are organized for travel writers, journalists, opinion leaders, travel and tour operators and other members of trade bodies so that they can be familiarized with the various products a hotel has to offer. It helps a lot in promoting the hotel.

### Publications

Hotels rely extensively on communication material to reach and influence their target markets. These include annual reports, brochures, cards, articles, hotel newsletters and magazines. Through brochures a hotel informs the target customers about a product, how it works and how it is to be assembled. Companies newsletters and magazines help in building its image and convey important news to target in markets.

### Speeches

This is another tool for creating product and company publicity which is done by giving tasks to trade association or at sales meeting or through media questionnaires. Hotels also participate in travel marts which provide them with an opportunity to exhibit their products and build up a relationship with the participants.

### Public Service Activity

Today hotels are engaged in community services to create a favourable image among the prospective clients for e.g., Mughal Sheraton has constructed number of toilets in Agra Fort; a hotel of Mumbai has undertaken the responsibility of maintaining the road link from where it is located to the Sahar International Airport.

### Sports and Cultural Sponsorship

This is carried out by the hotels to create a repetitive imagery in their target markets. These days some of the hotels are actively participating and sponsoring various sports and cultural events. Few hotels do cultural festivals sponsoring the event individually or in cooperative manner. A hotel in Delhi has a special club for special segment of clients. Some hotels conduct different types of contests and competitions with an intention to attract a certain segment of the market.

### Building PR Around the Owner/Operator

A chain of hotels in Delhi has one of its owners staying in one of its hotels for the last many decades and are not living in a separate building but using the same hotel along with its guests.

He shares dining along with other guests. This goes a long way in building a healthy relationship with the clients. The motive is to give the message that the hotel cares about the guests and each and every services and facilities provided by the hotel is being closely monitored by the owner/operator of the hotel. Perhaps, that is the reason why this chain of hotel has been able to place itself as the best in Delhi.

So we can say that public relations department plays a very important role in promoting and marketing the hotels product among the existing and prospective clients. Since tourist destinations are particularly influenced by negative publicity, it is the PR department that defends products that have encountered public problems. Hotels are now feeling that public relations can make a memorable impact on public awareness at a fraction of the advertising cost.

**PR in Airlines**

Generally, it is the Tourism Promotion Division of an Airline which caters to the PR activities of that airline. Airlines, be it domestic or International undertake a number of activities to attract individual tourists, special interest groups, conventions and congresses, and the whole idea of these exercises is to project the native land from where the airlines is operating as an attractive tourist destination.

**Public Relations Activities**

The airlines can make it much more convenient and meaningful to undertake their sales promotion activities through:

(a) Mainline Activities
(b) Ancillary Activities.

*Mainline Activities Include*

(i) Participation in major international travel trade shows and meets such as ITB (Berlin), WTM (London), JATA (Japan), FITUR (Spain), EIBTM (Switzerland). At the meets, promotional literature is distributed, audio-visuals are shown, press briefings are held so as to make the participants aware about the attractiveness of the destination and country.

(ii) Sponsoring visits to a country of promotion for travel agents and writers (FAM Trips), thereby increasing awareness of the country's various attractions for the foreign tourist.

(iii) Arranging cultural events and food-festivals and department stores promotions overseas, thus providing foreign countries, prospective clients a taste of country's cultural heritage and culinary range.

(iv) Nowadays, it is very common for an airline to promote/sponsor a cultural or sports events. Such activities entail the creation of a repetitive imagery in the mind of the people in the target markets, and in this way, the airline identifies itself with the public.

*Ancillary Activities Include*

(a) Organizing seminars overseas to update the travel trade about the country and its tourism products.

(b) Producing and screening of audio-visuals highlighting the different aspects of the country.

(c) Publishing a newsletter to bring about effective communication within the airlines offices.

(d) Airlines also resort to various schemes to attract foreign tourists into the country with attractive fares and whole lot of packages.

(e) Various Airlines in-flight magazines plays an important role in building a strong image about a particular airline and the country at large. These in-flight magazines are becoming a very popular medium of communication between a client and the organization and are invariably aimed at the corporate traveller.

**PR – Travel Agencies**

Most of the travel agencies do not have a separate division for public relation activities. But they do use various PR medium to promote the agency and its different range of products. Travel agencies are realizing day by day the needs for an effective Public Relation Department and are catching up with them. The conventional PR activities in the travel agencies are generally carried out by their marketing department.

The marketing department of a travel agency undertakes the PR activities like :

(a) Promoting their products through print, audio-visual materials distributing among target markets and in its clients. This ensures the visibility of their products in the markets. Each and every information in the brochures and newsletters are written and printed in such a way so that it creates a good image and attracts the prospective clients. So every care is taken to circulate such brochures.

(b) Through customer feedback cells, a travel agency is able to look after the complaints of the clients. This cell has a number of forms to be filed by their clients and related questionnaires which apprise a travel agency about their strengths and weaknesses in their services and facilities provided to the tourists and are very helpful in improving their image and product range.

(c) FAM trips are arranged by the travel agencies where they invite various suppliers, media persons and operators so as to gain favour from their part to gain business.

(d) Since many travel agencies do not have a full fledged foreign office, they have to have good trade relationships with their sales agents abroad. So to communicate with them effectively, they use brochures, newsletters and mailers to make their points.

(e) Participating in International fairs like ITB (Berlin), BIT (Milan), FITUR (Madrid), World Travel Mart (London), etc. and conferences give them an immense opportunity in promoting their products and country as a whole.

(f) Building and creating awareness about the travel package/product with the help of the travel writers/editors through write-ups and editorials in various local newspapers and travel magazines.

On the whole, we find that travel agencies do not pay great attention to effective use of PR medium in promoting their products and services as it is practiced in most of the developed countries. So, it is high time that they realize this fact and try to use this effective medium and PR strategies and tools in building up their image and promoting their products aligned with their marketing strategies.

To conclude we can say that as a matter of fact, it is the government and the department of tourism which has to play an important role as far as PR is concerned. This can be done through streamlining and rejuvenating its foreign offices abroad so that the message is clear and transparent that India is worth visiting and if you are not doing this, you have not discovered yourself.

Going by the experience gained, we have come across a very interesting fact that the role of Public Relations in tourism marketing is that the most of the PR departments of the hotels; airlines or travel agencies are basically handling complaints and are acting like a grievances cell. They have not resorted themselves to effective ways of public relations needs and strategies. To a great extent, these PR managers have failed in delivering their goods and are just sitting and waiting for a complaints/grievances to be made. It is same as an inspector waiting for the crime to happen. No ground work or very little ground work is done to create a favourable and good image about their products. The matter is still more worser in the department of tourism offices, where they just sit and watch the procedure and care little about the tourists. The tourist offices abroad also have a dismal picture. There the deputy directors, are just doing nothing to promote the cause of Indian Tourism and are simply having their holiday overseas.

So, it is high time that we should hear the death knell and wake up from our slumber if we have to make India a promising and worth visiting destination in the minds of the tourists of the world. And it is with the effective and righteous approach to PR strategies working in accordance with marketing strategies, which is going to change the face of Indian Tourism.

# Six

# Customer Information System and Effective CRM

Customer Relationship is now at the forefront of all businesses. With the vacation season on there is big scope for tourists to undertake travel to destinations like India. Yet deciding on a vacation is a tough task as involves not only choosing the location but also figuring out how to get there. Conventionally most people would approach a travel agent for this. In such circumstances there is a possibility of receiving biased and limited information from an agent for his personal profits. However, with the rapid growth of internet based technologies there has been a major impact on managing customer relationships where companies are establishing one to one customer relationship on line to provide complete range of information.

At the core of effective Customer Relationship Management (CRM) lies a good Customer Information System (CIS) to provide customer insight. There is a regular flow of information on various aspects of customer in CIS which is evaluated and compared with other points from time to time. The sole objective is to understand the customer and anticipate the behavioural pattern of customer. The CIS helps the agency to plan, implement and monitor customer contact. Strategy of CIS focuses upon gaining, retention and regaining of customers. In other words to develop an everlasting relationship with customers.

**Six Stage Model**

In the early 90s the concept of relationship marketing was formally introduced with a six stage model for developing relationship.

Contact→Involvement→Intimacy→Deterioration→Repair→Exit→Dissolution

It was believed that building a closer relationship with customers resulted in better returns in form of—

(a) Charging of price promised
(b) Increased use of company's services by hardcore loyalist to company.
(c) Referral role to bring new customers.

These relationships are not formed overnight. Even in ordinary man's life his relationship with a woman passes through various stages — like first meeting (first eye contact) dating, romance (affairs), marriage, honeymoon, followed by either of two routes either divorce or continuation of marriage (loyalty). Behavioural scientists have commonly used the above discussed six stage model in forming and consolidating the relationships. This process of transition from customer acquisition to customer retention can be summed up as :—

(1) Customer Acquisition
(2) Customer Personalization or Customization
(3) Enhancement of Mutual Economic Values
(4) Customer Retention and Referral.

In the first stage customer is acquired either through referral or through advertisements. In the second stage customer development takes place through personalized communication and customization of products and services through a mutual learning process. This stage leads to third stage wherein enhancement of mutual values takes place and as a result seller tries to maximize his revenue by exploiting his relationship with his customers. The sole objective of this entire exercise is to create customer referral group as well as increased base of customer retention. This customer acquisition to customer retention cycle goes on in case of every seller and customer product relationship. In the present age of global competitiveness this is called CRM (Customer Relationship Management).

The transition from conventional CRM to modern CRM is purely due to its integration with technology and this is why CRM today is called an E-enabled and integrated approach.

Today CRM is a core business process. It is not just the concern of sales or operation department but is a process that imparts all functions of an organization. This process to a large extent has capitalized on internet, which is not only inexpensive but also available anytime, anywhere. There is a strong belief that CRM suits best the companies that are engaged in business on the Website. No doubt it is correct but it can also help other small and big organizations in making their customers happy. Before arrival of CRM a grocer in the neighbourhood well aware of the tastes and liking of each member of your family or a owner of a bookstore could inform you personally about the arrival of new title of your favourite author but as their businesses grow such manual methods of delivering that personal touch have become impractical and impossible.

| *Conventional Approach to CRM* | *E-enabled and Integration approach* |
|---|---|
| • Customer acquisition by preparing/ contacting customer on phone | • Customer database |
| • Personal selling (Sales free management) | • Use of customer Information system. |
| • After Sales Services | • Electronic Point of Sales (EPOS) |
| • Customer complaints handling | • Use of computers in customer support. |
| • Extra care of customer | • Call centres |
| • Ultimate customer satisfaction | • Life time value of a customer |
| • Customer's account management | |

In other words, the days of the unsophisticated, uninformed, easily led customer are over. Service delivery method and price have become predominant factors influencing consumer decision making. In such a scenario, Customer Relationship Management enables a return and win-win thinking, transforming information in to services that can cover the buyer's cost without easing the vendor's profits. But it is difficult to understand why Indian Corporate Houses are skeptical about transforming from there customer interactions to relationship-based customer interactions?

**Travel Related Websites**

In travel business it is perceived to be a profitable business that is why many travel websites have sprung up. In the year 2000 online business travel industry was worth 4 billion dollars expected to go up to dollar 16.6 billion by 2003 representing a 9.6 per cent overall travel sales as compared to just 3 per cent of overall sales in 1999-2000. In the year 1999-2000 air travel represented an estimated 70 per cent of booking dollars spent via business online services compared to 20 per cent by hotel bookings and 9 per cent of car rentals. (Source: e Marketer.com)

Travel Websites offer destination guides with attractive pictures and travelogues to give the customer a feel of the destination. One of the prominent and most frequently visited travel website is Traveljini.com, covering almost 200 destinations with every possible information on shopping, sites, eating, lodging, socializing and services and many more.

On the other hand to offer variety another travel website Outlooktraveller.com has segregated the destination into two parts viz. 'Trip out' and 'Inside India'. 'Trip Out' aims to cover India and the World with special focus on theme vacations, e.g., Austrian Symphony or Malaysian circuit whereas 'Inside India' covers approximately no destination with every information possible on each aspect of these destinations.

Besides, there are other travel websites which serve the purpose of being a travel guide on the net. This may include Net2travel.com and Shubyatra.com. To compliment the efforts of these large size travel websites there are also some specific destination based travel websites for instance Kerala tourism.org, a site being run by State Department of Tourism.

The story of travel websites does not end here. Having decided where one wants to go, these sites also offer services like how to get there, either through purchase of readymade (tailor made) packages or by using customized packages. For instance the travel centre of Outlooktraveller.com is connected to Amadens allowing online reservation on all domestic and almost all international airlines. Similar services are offered by Net2travel.com. However, traveljini.com offers customized services with a wide range of packages to choose from keeping in view the varied nature and demand for traveller and travel. This being the largest travel website in India, it has over 40 business partners list which includes the Taj Group, Cox and Kings, Club Mahindra, Rent-a-Car, and so on.

In the race of e-business these travel websites are also offering specialized services like high utility designers map with tourist landmarks and locations, weather forecast, etc. (Outlooktraveller.com); WAP, Visa services auctions and online puja round the clock (traveljini.com); Comprehensive travel finance options ranging from Rs. 20,000 to Rs. 300,000 on outbound tours, medical insurance, exchange calculations and world hotels at Net2travel.com.

Over these years Net's true advantages have become apparent more particularly in terms of time saved and efforts required to physically interact with travel services providers. In short, it provides the best opportunity to compare package rates at just a click of a mouse. All this makes the customer feel truly in control in relation to the customized holiday plans. Customer loyalty has always been valuable but today it has become vital for success.

*Seven*

# Role of Incentives in Tourism Development

## Incentives Available for Travel and Tourism Industry

One of the major hurdles that all tourism projects face before they are realized is that of securing the financing needed for their development. Many tourism projects have been proven to be economically feasible but have not been developed because their promoters have been unable to attract the right amount or type of financing. The number of government agencies providing specific financial incentives for tourism projects has increased rapidly in recent years on a world wide basis. In this respect, these agencies are playing their dual roles as 'stimulators' and 'entrepreneurs'.

In Canada, for example, almost all of the provincial and territorial governments have financial assistance programmes specifically tailored for tourism development projects. The federal government has played an active role in this process by sharing the costs of some of these programmes with individual provinces.

Government financial incentive for tourism projects can be classified into two broad categories. Fiscal incentives are special allowance for income tax or other tax purposes. Direct and indirect incentives constitute the second main category, and include a wide variety of programmes aimed at easing the financial requirements of projects. The basic objective of most of these incentive programmes is to help business carry out tourism development projects that, without assistance, might have been completely abandoned or seriously delayed. On a global basis, all levels of governments get involved in providing these types of incentive programmes. The following is a list of some of the types of financial incentive programmes provided by government agencies to tourism projects:

**Government Incentives**

(i) Financial Incentives
  (a) Foreign Exchange and NRI related
    - Fiscal Incentive
    - Direct/Indirect Incentives.

(ii) Non-financial Incentives.

**Government Financial Incentives**

*Fiscal Incentives*

They are special allowances for income tax or other purposes. Further they can also be classified in three categories namely, tax holidays or deferrals, remission of tariffs and tax reductions.

(I) *Tax Holidays or Deferrals:* It implies the government agency defers the payment of income taxes or other taxes for a predetermined time period. In India tourism industry is entitled for following tax deferrals:

(a) Under Section 80 of Income Tax Act 25 per cent of the profits derived by an Indian company from hotel business is exempted from income tax for a period of eight years.

(b) All new approved hotels set up in hilly areas, rural areas, pilgrim centres and all places identified by the Ministry of Tourism where tourism is intended to be developed, will be exempted from expenditure tax for a period of ten years. These hotels will be given 50 per cent exemption from income tax under Section 80 (i) of the Income Tax Act. This concession will be available at places where adequate hotel room accommodation of reasonable on the assurance that the hotels should have become operational by December 1993.

(c) Under Section 80(i) of the Income Tax Act, any hotel which starts functioning after 31.3.1990 but before 1.4.1995 is eligible for a deduction of an amount equal to:

(i) In the case of company, 30 per cent of the profits derived from the business of hotel, for a period of ten assessment years.

(ii) In the case of a co-operative society, twenty five per cent of the profits derived from the business of hotels, for a period of twelve assessment years.

(iii) In other cases, 25 per cent of the profits derived from the business of hotel, for a period of ten assessment years.

(iv) Under Section 80 HH of Income Tax Act, 20 per cent of the profits from hotels set up in specified backward areas are deductable from the taxable income for a period of ten years.

(II) *Tax Reduction:* It means the government lowers the norms tax rates that would be paid by the project.

(a) To encourage equity participation in new tourism projects the shareholders should be entitled to the benefits under Section 80 CC of the Income Tax Act in respect of investment in new equity for new capital issue. The concession is available to the extent of 50 per cent of the cost of the share purchased (or 20,000 whichever is least ) subject to maximum of Rs. 20,000.

(b) Under the provision of section 80HHC. 50 per cent of the income attributable to the foreign exchange earnings is allowed as deduction straightaway. For the remaining 50 per cent no benefit of tax exemption is available so that income is taken to a reserve fund for investment in tourism industry.

(c) Under Section 80 HHD of the Income Tax Act, any Indian company or a person resident in India, engaged in the business of a hotel or of a tour operator, approved by the presecribed authority in this behalf of a travel agent, is allowed a deduction of a sum equal to the aggregate of:

(i) 50 per cent of the profits derived by them from services provided to foreign tourists; and

(ii) the balance amount of the profit if such balance is credited to a reserve account for reinvestment in activities related to tourism industries. Subject to the condition, inter-alia that the receipts from the foreign tourists are received by the assessee in convertible foreign exchange.

(d) Under Section 88A of the Income Tax Act, an individual or a HUF or an association or a body of individuals, consisting in either case, only of husband or wife governed by the system of community of property in force in the state of Goa or the Union Territories of Dadra and Nagar Haveli and Daman and Diu is allowed a tax rebate of an amount of investment if the new shares eligible for tax rebate is Rs. 25,000/-

(III) *Remission of Tariffs:* Remission of tariffs implies that the government relaxes or removes import duties on goods and services required by the project. Concession in relation to custom duty given by Indian government are enlisted below:

(a) Custom Duty on items included in the Ministry of Finance (Department of Revenue) Notification dated 2.1.86 and 1.3.88 has been reduced to the level as applicable to project imports provided the goods imported are required for initial setting up of a hotel or for substantial expansion of a hotel.

(b) New schemes have been launched for the promotion of adventure tourism including duty reduction in the import of specialised equipment.

(c) Indian Tourism Development Corporation has been permitted to import 300 air-conditioning units to be used in tourist coaches at concessional duty of 50 per cent.

(d) Tour operators were allowed to import 200 luxury cars and buses at soft rates on a one time basis. (1989-90).

*Foreign Exchange and NRI Related Incentives*

1. Approved hotels are eligible for (Foreign Exchange Incentive Quota) which is determined @ 10 per cent of their direct foreign exchange earnings. This quota is available to respective hotels for essential imports

including vehicles, overseas promotional tours, publicity and advertising, etc.

2. Hotels are also eligible to the release of foreign exchange at the rate of 2.5 per cent of their foreign exchange earnings during the preceding licencing year, subject to a maximum of Rs. 15 lakhs, for tourism promotion and travel abroad.
3. Foreign collaborators can invest in equity participation upto 5 per cent in foreign exchange. The principle and interest is reportable.
4. The foreign collaborators are entitled to receive a lumpsum payment for transfer of technology planning, designing and equipping, etc.
5. The fee payable to the foreign party for sales, publicity and marketing will normally relate to the room projects. But all such related payments will be subject to the operating Indian taxation laws and foreign exchange regulations. The major international chains who have entered into an agreement with Indian companies are Intercontinental, Holiday Inn, Ramada Inn, Ouality Inn, Le Meridian, Hyatt and Kempinski, etc.
6. The foreign investors are free to repatriate the dividends on any other payments due to him on his investment in foreign exchange after payment of Indian taxes.
7. It is proposed to impose a minimum payment of US$ 350 on foreign charter operators for a charter which must operate in India for a minimum period of seven days.
8. Loans to Indian parties in case of foreign collaborations upto 50 per cent of the project subject to the conditions to be approved by the government.
9. Non-Resident Indians can invest in 3, 4, 5 star or resort hotels category.
10. Investment by non-resident Indians can be made in two ways: (i) either on repatriable or (ii) on non-repatriable basis.
    (i) In the case of investment on repatriable basis, there are two schemes, investment can be made in the (new and existing companies) other than a FERA company). For permission to invest under the 40 per cent scheme,

the investor is to apply to the Indian company. Under the 74 per cent scheme only a new investment can be made including expansion and diversification of existing industrial undertaking.

(ii) In case of investment on non-repatriable basis NRI can freely invest in any public or private company in India (except which is engaged in real estate, agricultural and plantation business) up to 1000 per cent without any obligation to associate Resident Indian in it any time.

11. NRIs can import raw material as well as machinery under the open General Licence Scheme of Government of India.

*Direct and Indirect Incentives*

These incentives include a wide variety of programmes aimed at easing the financing requirements of projects.

1. Remittances to India out of foreign incomes are exempted from income tax.
2. Exemption from wealth tax in case of investment in new equity issues of companies in the priority sectors. Income tax on the earnings from these investments is to be charged on a flat rate of 20 per cent.
3. Interest subsidy of 3 per cent on loans for tourist vehicles.
4. Increase in the depreciation rate from 40 per cent to 50 per cent on tourist vehicles.
5. Low Interest loans: A Tourism Finance Corporation has been set up with a capital of Rs.100 crores to provide loans to Tourism Industry at soft rates. (April 1989).
6. Interest Rebates: Tourism Finance Corporation of India, Industrial Finance Cooperation of India, IDBI and ICICI grant an interest rebate to hotels on the foreign exchange earnings. This interest rebate is equal to 20 per cent of the interest payable by them on institutional loan during any year. The interest rebate on foreign exchange earnings for hotels has been evolved on the basis of type of hotel whether Five Star or any other.

   (i) Five Star Hotels: They are entitled for 20 per cent interest rebate if their foreign exchange earnings in the particular year exceed 50 per cent of their total earnings.

(ii) Other hotels (2/3 Star-hotels): They are eligible for an interest rebate of 20 per cent if their foreign exchange earnings constitute 25 per cent more of their total turnover during the particular year.

7. Infrastructure Assistance:

   (a) Under Appendix I of the Income Tax Rules, 1962—buildings used as hotels are eligible for depreciation at the rate 20 per cent with effect from 2.4.1987 (assessment year 1988-89). In respect of furniture and fitting used in hotels, a higher rate of depreciation of 15 per cent has been provided under item II92) of Appendix I to the Income Tax Rules,1862 as against the general rate of 10 per cent.

8. Lease backs: The Chief Controller of Imports and Exports has made the lease financing facility available now to hotels for imports of equipments. This would be applicable to hotel approved by the department of tourism.

9. A market development fund has been approved in principle by the Ministry of Tourism. This would be a major budgetary support extended to hotels and travel agencies in setting up the required infrastructure.

10. Interest subsidy: In order to encourage construction of budget hotels, the government has decided to increase the rate of interest subsidy presently admissible on loans granted by the Industrial Finance Corporation of India for hotel projects from 1 per cent in the case of 1 and 2 star category hortels. The interest subsidy on 3-star hotels will continue to be 1 per cent while in the case of 4 and 5 star categories. It has been discontinued. The ceiling of Rs. 75 lakhs on which interest subsidy is presently admissible in the case of each loan remains unchanged.

11. Budget Allocation: Government has increased the plan outlay tremendously for tourism development. It was Rs. 21 lakhs in Second Five Year Plan (1956-61), Rs. 34 crores in Fourth Five Year Plan (1969-74) and Rs.120 crores in the Seventh Five Year Plan (1985-90).

12. MRTP Act: Hotels are exempted from the purview of section 21 and 22 of the MRTP Act.

Applications for automatic approval for foreign investment or technology agreements and/or management contracts can be made to the Reserve Bank of India who will accord automatic approval and the entrepreneurs can approach authorised dealers for release of foreign exchange. Agreements which involve a variation in the parameters will be considered on merits by the Foreign Investment Promotion Board.

**Incentives Announced by the Finance Minister during Budget Speech (1997-98)**

1. Section 80 IA of Income Tax Act 1961 has been reintroduced. Consequently all hotels which start operating between 1.4.1997 and 31.3.2002 will be eligible for income tax deductions as under:-
   (a) Hotels located in the hilly areas, rural areas, places of pilgrimage or a specified place of tourist importance will be eligible to 50 per cent deductions from the profits/gains.
   (b) In respect of hotels located in other places, the deductions allowed are 30 per cent only.

   The above benefits have been extended to the hotels for a period of 10 years and these benefits are not available for the hotels located in the metropolis like Mumbai, Delhi, Chennai and Kolkata.
2. The Expenditure Tax has been waived off in respect of the hotels located in hilly areas or rural areas or a place of pilgrimage or a specified place of tourist importance w.e.f. 1.4.1999.
3. The Import duty on the project equipment needed by the hotels was 35 per cent, which has now been reduced to 25 per cent.
4. The Import duty on specified speciality food items used by the foreign tourists have been reduced from 50 per cent to 25 per cent.

The Finance Minister in his Budget speech has also made a mention for simplification of the section 37 of Income Tax Act which would also help in the promotion of Tourism amongst other sectors of the economy. Further reduction in Capital Gains

Tax from 20 per cent to 10 per cent in respect of NRIs and financial Institutions will give impetus to the investment in tourism sector. There is also a reference to the proposed amendment in the Urban Land Ceiling Act, which could indirectly help in the identification of the Hotels sites.

The Budget 2002 has made further advancements towards this direction. Through this budget it appears that—

India's hospitality industry, after years of deliberation with innumerable bureaucrats and government babus, now has the right to wear that satisfied smile proudly for it has achieved the inevitable, a decent enough mention in the budget speech. It was a pleasant surprise for the fraternity, as there was not only a mention of this industry in Yashwant Sinha's 2002 Budget, but also an offering of more sops and opportunities than it has ever received in its long history. Many feel that this definitely is an affirmation of the fact to what the Indian government seems to have woken up to - the reality that tourism and hospitality are the 'growth sectors' of the future.

If we take a look at the factors that will directly or indirectly effect Indian hospitality and in doing so also puts a simple question out to the industry; 'What does the Budget mean to us?

We find in general the increase in the plan outlay for tourism by 50 per cent crore in 2002-03 and the proposed development of six tourism circuits is expected to have a positive impact on the hospitality industry.

The increase in the outlay, is Sinha's only sop that will have effect right through the industry. Considering the size of the country and industry it has to cover, the increase is realistically insignificant. But still, hospitality operations, big and small, in some way or the other are expected to benefit from it.

- The income tax incentive under section 80-IB of the Income Tax Act, for units setting up and operating large convention centres constructed during April 1, 2002 to March 31, 2005 offers a deduction of 50 per cent of the profits for the first five years from the date of commencing operations.

The 80-IB rebate is expected to have a strong and positive impact on a limited number hotel companies, especially those in the four and five-star categories. From incentives offered under

80-IB, of the major hotel companies, East India Hotels Ltd (EIH) with its Trident, Bandra Kurla Complex, Mumbai and the Indian Hotels Company Ltd's (IHCL) upcoming properties in New Delhi and Hyderabad, are expected to benefit. Other players in the industry, like Le-Meridien in Kochi, Jaypee Hotels' Agra venture and the Marriott International's recently inaugurated Renaissance, Mumbai, are some of the other operations with large convention centres most likely to benefit from the rebate.

- Additional depreciation of 15 per cent is allowable for new plant and machinery acquired on or after April 1, 2002, for the setting up of a new unit or for expanding the installed capacity of an existing unit by at least 25 per cent.

While the April 1 time frame may look to have escaped many properties currently under construction or renovation, the reverse may actually be true. For once promoters may be grateful for September 11, whose effect on business cause many to postpone planned renovations and repairs.

All new hotel projects are expected to benefit from this as it will give them the additional flexibility of writing off carried forward losses and thus improving profitability in the long run. It is also expected to have a direct impact on the bottom-line of new hotel properties and hotels undertaking major renovations.

**Accommodation**

*Budget Hotels*

- Sections three and five (Hotel Expenditure Tax, HET) of the Expenditure-tax Act, has been amended to make the provisions of the Act applicable only to rooms charges and only where such charges for any unit of residential accommodation are Rs. 3,000 or more per day. This amendment will take effect from June 1, 2002.

The increase in the lower threshold limit of the HET to a room tariff of Rs. 3,000 per day from Rs. 2,000 per room per day, is expected to have a positive impact on budget segment of hotels. The profit margins of this segment of hotels are expected to improve for two direct reasons; an expected increase in the tariff rates, a resultant increase in the average room rates.

Even-though budget hotels offering rooms on single occupancies are expected to benefit from this, a majority of hoteliers have called this move an eyewash because of a change in the language used in the amended provision. Sinha dropped the term 'per person' in favour of 'per room', which has actually brought down the per person per room rate down to Rs 1,500 from the earlier of Rs 2,000. However, the benefit is undoubtedly there and lies with those accommodation operations that have high corporate guest turnover as these guests usually travel in singles. The amended HET allows for a hike in the rack rate (which is expected across the board) with no fear of competition and tax.

*Luxury Hotels*

- Section 80HHD is a percentage deduction available to the business of a hotel, tour operator or travel agent, in respect of earnings in convertible foreign exchange from services provided to foreign tourists. The new bill seeks to enhance the rate of deduction of section 80HHD in the following manner, for assessment year 2003-04, 25 per cent of profits from services to foreign tourists and further 25 per cent of such profits as are transferred to the reserve, thereby raising the overall deduction from 40 to 50 per cent. For assessment year 2004-05, the enhancement is for 15 per cent of profits and 15 per cent of reserve, thereby taking the overall deduction from 20 to 30 per cent. This amendment will take effect from April 1, 2003.

The increase in the 80HHD deduction which is an income tax concession is expected to have a positive impact on the net profits of hotel companies, as close to 50 per cent of total properties which are actually dependent on international guests, is in foreign currency.

An amended Section 80HHD will go down extremely well with two big players; Asian Hotels and Hotel Leela Venture, as compared with the other major players in the industry. These two earn cent 70 per cent of their revenue in foreign currency.

**Food and Beverage**

- The exemption of service tax on services provided by hotels has been extended by another year to March 31, 2003.

The extension will most definitely have a positive impact on hotel companies as it will help release some of the tax pressure for another year. Most hotels stand to benefit from this, even though the industry average on percentage of earnings from such services is around five to six per cent, the final amount is quite substantial.

The exemption of the HET of 10 per cent on F&B and minor operating divisions such as telephone services, laundry, health club and the business centre, is expected to have a positive impact on hotel companies, albeit limited (F&B and others account for around 45 per cent of a hotel's total income.) As a result, margins on these services are expected to improve.

Of the major hotel companies, ITC Hotels is expected to benefit more from exemption of the hotel expenditure tax, as it derives over 55 per cent of its total hotel income through the F&B and MOD segments.

**Wine and Spirits**

The reduction in the customs duty on imported liquor from 210 per cent, to 182 per cent, and the rationalization of the countervailing duty (CVD) on wine and liquor, is expected to have a positive impact on hotel companies, especially those in the premium segment.

# Eight

# Fundamentals of Research in Tourism and Leisure Planning

In this study we examine what Research is, who does it and why and what is the role of Research in Tourism and Leisure Planning and Management process. To become familiar with world of Research it is important to know how it is structured and how it is produced. What is Research and what are its fundamentals? Most relevant and applied definition comes from sociologist Nerbert Elias in 1986 and much has been added afterwards by succeeding researchers. According to Elias, the aim of Research is the same as in all sciences, i.e., to make known something previously unknown to human beings. In other words, it is advance and improve human knowledge or make it more certain or better fitting.

Making known something unknown could cover a number of activities varying from job of a journalist to a detective. In his definition Elias also mentions that it is a scientific tool which is used to advance or improve human knowledge. This feature probably distinguishes it from other investigating activities that is of journalists and detectives.

## Perspectives of Research

Research with this aim can be studied in three perspectives:

*1. Social Science Research*

Research which is carried out using the methods and traditions of social sciences particularly if they are related to tourism and leisure management. Social sciences differ from natural sciences like chemistry, physics in a sense that social sciences deal with people and people are less predictable than non-human phenomena. If we put it differently study of people is not purely passive subject because people can be aware of the research being conducted about them and they can also affect the results of the Research as they may change their behaviour accordingly.

*2. Scientific Research*

This kind of research is carried out within rules and conventions of sciences. This means it is based on logic and reason as well as systematic examination of evidence. It contributes to a cumulative body of knowledge about a field or topic.

*3. Applied Research*

This is carried out in a situation where we need to find out solution to problems arising in field of policy, planning and management and these are also closely related to tourism and leisure management.

Over the years three types of Research are being practised by researchers, viz.:

| | *Kind of Research* | *Job Performed* |
|---|---|---|
| (i) | Descriptive Research | Finding out |
| (ii) | Explanatory Research | Explaining |
| (iii) | Evaluative Research | Evaluating. |

In some cases only one of these is applied but in majority of cases two or more of approaches are applied in the same project. In Tourism and Leisure Descriptive Research is more common because this is a relatively new field and there is a need to 'map' the territory. In this field, therefore, much of descriptive research can be described as 'exploratory' for it merely discovers patterns of behaviour and explanation is left util later or to other researchers.

Another reason for so much of application of Descriptive Research in Tourism and Leisure is due to the fact that levels of participation in different Leisure activities change over time; importance of different tourism markets changes; the pattern of participation among different social groups changes. Therefore, a lot of focus is laid upon monitoring basic pattern of behaviour. It is mandatory of providers of services in tourism and leisure and respond to rapidly changing market conditions whether or not they can be explained or understood, although understanding and explaining of these rapid changes in patterns is welcomed by all concerned. Why is there not much use of Explanatory or Applied

Research. Because in Applied Research often, though not always, there exists a gap between research project and policy planning or management activity. It means a company may initiate a market profile study but when it comes to use of the results of this research for marketing or planning purposes, it would be a separate exercise and research team is not involved. Role of research team is simply limited to a descriptive study.

Explanatory Research moves beyond description to the alarming issue of casualty. It is only one side of same coin to discover that 'A' has increased and 'B' has decreased but to establish that rise in 'A' has been the result of fall in 'B', is much more a rigorous and demanding task. To establish casualty or likelihood of casualty researchers need to collect, analyze and interpret data carefully.

However, most relevant or applied is Evaluative Research which arises from the part of policy and management decision-making process, making judgements on the success or effectiveness of policies or programmes, i.e., whether a particular leisure activity is meeting desired satisfaction level; or whether a particular tourism promotion campaign has been cost-effective Evaluative Research is yet to well develop in field of leisure and tourism.

**Role of Research in Planning and Management**

All organisations engage in planning what to do in future and managing resources to achieve their goals. Research has a specific role to play in all six steps of planning management process:

1. Setting up of goals and objectives
2. Identification and evaluation of alternative course of action
3. Choosing preferred alternatives
4. Implementing the preferred course of action
5. Controlling and monitoring the implementation process
6. Feedback and adjustment.

Planning in Management of Tourism and Leisure activities can be seen as a process of deciding what tourism/leisure services should be provided in future (Step 1-3). Step 4-6 can be termed as management or implementation of plans. Although planning is usually associated in public perception with government bodies, it is also an activity undertaken by private sector while the latter are only concerned with their own activities, government bodies often have a wider responsibility to provide a planning framework as well as management approaches for activities of many public and private sector organizations. Research certainly has a role to play certainly at each step:

*Step 1*

To help decision makers in deciding what they wish to achieve by providing information on current problems.

*Step 2-3*

By identifying and evaluating alternative courses of action best suited to achieving the set goal and objectives Research can also provide vital information on view of public and likely consequences of alternative courses of action.

*Step 4-6*

Through monitoring and evaluating the implementation process and its effects in the form of providing feedback by either confirming the success of the operation or indicating need for modifications.

**Role of Academics in Research for Leisure and Tourism**

Generally academics become involved in funded research of a practically orientated nature when their own interests coincide with those of the agency concerned. For instance an academic may be interested in ways of measuring what motivates people to engage in certain outdoor recreation activities and this could coincide with an outdoor recreation agency's need for research to assist in developing a marketing strategy. Some academics specialize in applied areas, such as marketing or planning, so they are very often in a better position to attract funding from the 'practical world'. Academics may use funds to employ one or more research assistants who may also be registered for a higher degree, usually a PhD. This leads to the second academic source of research, namely students.

PhD and Masters degree students can be a major source of research. Journals periodically publish lists of thesis and dissertations completed in the area (Van Doren and Stubbles 1976, Van Doren and Solan 1979, Jafari and Aaser 1988). Thesis from most USA and UK universities are available on microfiche.

PhD theses are the most significant form of student research, but research done by Masters degree and graduate diploma students and even undergraduates can be a useful contribution to knowledge. Leisure and tourism are not generally well endowed with research funds, so even, for example, a small survey conducted by a group of undergraduates on a particular leisure activity or in a particular locality, or a thorough review of an area of literature, may be of considerable use or interest to others.

Government and commercial organizations often have their own in-house research organizations – for example, the UK Office of Population Censuses and Surveys, the Australian Bureau of Tourism Research and the US Forest Service Experiment Stations. Commercial organizations in leisure and tourism tend to rely on consultants for their social, economic and market research, although equipment manufacturers, for instance in sport, may conduct their own research for product development.

Research conducted by commercial bodies is usually confidential but that conducted by government agencies is generally available to the public. Research reports from these organizations can therefore be important sources of knowledge, especially of a more practically orientated nature. For example, in nearly every developed country some government agency takes responsibility for conducting nation-wide surveys of leisure participation rates and tourism patterns. This is research which no other organization would have the resources to undertake.

Consultants exist to offer their research and advisory services to the leisure and tourism industries. Some consultancy organizations are large, multinational companies involved in accountancy, management and property development consultancy generally, who establish specialized units covering the leisure and/or tourism field. Examples are Coopers and Lybrand and Price-Waterhouse. But there are many other, smaller, specialized organizations in the consultancy field. Some academics operate consultancy companies as a 'side-line', either because of academic interest in a particular area or to supplement incomes or both.

Managers in leisure and tourism who recognize the full extent of the management process should see research as very much part of their responsibilities. Since most of the readers of this book will be actual or trainee managers, this is a most important point to recognize. Successful management depends on good information. Much information—for example, sales figures—comes to the manager as a matter of routine and does not require 'research'. However, the creative utilization of such data—for example, to establish market trends—may amount to research. Other types of information can only be obtained by means of specific research projects. In some areas of leisure and tourism management even the most basic information must be obtained by research. For example, while managers of theatres or resorts routinely receive information on the level of use from sales figures, this is not the case for the manager of an urban park or a beach; to gain information on the number of users of the latter it is necessary to engage in a specific data gathering exercise. Such data gathering may not be very sophisticated and some would say that it does not qualify as 'research', but in the sense that it involves 'finding out', and sometimes 'explaining', it is research for the purposes of this book.

Most managers need to carry out—or commission—research if they also want to find out additional information about their users or customers, for example, where they come from (the 'catchment area' of the facility) or their socio-economic characteristics. Research is also a way of finding out customers' evaluations of the facility or service.

It might be argued that managers do not themselves need research skills since they can always commission consultants to carry out the research. However, managers will be better able to commission good research and evaluate the results if they are familiar with the research process themselves, and not all managers work in an ideal world where funds exist to commission research: often the only way managers can get research done is to do it themselves.

To conclude we can say that Research in Tourism and Leisure is still to play its role as it has done in other fields. Although lot of funds are being provided by universities as well as commercial organizations but results of such researches are very focussed to suit only the interests of the funding organization. To obtain maximum results we need to look towards research as a tool with solutions to all problems related to development and promotion of tourism. If this tool is used in right direction it can end up in giving limitless results but if not used properly can lead our efforts to wrong direction and as a result we will miss our target.

*Nine*

# Tourism through Plans, Expectations and Apprehensions

Tourism industry is a limitless industry with immense growth potential. It is number two next only to oil industry and third in India next to Gems and Garment industry. Tourism has tremendous positive impacts on the economic and social aspects of the host country specially in case of developing countries. So, to reap the economic and social benefits of tourism every country is vying with each other to woo more domestic and international tourists. India is no exception, though her achievements are not astonishing. But if we see the figures available we can see that tourist arrivals have increased manifolds from 1960 to1993 and from a meagre figure of 16829 in 1960 to 2.12 million in 1993. But this growth which has been achieved does not seem remarkable as compared to other South-East Asian nations like Singapore, Malaysia, Hong Kong and Thailand, etc.

**First Five Year Plan (1951-556)**

During the First Five Year Plan (1951-56), tourism was not a conspicuous economic activity and that tourism was not given a specific allocation. However, during this period many new promotional schemes for tourism were taken up. During this period, tourism promotion offices of India were established at places like: New York, Sri Lanka, Australia, London and Paris. This was as a result of Sir Sarjent Committee report. This commission was set up in 1945 by Government of India under the chairmanship of Sir John Sarjent, the then Educational Advisor to Government of India. With the main objective to survey the potentialities of developing tourist traffic in the country.

The committee submitted its report in 1946 suggesting that it would be in the interest of our country to promote tourism from both within and overseas by all possible available means. The report opined that every aspect of business could benefit greatly by an influx of tourists. One of the major recommendations of the committee was to undertake tourism promotion on a methodological basis by a separate organization. As result of this a separate tourist traffic branch was set up in the Ministry of Transport in 1949 with the main objective of development of tourist in India.

**Department of Tourism and Its Branches**

During 1955-56 the tourist traffic wing had four branches:

(A) *Tourist Traffic Section*—to look after subjects like development of both internal and external tourist traffic, legislative matters, five year plans, travel agencies, hotels, rest houses, facilitation, tourist statistics and International conferences on tourism and references relating to UN and it's agencies.

(B) *Tourism Administration Section*—to deal with administrative work of tourist offices in India and abroad, budgeting, delegation of financial powers to tourist officers, opening of new tourist offices abroad and their periodical inspection.

(C) *Tourist Publicity Section*—to deal with publication of tourist literature such as pamphlets, guide books, posters, issuing of advertisement, and participation in exhibitions and fairs.

(D) *Distribution Section*—to deal with the distribution of publicity material published by publicity section.

These branches were functioning under the Deputy Secretary and two Under Secretaries with Ministry of Shipping and Transport. At this stage there was a proposal for setting up a Directorate General of Tourism. During this period foreign tourist arrivals registered a compound growth of 8.6 per cent per annum and foreign exchange earnings from tourism registered 10 per cent growth.

**TABLE 9.1**
**PERCENTAGE CHANGE IN TOURIST ARRIVALS**

| *Year* | *Tourist arrivals* | *Increase* |
|---|---|---|
| 1951 | 16829 | |
| 1955 | 33269 | 29.7 per cent |

*Source*: Department of Tourism, Government of India, New Delhi.

### Second Five Year Plan (1956-61)

The Second Five Year Plan (1956-61) recognized tourism as a significant industry and made a small but specific allocation for tourism. A modest allocation of Rs. 3.36 crores was made for the development of tourism infrastructure.

**TABLE 9.2**
**BUDGET ALLOCATION FOR TOURISM**

*Rs. In Lakhs*

| *Year* | *Total Outlay* | *Central sector* | *State sector* | *Exp.* | *Central sector* | *State sector* |
|---|---|---|---|---|---|---|
| 1957-62 | 336-38 | 157.94 | 178.44 | 221.31 | 86.885 | 134.425 |

*Source*: Department of Tourism, Government of India, New Delhi.

The plan adopted a method of classification of tourism projects into categories.

The most remarkable achievement during this plan was the establishment of Department of Tourism at centre in 1958. The new department was put under the charge of Director General and 4 Directors in Charge of Administration, Publicity, Travel Relation and Planning and Development.

**TABLE 9.3**
**TOURISM GROWTH DURING SECOND FIVE YEAR PLAN**

| *Year* | *Tourist Arrivals* | *Percentage growth* |
|---|---|---|
| 1955 | 33,269 | |
| 1960 | 1,23,095 | 27.0 |

*Source*: Department of Tourism, Government of India, New Delhi.

**Third Five Year Plan (1961-66)**

The Third Plan made an allocation of Rs. 8 crores, against a small allocation, considering the vastness of the industry.

**TABLE 9.4**
**TOURISM OUTLAY AND EXPENDITURE (1962-67)**

*Rs. In Lakhs*

| *Year* | *Total Outlay* | *Central Outlay* | *State Outlay* | *Actual Exp.* | *Exp. Central* | *Exp. State* |
|---|---|---|---|---|---|---|
| 1962-67 | 800 | 350 | 450 | 510.45 | 145.12 | 365.15 |

*Source:* Department of Tourism, Government of India, New Delhi.

During this Plan the infrastructural facilities that were commissioned in Plan II were completed. New works at selected centre initiated after the recommendation of the Jha Committee.

**TABLE 9.5**
**TOURISM PROMOTION AFTER JHA COMMITTEE IMPLEMENTATION**

| *Year* | *Arrival* | *Percentage increase over year* |
|---|---|---|
| 1963 | 147900 | |
| 1966 | 159603 | 7.9 |
| 1967 | 179563 | 12.5 |
| 1968 | 188820 | 5.2 |
| 1969 | 244729 | 29.6 |

*Source:* Department of Tourism, Government of India, New Delhi.

More significant event took place during this period. The India Tourism Development Corporation (ITDC) was set up and the Ministry of Tourism and Civil Aviation was established with two full fledged departments viz—

Department of Tourism and
Department of Civil Aviation

India Tourism Development Corporation was set up on the recommendations of the Jha Committee (1963). It recommended that the public sector should assume a more active and positive role in promoting tourism. The Ministry of Tourism was put under the charge of a full time minister. So, roughly after 18 years that the subject of tourism was accorded a separate entity and became independent of Transport and Shipping Ministry.

**Fourth Five Year Plan (1970-75)**

Under the Fourth Plan broad approach was to improve the tourist facilities with a view to promoting destinational traffic as distinct from transit traffic. Integrated development of selected areas and encouraging charter traffic was adopted. Emphasis was laid down on provision of accommodation, transport and recreational facilities. Efforts were concentrated in areas where there was an identified large flow of foreign tourist traffic.

**TABLE 9.6**
**ARRIVAL OF TOURISTS DURING THE FOURTH FIVE YEAR PLAN**

| *Year* | *Arrivals* | *Percentage increase over past year* |
|---|---|---|
| 1969 | 244727 | |
| 1970 | 280821 | 14.8 |
| 1971 | 300995 | 7.2 |
| 1972 | 342950 | 13.9 |
| 1973 | 409895 | 19.5 |
| 1974 | 433161 | 3.2 |

*Source:* Department of Tourism, Government of India, New Delhi.

Under this plan new guidelines were prepared wherein the central Department of Tourism completely took over the planning and development of facilities suitable for overseas tourists. While the state governments were assisted to develop facilities for domestic tourists. State governments were free to shape their plans the way they liked. No matching subsidy of 50 per cent was given by the centre to the state departments of Tourism. The arrangement was not only good for the states to develop their domestic plans (as a result we see that the total outlay for the state was 1168 lakhs but the actual expenditure was 1631 lakhs) but it also gave central government Department of Tourism an opportunity to concentrate on international markets and enhance its share in total tourism market.

Besides several constraints, 16 more youth hostels on international standard were constructed and furnished in different parts of the country to serve as catalystic models to the states to construct similar hostels elsewhere. Similarly several forest lodges, tourist bungalows were built.

### Fifth Five Year Plan (1974-78)

The preamble to the Fifth Five Year Plan for tourism explained the role of the centre and state governments. In this plan the centre concentrated on issues related to promotion of international tourism and state concentrated on subject related to development of projects regarding domestic tourism.

**TABLE 9.7**
**THE TOURIST ARRIVAL DURING FIFTH FIVE YEAR PLAN**

| *Year* | *Arrivals* | *Percentage increase over past year* |
|---|---|---|
| 1973 | 409895 | |
| 1974 | 433161 | 3.2 |
| 1975 | 465275 | 10.0 |
| 1976 | 533951 | 14.8 |
| 1977 | 640422 | 19.9 |
| 1978 | 747995 | 160.8 |

*Source:* Department of Tourism, Government of India, New Delhi.

**TABLE 9.8**
**FOREIGN EXCHANGE EARNINGS DURING FIFTH FIVE YEAR PLAN**

*(In Rs. millions)*

| *Year* | *Earnings* | *Percentage increase over past year* |
|---|---|---|
| 1972 | 577 | |
| 1973 | 711 | 23.2 |
| 1974 | 932 | 31.1 |
| 1975 | 1024 | 11.8 |
| 1976 | 2250 | 115.9 |
| 1977 | 2830 | 25.8 |
| 1978 | 3300 | 16.6 |

*Source:* Department of Tourism, Government of India, New Delhi.

**TABLE 9.9**
**TOURIST ARRIVAL FIGURES FOR 1977-80**

| *Year* | *Arrival* | *Percentage change* | *Foreign* | *Percentage change* |
|---|---|---|---|---|
| 1977 | 640422 | | 2830 | |
| 1978 | 747995 | 16.8 | 3300 | 16.6 |
| 1979 | 764781 | 2.2 | 3840 | 16.3 |
| 1980 | 800150 | 4.6 | 4820 | 25.5 |

*Source:* Department of Tourism, Government of India, New Delhi.

**Sixth Five Year Plan (1980-85)**

The major objectives of the investment in the tourism sector were to optimize the use of existing capacity and to increase substantially the tourist accommodation in public and private sectors. It was decided to adopt a selective approach with a view to maximize the returns on investments. In the development of tourism, selected travel circuit approach was followed and marketing facilities were sought to be provided. A close coordination in regard to provision of facilities in the central states and private sectors in the same areas and location was to be maintained to obtain optimum results from the available resources. This approach would provide flexibility in offering a mixed tourism package, help to recognize traffic and promote repeat visits to increase the overall volume of traffic. The broad divisions of responsibility between central and state governments continued to be on the basis that larger schemes meant for foreign tourism were to be cared by the central government and the schemes meant for the domestic tourism to be developed by the state government concerned. An outlay of 187.46 crores had been made in the plan. The first ever Tourism Policy of the country was announced during 1982 which specified development objectives and provided an action plan based on "travel circuit" concept to maximise the benefits of tourism.

Some of the important features of the sixth plan were :

(a) for the first time integrated approach was adopted for the promotion of tourism, i.e., infrastructural facilities of Rail, Road and Air so as to smoothen the movement of tourism in and from India.

(b) for the first time tourists figure was projected although highly unfeasible.

(c) Concept of travel circuits (16 travel circuits were identified) and that of tourist centres/villages were identified.

The travel circuits approach aims at spreading tourism geographically and to enable every state in India to offer something to the visitor.

**TABLE 9.10**
**TOURISTS ARRIVAL IN 1980-85**

| *Year* | *Arrival* | *Percentage change* |
|---|---|---|
| 1979 | 764781 | |
| 1980 | 800150 | 4.6 |
| 1981 | 853148 | 6.6 |
| 1982 | 860178 | 0.8 |
| 1983 | 884731 | 2.9 |
| 1984 | 835803 | 0.6 |
| 1985 | 836908 | 0.2 |

*Source:* Department of Tourism, Government of India, New Delhi.

**Seventh Five Year Plan (1985-90)**

The travel sector was accorded the status of an industry and a National Committee on Tourism was set up by the government in 1986 to evaluate the relevance of tourism and draw up a long-term plan for its development. It submitted its recommendations on the basis of which TFCI (Tourism Finance Corporation of India) was set up to finance tourism projects.

During the Seventh Five Year Plan tourism received significant notice and greater importance was attached. An approach paper approved by National Development Council in July 1984 included the following thrust areas for development :

(a) Development of selected tourist circuit centres which are popular with the tourist instead of spreading limited resources then over a large number of circuit centres.

(b) Diversification of tourism to India from traditional sightseeing tours centred primarily on places of cultural tourism interest towards the most rapidly growing holiday tourism market within the framework of the country's milieu, environmental and socio-cultural implications of tourism projects.

(c) Development of non-traditional areas such as – trekking, winter sports, wild life tourism, beach resort tourism. To exploit the tourism resources of the Himalaya, the vast coast line with sandy beaches and abundant sunshine and wild life to attract more tourists and to stretch their period of stay in the country.

(d) To exploit advantages of India's unique places as cultural tourism destination and to utilize tourism as a major force in support of conservation of national heritage.

(e) Exploration of new tourist generating markets, particularly, in the Middle East, South East and East Asian countries who have a broad spectrum of cultural affinity with Indian providing scope for longer ethnic tourism.

(f) Launching of a national image building and marketing plan in key markets by pooling resources of the various public and private agencies in spite of independent and disjoined efforts presently undertaken by these organizations to project a better image of the country which could yield abundant fallout for tourism growth and also be of advantage in trade and commerce.

(g) Provision of inexpensive but clean accommodation at different places of tourists interests.

(h) Consolidations of operations rather than expansion and improvements in the service efficiency of public sector corporation in the tourism sector.

(i) Streamlining of facilitation procedures for passengers at the airports, so that formalities and time taken to complete them is minimal.

In 1988 National Committee on Tourism (NCT) was set-up by the Planning Commission. The objectives were:

(i) Potential of tourism should be fully exploited for economic development of the country.

(ii) Expansion of the movements from developed to developing countries must be included in the international programme of development coordination.

(iii) The development of this industry should best be left to the initiative of private sector.

(iv) State should concentrate on planning broad strategies of tourism development, provision of fiscal and monetary incentives to catalyse private sector investment and to devise an effective regulatory and supervisory mechanism to protect the interest of the individual.

(v) The interaction between tourism and cultural pollution and environmental spoilation is complex and requires sensitive handling.

(vi) To formulate policies on tourism special attention is required.

(vii) Since dynamics of tourism are unique so it requires a high degree of coordination and efficient delivery system.

(viii) Development strategy for tourism sector should be based on the principal of low cost economy, higher levels of productivity and promoting competition.

(ix) Selective approach must be adopted since it is multi-destination country.

(x) New emerging markets like West Europe and North America must be tapped to increase the share from 0.33 per cent.

(xi) Projected 7 per cent of per annum growth in arrival during the eight and ninth plan. Only then 2.75 to 3 million target can be achieved.

The main thrust in the seventh plan of the centre is to vigorously promote domestic tourism and move towards diversification of overseas tourism. In India instead of merely concentrating on cultural tourism interests, greater emphasis on leisure and action oriented tourism should be made.

The Department of Tourism is paying special emphasis on creation of facilities for domestic tourists so as to promote movement of people from one region to another. To provide budget accommodation for domestic tourists, Yatri Niwas are being constructed at a number of places in the country to provide clean functional accommodation available to budget travellers at reasonable price. Since pilgrims constituted a fairly large chunk of the domestic tourists, neat functional and low priced accommodation is being provided for them in the form of *Yatrikas* by the Bhartiya Yatri Vikas Samiti. Under cultural tourism, to avoid unplanned and irregular growth to maintain the environmental characteristics of the Archaeological centres, the land use master plans of major historical monuments were got prepared through Town and Country Planning Organizations and the National Institute of Designs, Ahmedabad.

**TABLE 9.11**
**TOURISTS ARRIVAL IN 1986-90**

| *Year* | *Arrival* | *Percentage change* | *Foreign exchange* |
|---|---|---|---|
| 1984 | 835803 | | |
| 1985 | 836908 | 0.2 | 1189.0 |
| 1986 | 1.08 m | 29.1 | 1607.0 |
| 1987 | 1.16 m | 7.8 | 1856.0 |
| 1988 | 1.24 m | 6.5 | 2103.0 |
| 1989 | 1.32 m | 7.8 | 2456.5 |
| 1990 | 1.79 m | 0.5 | 2444.1 |

*Source:* Department of Tourism, Government of India, New Delhi.

Besides promotion of domestic tourism in the sixth and the seventh plans number of measures were taken up including wide publicity abroad, establishment of equipment hire shops, training of guides, setting up of mountain communication network system and rescue patrols, etc.

**Eighth Five Year Plan (1991-95)**

The most important event of Eighth Five Year Plan was Visit India Year 1991 – aimed at future development.

To project India as a destination of tourists. With the aim of replenishing the traditional image of India as a cultural destination, with more vibrant image of a country with a diversified tourism product.

*Objective of the Plan*

(a) national awareness of the socio-economic benefits of tourism;
(b) improvements of international image of India;
(c) removal of bottlenecks in promotion of international tourism in a concerted manner.

In order to achieve these objectives and to promote all parts of India as a tourist destinations emphasis was laid on:

(i) To project new tourist destinations and activities;
(ii) To promote shopping as a major attraction;
(iii) To stress the cultural richness of India and also highlight its suitability as a year round destination.
(iv) To promote India as a major conference/convention centre.

During February 1994 the Union government opened up the skies for private operators by repealing the Air Corporation Act and help promote tourism industry a big foreign exchange earner which will still remain to be fully explored and exploited. This repealment of ordinance enabled Air Taxi Operators (ATO's) to turn themselves into scheduled airlines with effect from 1st March 1994. This will not only create an atmosphere of competition but also ensure that the services offered are the best and for this the airlines and the related agencies are sought to play a very vital role.

## Planning Tourism

*9th 5-year Plan Takes Stock of Tourism Industry*

Tourism has emerged as one of world's largest industries and the fastest-growing sector of the world economy; tourism receipts account for a little over 8 per cent of world export of goods and more than 34 per cent of world export of services. In India, however, the sector has failed to receive due importance on the country's development agenda.

Employing only 2.4 per cent of the Indian workforce, the vast potential of tourism as an instrument of employment generation and poverty alleviation has tended to remain largely unutilised. Of the 625 million world tourist arrivals in 1998, India received a meager 2.36 million or 0.38 per cent of the total world tourist arrivals and only 0.62 per cent of world tourist receipts.

Compared to other countries in the region, India's performance in the sector has been rather poor. Major causes cited for this are lack of professionalism, unhygienic conditions, poor infrastructure, lack of easily accessible information, lack of safety, poor visitor experience, restrictive air transport policy, inadequate facilitation services multiplicity of taxes and the low priority accorded to tourism. However, despite its tiny share of world tourist arrivals, tourism in India has emerged as the second-largest foreign exchange earner for the country, even through the mainstay of the tourism industry in India continues to be domestic tourism.

Domestic tourists (excluding religious tourists), who stayed in accommodation establishments, increased from 109.2 million 1993 to 159.9 million in 1997, registering an annual rate of growth of 10 per cent. That growth rate declined to 9.35 in 1999 when an estimated 175.4 million domestic tourist visits were recorded. Foreign tourist arrivals to India grew from 1.82 million in 1992-93 to 2.33 million in 1996-97, registering an average annual growth rate of 6.37 per cent during the Eighth Five Year Plan Period. In the first two years of the Ninth Plan, the growth rate declined to 1.49 per cent and an estimated 2.40 million foreign tourist arrivals were recorded in 1998-99.

A very large proportion of the foreign tourists, that is, around 91.7 per cent, visited India for holidaying and sightseeing, followed by business travellers who constituted approximately 5.1 per cent of the visitors. Although international arrivals are a small proportion of world tourist arrivals, international tourists have the longest stay of 29 days in India. This is reflected in the proportion of revenues being higher than percentage of world tourist arrivals. Foreign exchange earnings during the Eighth Plan period surged from Rs. 6,060 crore in 1992-93 to Rs. 10,231 crore in 1996-97, achieving an annual growth rate of 13.99 per cent in the first two years of the Ninth Plan and earnings in 1998-99 were estimated at Rs. 12.604 crore. The sector provided direct employment to about 14.79 million people during 1998-99.

The Ninth Plan envisages the government playing a role of facilitator for private sector participation in the development of tourism. The Plan seeks to diversify the tourism product by encouraging rural and village tourism, pilgrim and spiritual tourism, adventure and eco tourism, indigenous and natural health tourism, heritage tourism and youth and senior citizen's packages. The outlay for the Central Sector in the Ninth Plan is Rs. 793.75 crore, comprising a budgetary support of Rs. 485.75 crore and internal and extra budgetary resources of Rs. 308 crore. The main schemes of the Ministry of Tourism relate to infrastructure development, human resource development and publicity and marketing.

To Conclude during 9th 5-year plan period following steps were undertaken:

- A National Policy on Tourism was formulated in 1982, focussing on the development of travel circuits, and assigned the responsibility of promoting international tourism to the central government and domestic tourism to the state governments.
- Tourism was given the status of an 'Industry' in 1986 and became eligible for several incentives and facilities including tax incentives, subsidies, priorities in the sanctioning of loans by the state and financial institutions, and preferences in providing electricity and water connection.
- Tourism was made a priority sector for foreign direct investment in 1991, making it eligible for automatic approvals up to 51 per cent of the equity.
- A National Strategy for Tourism Development was evolved in 1996, which advocated the strengthening of institutional set-ups in human resource development, setting up of an Advisory Board of Tourism Industry and Trade (which has since been set up), the integrated development of tourist destinations and the promotion of private sector in tourism development.
- Tourism was granted 'Export House' status in 1998 making

hotels, travel agents, tour operators and tourist transport operators eligible for such recognition entitling them to various incentives.

- In order to take advantage of the liberalised economic regime and the developments taking place around the world, a new National Tourism Policy is under consideration by the government.

# *Annexure 9.1*

# Draft of National Tourism Policy - 1997

The development plan for tourism during Eight Plan (1992-97) was based on the "National Action Plan for Tourism" presented in the Parliament on 5th May 1992. It proposed to achieve diversification of tourism product, accelerated growth of tourism infrastructure, effective marketing and promotional efforts in the overseas markets and removal of all impediments to tourism. A major component of the Action Plan was the development of all inclusive "Special Tourism Areas" and intensive development of selected circuits. The Action Plan did not specify the infrastructural requirements and the investments needed to meet the targets and the sources of funding for the same. The "Tourism Synergy Programme" enlisting the activities and infrastructural components to be provided by various agencies including the private sector and State Governments was thus prepared in 1993. It was further modified and converted into a "National Strategy for the Development of Tourism" during 1996. These documents were aimed at achieving a greater realisation of the importance of tourism, a consensus on the developmental needs, positive contribution of all the Infrastructural Departments on a coordinated manner, higher plan allocations and introduction of new schemes for accelerated development of tourism.

### Types of Tourism

*Domestic Tourism*

Travel for pilgrimage and learning has been an integral part of Indian culture ever since the beginning of its civilization. Several centres of learning and religious worship developed all over the country since ancient times. This gave further impetus to the mass movement of people from one place to another. Development of traditional industries and trade created the stream of business travellers. Several trading routes were established and traders started frequenting the centres of trade from distant places. The ancient rulers gave due recognition to these travellers and created many wayside facilities like inns, *sarais*, *dharamshalas* and caravans for their benefit. These formed the tourism infrastructure of India in those days. Thus, India has been experiencing massive movement of domestic tourists for several centuries.

A few centuries ago the Moghul rulers built luxurious palaces and enchanting gardens in places of natural scenic attraction. During the period of British rule in India, domestic tourism received a new direction and meaning due to the establishment of Railways and Export/Import houses at port towns introducing qualitative and quantitative changes in the Indian business tourism. In addition, the construction of circuit houses, dak bunglows and forest lodges provided the infrastructure for leisure and wild life tourism. Several hill stations were also developed during the period which became the core of Indian leisure tourism. The emergence of a large 'urban middle class' coupled with better transport and communication facilities has created a new class of holiday and leisure tourists in contemporary India. The National Action Plan for Tourism-1992 thus gave considerable emphasis on the development of domestic tourism including pilgrim tourism. Thus, domestic tourism has become the main stay of Indian tourism and it is likely to grow substantially during the coming years. The economic, social and cultural advantages of domestic tourism are:

- Domestic movement of people for non-migratory purposes constitutes shifts in consumer markets of variable importance and are catalysts of the national economy.
- It has extremely high social, cultural, educational and political value and true economic value, although still embryonic in some cases.
- It generates large-scale employment opportunities particularly in rural areas and restrains the exodus of people to large towns.
- The new job created to meet the needs of domestic tourists have a relatively low unit cost per job and it helps increase the number of jobs.

- Production methods for services demanded by domestic tourist generally remain simple and based on local materials.
- It also requires only simple installations infrastructure in transport, accommodation and catering which would take into account local cultural, political and historic traditions.
- It has the ability to sustain and maintain the tourism industry during lean periods of international tourism by providing an alternative for demand substitution.
- It contributes to an improved balancing of national economy through redistribution of national income and thus provides a better environment for the growth of both domestic and inbound tourism.
- It is the single unifying force which helps to achieve understanding between various linguistic, religious and communal groups living in different parts of the country. It, thus, contributes towards strengthening the fabric of national unity and cultural integration.

*Inbound Tourism*

Tourism is the world's largest export industry. In India also the foreign exchange earning from tourism is the third largest after readymade garments and Gem and Jewellery. Tourism receipts have been growing at a phenomenal rate in the recent years and it has become the single largest component of the services export. The projections available indicate that tourism would become the largest export industry in India too as it has already attained the top position in the world context. The other benefits of inbound tourism are:

- The projection of national image abroad, reduction of ideological gaps and enhancement of international understanding are generally better achieved through inbound tourism.
- Inbound tourism generates larger employment opportunities per tourist and leads to more income to local community.
- International tourists visiting interiors of the country for reasons of purity of environment and nature contributes

to the development of such areas particularly in backward regions.

- Inbound tourism has significant linkages with the art and artefacts of the country including handicrafts and thus contributes to the improvement of living conditions of village artisans.
- Expansion of inbound tourism also leads to the provision of better infrastructural facilities in specific areas and thus stimulates diversification and development of other industries.

Though India achieved substantial growth in international tourist arrivals since 1951, the share of India in the world tourist traffic still remains to be less than 0.4 per cent. It is, however, encouraging to note that the average duration of stay of inbound tourist in India is one of the highest in the world. Considering the dimensions of the country and the multitude of attractions it possesses the potential of India in attracting international tourist is yet to be realized. The perceived constraints in the expansion of tourism are inadequate infrastructure including poor accessibility and non-availability of trained manpower in sufficient number.

*Outbound Tourism*

A large number of Indians go abroad every year for various purposes including business, study, pilgrimage, pleasure, etc. The process of economic liberalization and growing affluence of people are likely to accelerate the outbound tourist traffic from India considerably. Though this aspect of tourism has not been the concern of the Department of Tourism so far, it has become necessary to recognize the phenomenon and evaluate its social and economic consequences. The volume of inbound traffic is also often linked to outbound tourism as international carriers have to depend on both for their operations.

**Objectives of Tourism Development**

The national objectives of tourism development are:-

(i) It becomes a unifying force nationally and internationally fostering better understanding through travel.

(ii) It gives a direction and opportunity to the people of the country through inbound, outbound and domestic tourism to understand the geographical and cultural diversity of nations and regions as well as the aspirations and viewpoints of others so as to bring about a greater national integration and cohesion.

(iii) It offers opportunities to the youth of the country not only for employment but also for taking up activities of nation building character like sports, adventure and the like.

(iv) It brings socio-economic benefits to the community and the State in terms of faster economic growth, larger employment opportunities, better income generation and foreign exchange earning, balanced development of backward areas and weaker sections, higher tax revenue to the State and causes sustainable human development.

(v) It becomes a positive force for the preservation and enrichment of our cultural heritage in all its manifestations and causes accretion and strength rather than damage to our social and cultural values.

(vi) It should also become a reason for better preservation and protection of our natural resources, environment and ecology.

(vii) It should become a major avenue for the people of India and other countries to see, feel and admire its magnificent attractions and achievements including natural beauty, geographical and cultural diversities, heritage of arts and crafts and industrial and scientific progress.

(viii) Above all, tourism should be able to project the quintessence of our culture so as to give our people a sense of unity and identity, a broadening of their intellectual, emotional and cultural horizon and a sense of belonging and pride and for the international traveller, tourism should create a better understanding of our land, people and culture.

**The Policy Framework — Guidelines**

The national policies with regard to tourism for achieving the objectives enumerated in this statement have to be consistent with the existing global scenario as well as national priorities and ethos. The policy should also take care of all.possible conflicts and ensure sustained growth of tourism on desired lines. Taking into account these considerations, the following policy guidelines have been formulated.

*Recognition*

The economic and social benefits of tourism and its importance as an instrument of economic growth have to be fully recognized by all sections of the society. There is still a belief that the potential of the tourism would be determined by the income levels of inhabitants and is basically a leisure industry not requiring the attention of planners and administrators. This belief based on information gap has systematically constrained the development of tourism in the country over the years. It would, therefore, be the policy of the Government to bridge this information gap through proper statistical documentation of the impact of tourism and its wide publicity to create awareness so that tourism is given due recognition and national priority.

*The Product*

Persons travelling to other places invariably seek a pleasant detectable experience on their trips. The most desired tourism product thus consists of :

- an environment of peace and stability.
- an assurance of safety and security.
- a friendly host society.
- an industry and a government that provide the requisite facilities promptly and efficiently.
- absence of extortion and hostility
- accessible tourist attractions
- an integrated system of physical infrastructure that does not fall. These include :
  - International air seat capacity
  - Internal transport system
  - Hotels and restaurants of quality
  - Entertainment and recreational avenues
  - Shopping and communication facilities
  - Well preserved monuments with tourist amenities

- Basic amenities like drinking water, toilets, refreshment centres, etc. at the tourist sites.

*The policy, therefore, will be to work towards creating such a tourism product to the extent possible.*

*The Responsibility: A Multi-Dimensional Activity*

Tourism consists of several goods and services consumed by the tourists at their places of visit. These are provided by a multitude of establishments and agencies functioning at various levels. Tourists also have to come in contact with various government agencies and a number of infrastructural facilities are being provided by them. The development of tourism, therefore, can not be the responsibility of any single agency. It is also not possible to have any artificial demarcation of responsibilities between the Central and State Governments as most of the delivery systems are primarily within the control of State/UT Governments. The policy, therefore, will be to develop tourism as a common endeavour of all the agencies vitally concerned with it at the Central and State levels, public sector undertakings and the private sector.

*The Need for Co-ordination and Synergy*

The infrastructure for tourism consists of not only the on-site facilities like hotels, restaurants, entertainment facilities, etc. but also includes all forms of transport and communications infrastructure and basic amenities. The provisions of an integrated system of physical infrastructure including air, rail, road and water transport facilities, communication systems and basic amenities like electricity, water supply, drainage and solid waste disposal systems is a pre-requisite for the development of tourism in any area identified for the same. All the departments/agencies involved in infrastructure development have to, therefore, adopt a joint approach and establish synergy in the development of infrastructure for tourism. The policy, therefore, would be to ensure the necessary linkages and synergies in the policies and programmes of all such departments/agencies by establishing effective co-ordination mechanisms at Central, State and District levels.

*The Approach*

Tourism policy 1982 envisaged a selective approach based on travel circuit concept in the provision of tourism infrastructure to achieve intensive development of selected centres. The National Action Plan for Tourism 1992 also reiterated the need for such a policy to achieve significant impact on infrastructural development with the limited resources available. These policies, however, did not succeed in view of persistent demands for several small projects to meet the needs of domestic tourists in almost every place of tourist interest. Even the Government of India essentially followed a scheme approach instead of area approach in providing financial assistance for the development of tourism infrastructure. The approach for the future development of tourism has to, therefore, take into account both the needs for selective development and the demands of a wide cross-section of domestic tourists. The policy will be to encourage peoples' participation in tourism development including Panchayati Raj Institutions, local bodies, non-governmental organizations and enterprising local youth to create public awareness and to achieve a wider spread of tourist facilities. The Central Government Investment would be concentrated to a large extent in centres selected for integrated development.

*The Choice*

International tourist traffic to the country is largely confined to certain selected centres and destinations at present. There is also a fair level of seasonality in the international tourist arrivals. As a result there is a good deal of congestion and scarcity of facilities in some of these centres during peak seasons. The tourist traffic to some of the centres have even exceeded the carrying capacity with the attendant problem of environmental degradation. Even the metro cities like Mumbai and Delhi have started experiencing scarcity of accommodation and other facilities in peak seasons. It has, therefore, become necessary to go beyond the beaten tracks and to facilitate direct visit of tourists to new destinations. However, the choice of such new destinations for development will have to be based on their intrinsic attractions, potential for development and the carrying capacity as well as availability of resources. The policy would be, therefore, to identify such destinations and work towards their integrated development with the involvement of all the infrastructural departments, State Governments and the private sector and to facilitate direct and easy access to those destinations.

*Forms of Tourism*

The main strength of Indian tourism at present is its cultural attractions particularly, the large number of monuments and archaeological remains scattered throughout the country, its art and artefacts and colourful fairs and festivals. The country is also endowed with a number of other tourist attractions and options including beach tourism; forests, wild life and landscapes for eco-tourism, snow, river and mountain peaks for adventure tourism, health resources and farms for health tourism, technological parks and science museums for science tourism, centres of pilgrimage for spiritual tourism, etc. There are also facilities for conference and convention tourism and shopping tours. The policy, therefore, would be to diversify the tourism product in such a way that it supplements the main stream of cultural tourism. It would also be ensured that the appropriate form of tourism based on specific features of attraction and ecological considerations is developed in each identified area.

*Levels of Development*

The principle of sustainable development stipulates that the level of development does not exceed the carrying capacity of the area. The policy would be to ensure adherence to such limits through appropriate planning instruments, guidelines and enabling regulations.

*Role of the Government*

Tourism is a multi-sectoral activity and the industry is affected by many other sectors of the national economy. The State has to, therefore, ensure intergovernmental linkages and co-ordination. It also has to play a pivotal role in tourism management and promotion. In particular, the government has to:

(i) Provide public infrastructural facilities including local planning and zoning arrangements;

(ii) Plan tourism development as a part of the over all area development strategy;
(iii) Create nucleus infrastructure in the initial stages of development to demonstrate the potential of the area;
(iv) Provide support facilities and facilitation services to private enterprises along with appropriate incentives and land policies;
(v) Introduce regulatory measures to ensure social, cultural and environmental sustainability;
(vi) Ensure that the type and scale of tourism development is compatible with the environment and socio-cultural milieu of the area;
(vii) Ensure that the local community is fully involved and the benefits of tourism accrue to them;
(viii) Facilitate availability of trained manpower particularly from amongst the local population jointly with the industry;
(ix) Undertake research, prepare master plans and facilitate formulation of marketing strategies;
(x) Organize overseas promotion and marketing jointly with the industry;
(xi) Facilitate the growth of a dynamic tourism sector.

*Role of Private Sector*

As tourism has emerged as the largest export industry globally, the private sector has to consider investment in tourism from a long-term perspective and create the required facilities including accommodation, restaurant, entertainment facilities, shopping complexes, etc. in areas identified for tourism development. In general the private sector has to :

(i) Build and manage the required tourist facilities in all places of tourist interest.
(ii) Assume collective responsibility for laying down industry standards, ethics and fair practices.
(iii) Ensure preservation and protection of tourist attractions and give lead in green practices.
(iv) Involve the local community in tourism projects and ensure that the benefits of tourism accrue to them in right measure.

(v) Undertake industry training and manpower development to achieve excellence in quality of services.
(vi) Participate in the preparation of investment guidelines and marketing strategies and assist in database creation and research.
(vii) Ensure safety and security of tourists; and
(viii) Endeavour to promote tourism on a sustained and long-term perspective.

*Facilitation Services*

Tourists have to pass through several government agencies so as to meet the requirements under various laws. These include obtaining visas, undergoing immigration checks, obtaining permits to visit certain areas, payment of fees for certain facilities, etc. The endeavour of the government would be to improve efficiency in providing such facilitation services and make travel a pleasant experience.

*Foreign Investments and Incentives*

In view of large investment requirements in the tourism sector and the need for maintaining high quality standards in services, hotels and tourism related industries will continue to be in the priority list of industries for foreign investment. Further, in order to off-set the specific constraints of tourism industry and to put in place the required infrastructure as quickly as possible, particularly in less developed areas, appropriate incentive schemes would be considered. It would also be the endeavour of the government to put in place uniform taxation and land policies in all the States/Union Territories.

*Resources for Development*

Development of tourism to the extent desired would involve heavy investments in infrastructure. The resources for such investments have to come mostly from private investors, financial institutions and external borrowing. Financial viability and commercial returns are the guiding factors in such investments. Very often, it would depend on investments to bridge certain critical gaps in infrastructure which by itself may not be commercially remunerative. Special funds have to be therefore, created for such investments. It would be thus the policy of the government to facilitate larger flow of funds to tourism infrastructure and to create a Tourism Development Fund to bridge critical infrastructure gaps.

*Regions of Special Interest*

The seven States of North East with beautiful landscapes, lush green forests, exotic wildlife, unique forms of art and culture and affable tribal societies have hitherto remained backward due to various reasons including poor infrastucture. These States along with other States in the Himalayan Region offer enormous potential for the development of ecotourism. Similarly the islands of Andaman and Nicobar as well as Lakshadweep are ideal for sustainable development of island tourism. It is also important to revive and strengthen tourism industry in Jammu and Kashmir to accelerate the economic growth of the State. It would, therefore, be the policy of the government to initiate and support special programmes and schemes for the development of tourism in these regions with a view to achieve overall economic development of the region.

*Conservation and Development*

Tourism development needs to be properly guided and regulated to avoid adverse impact on the natural environment and cultural heritage which constitute the tourist attraction. Despoilation of natural environment, archaeological monuments, beaches, mountains and places of natural beauty; disruption in the culturally sensitive areas; clandestine selling of antiques and vandalism are some of the negative aspects of tourism. A judicious balance, therefore, needs to be maintained between conservation and development. The policy, therefore, would be to maintain balance through planning restrictions and by educating the people in appreciating their rich heritage and by eliciting their co-operation in preserving and protecting it.

*Adoption of New Technologies*

The revolutionary changes that are taking place in the computer and communication technologies, and other relevant sectors would be adopted in the tourism sector to provide better facilities to tourists and to market the tourism product.

**Plan of Action**

The broad plan of action for the implementation of the policies to achieve the objectives would consist of the following :

(i) Preparing an action plan specifying short, medium and long-term strategies and the role of each of the players in the development of tourism.

(ii) Strengthening the statistical machinery, reporting systems, research and database on tourism to measure the economic and social benefits of tourism, identify potential tourist destinations for integrated development, plan infrastructure development, formulate marketing strategies and monitor the progress of implementation and impact of various programmes and projects.

(iii) Creating public awareness about economic and social benefits of tourism amongst administrators, planners and the masses through seminars, workshops, presentations, etc.

(iv) Launching of campaigns through local bodies, non-governmental organizations, youth centres, etc. to create awareness about the traditions of Indian hospitality and the importance of extending warmth and affection to tourists so as to control touting, extortion and harassment to tourists.

(v) Initiating measures for ensuring public participation by encouraging Panchayati Raj Institutions, local bodies, religious trusts, etc. to achieve a wider spread of tourist facilities.

(vi) Strengthening the institutional set-up for human resource development and improving the standards of training in private institutes through accreditation and quality control. It will include the setting up of an Advanced Institute of Hotel Management and a Culinary Institute apart from strengthening the existing training infrastructure.

(vii) Setting up a National Tourism Documentation Centre equipped with modern technology systems to function as a repository of research findings and publications on tourism.

(viii) Setting up an advisory "Board of Tourism Industry and Trade" to achieve effective co-ordination with other Infrastructural Departments and the private sector. Such institutions will also be promoted at the State and District levels.

(ix) Strengthening the existing organizational structure to make it possible to perform its multifarious activities efficiently for the development of tourism. Setting-up of a National Tourism Authority will be considered in this regard.

(x) Giving guidance and financial assistance to State/ Union Territory Governments for preparing tourism Master Plans, identifying tourism resources, prioritising development circuits and projects and specifying the most suitable forms of tourism.

# Ten

# Management of Tourism Business: A Strategic Review

Tourism is a subject which is extremely complex as far as it touches not only the economic fabric of the society but also has a deep rooted effect on social norm and moral behaviour. On one hand, if tackled properly it can provide immense profits to mankind and on other hand unbalanced tourism development can also result in social upheaval which in turn let off a chassis of irreversible reactions.

In India we have made strides in so many areas, for example, new hotels are coming up everywhere, domestic airlines have mushroomed, more foreign airlines are coming into India. All this indicates that there will be a substantial growth. But a careful insight study reveals that we still lack certain basic facilities. Every country has beautiful mountains, rivers, and valleys but one must have the infrastructure to enjoy the beauty. Although a lot is being planned with regard to improvement in infrastructure and facilities for promoting tourism, the actual implementing is not keeping pace with the increasing requirements.

By 2010 AD World Tourism Organization (WTO) says that approximately 661 million will cross international borders for holidays. India's target for that year is 5 million or 0.75 per cent. To me even that tiny a number reflects optimism on the part of policy makers. There have not been any major policy announcement in the sector in spite of the importance this sector holds as the countries second largest foreign exchange earner.

Moreover, new investments in this sector have been hard to come. By upto 1995, 141 projects had been approved, only three have been implemented so far. The root of this neglect lies in the official attitude towards this industry as an activity for elitist rather than as a developmental industry. Another factor for the neglect is that tourism is a State subject, so there has never been any coordinated efforts either to promote the industry or, as importantly, market India abroad on. The Department of Tourism is responsible to do this. In Eighth Plan total plan outlay was Rs. 450 crores of which approximately Rs. 275 crores were spent on marketing tourism abroad and maintaining 18 overseas offices. But contribution of overseas offices in promoting tourism overseas is insignificant considering the amount spent there.

**Travel Scenario**

It is therefore the right time now to calculate an educated guess of travel scenario by 2010 AD. For this it would be imperative to take into account existing situation in areas of basic facilities like water, sanitation, sewage disposable, electricity, gas supply, transport modes, hygiene in service, general cleanliness, destination, hotels, airports, rail routes, agency businesses, tourism policies, investment incentives, foreign exchange regulations, as well as impacts of economic liberalization on tourism development.

With regard to the basic facilities, there have been no serious attempts made to improve facilities. Railways still carry people like cattle, in spite of computerization for reservation people still have to queue for long hours. For last number of years we have been talking about cable railways to connect our mountain resorts, yet nothing has been done about it. But let us not overplay our negative features, because no country has everything for tourism development, it has to be an integrated process. In other words there shall be a defined policy of integrated development road, rail, air, accommodation, local transportation, food, encompassing up till now in India no less then 6-7 ministries were involve in development of tourism project, i.e., customs, home affairs, transport, civil aviation, immigration, finance, defence and environment. For example, in 1995 in Orissa a huge area was earmarked for tourism development where leading hotel chains would have set up luxury hotels with variety of facilities for watersports. But the project was stalled because it has not received clearance from environment ministry. So, it is required that they must act together.

It was in 1996 that a National Strategy Plan for Tourism Development was prepared and submitted by Tourism Secretary G. Sundram. According to this plan it was acknowledged that the promotional efforts in overseas markets have been general in nature without identifying potential market segments and their demand profiles. And another bigger reason for India's failure to benefit from growing tourism traffic is lack of infrastructure. For this Department of Tourism projected an investment worth Rs. 31,350 crores. Rs. 7,500 crores for hotels; Rs. 15,000 crores for transportation, etc., but neither the Centre nor State Governments have this kind of funds. Keeping in mind this constraint in the Ninth Plan Ministry of Tourism has asked for an allocation of Rs. 4,500 crores but chances of such a hike look bleak. Now new draft on tourism policy has also been adopted and so this new thrust will pay rich dividends. Though one can debate surely on speed of developments. Yet one thing is very clear that post liberalization period is witnessing a fiercely competitive scenario leading to customers getting not only the cost benefit, i.e., where customer stands to gain but also improved quality of service and options available. For example, in the pre-liberalization period, Indian Airlines enjoyed monopoly on domestic skies but today this monopoly is challenged by private scheduled airlines, thereby giving air customers a choice for the first time. But this development has posed a serious challenge too. If the current growth rate with regard to domestic air travel remains at the level of 10 per cent per annum, the fleet size of all jet aircraft in India go up to132. This figure also represents a capacity increase of approximately 61 per cent. In order to operate such a fleet same infrastructural measures will become mandatory. These measures could be in direction of improved handling and parking facilities at certain airports (Delhi, Mumbai, Bangalore) and at other places upgradation of standard. So far no domestic import has ideal links to surface transportation like railway connection, express highways and parking facilities. Airports of new millennium should be well planned and built. Examples of most successful and efficient airport like Changi airport of Singapore where roads and express highways were already there before the airport became operational. Therefore, if we have the intention of opening up of some new International airports, road construction and improvement should start today to reap the benefits of all these efforts in the new millennium.

Tourism can not grow in a vacuum, it goes with general economic development. In other words our attempts shall be best in every possible field of endeavour to make India a good travel destination. India always had the potentials but its weak points deterred tourists from coming. These weak points are going to pose threats to development of tourism in India.

**Suggestions for Improvement**

The first and foremost important area, which not only requires careful planning but also an effective implementation is in the area of infrastructure. If plans are envisaged by Department of Tourism and implemented by travel industry, there should be a major thrust in development of infrastructure, which in turn will play an important part in attracting target number of inbound visitors to India. This would involve the development of efficient telecommunications, roads, rails, airlines, and clear, efficient and user friendly airports. Also the staff within these establishment should be well trained. These services will not only cater to the needs of visitors but also of local population. If basic facilities are upgraded habits will change and with education spreading the awareness of the need to be internationally competitive the most vital question which come to mind is that what steps will shape the future of tourism in India? With the liberalization and globalization on the front, only professional companies will survive as consumer is now demanding quality and value for money. As a result, travel agents handling corporate houses would move towards the travel management concepts, i.e., they would become travel managers for the consumers charging them a fee per transaction rather than merely being an agent for airline.

Policies regarding development of new hotels, the government should abolish income tax with regard to sales and not on food and beverage and other sales. The land costs are sky high. At present land cost accounts to 40 per cent of total project cost whereas to make a project feasible and successful it should not amount to more than 10 per cent of project cost, which is in case of other industries. Therefore, both existing and new hotel projects should be granted higher floor area ratio to enable them to add more rooms. Though the process of allotting land is slow, as a result, some established locations lose tourist traffic for want of good accommodation with basic requirements like hygiene, security, god food and water. So, all these constraints call for a standard land policy which may be altered only for regions with special problems. Besides, the bottleneck situation with regard to hotels at India's major gateway points needs to be improved. Until now India is the most expensive destination for tourists who can see Malaysia, Singapore and Indonesia at half the cost. Under Dual Tariff System, i.e., in rupees and dollars, dollar tariff is30 per cent to 40 per cent higher. We should, therefore, have a common tariff with maximum of taxes to make India attractive and competitive destination.

Alongside to infrastructure and accommodation, transportation would be another important component calling for special attention from planners of tourism development. Now, concept of Leisure travel is changing. Earlier it meant Visiting Friends and Relatives (VFR) now we go abroad to shop as well as for sight seeing involving mobility and in return efficient transport system. Besides, planned development of air transport, we also need to plan for surface and water transport. At present surface transport is hampered by infrastructural constraints like poor roads and capacity, lack of professionalism, absence of underground railways to city centre, if proper thought is not given to this sector the scenario is unlikely to change in future, i.e., demand will always chase inadequate supply.

There is also a great scope to development of destinations especially in coastal areas. For development of coastal areas we need to develop our waterways for cruises which will also decongest our transportation system and we can do this without disturbing the daily routine life of a city. Take the example of Egypt which virtually lives off the Nile for cruises with dinner and entertainment. Of course, in recent years many States Governments have identified tourist destination for development. Even some states for instance, UP, MP, and Bihar are permitting the participation of foreign capital in this development. Incentives being offered by these States seem to be quite attractive. So far

India has managed not to become a mass tourist destination. However, care should be taken by the government to protect certain areas of tourist importance like Taj Mahal, visited by hundreds of thousands of tourist every day. But this does not mean that we become rigid about our policies on environment. One should preserve the environment but leave areas of tourist interest out of its domain. For example, if a beach resort is not constructed within 500 metres from the beach why should tourists come for a beach holiday. There are other areas to consider for environment preservation like wild life, forest, monuments, historical remains, etc.

To conclude, we can say that now when India's is all set to become a favoured destination, it will take some time to ensure that India is a clean place. Awareness will be followed by action. We have already reached the stage of awareness and action will follow in coming years. Only a line of caution would save the industry from collapsing, i.e., whatever is promised shall be delivered in the same manner as is committed. Only this line of action can help in improving and restoring the image of our country consequently making it the destination of 21st century.

# Eleven

# Tourism Organizational Setup in India

For any industry to develop, an organization is a must as it plays a vital role in the planning, development and growth. An organization consists of individuals whose primary role is the achievement of a common objective for which it has been set up. The aim of the organization is to arrange people into working groups, associating those with similar functions or purposes in order to move efficiently to obtain a desired result. It is the framework within which an industry works. It relates to the structure of the industry and is concerned with issues involved in, and the approaches to it. This industry could be any including tourism industry.

The organization of tourist industry in any country varies widely, as there are a number of considerations, which influence the nature of organizational set up. Today almost all countries have tourist organizations to deal specifically with the subject of tourism. However, the pattern and nature of these organizations differ widely from one country to another.

A study of tourism organizations should logically begin with the official tourist organization called the National Tourist Organization followed by other semi-official or private organizations, which together serve the objectives of tourism. The United Nations Conference on International Travel and Tourism held in Rome in 1963 recommended that National Tourist Organization should be granted the authority and resources necessary to enable them to take effective action, as desired by governments for development and promotion of national and international tourism.

## National Tourist Organization

The National Tourist Organization is the body responsible for the formulation and implementation of national tourist policy. All countries which are engaged in tourism have a National Tourist Organization which plays a leading role in direction and promotion of tourism. The National Tourism Organisation may be a full-fledged Ministry, a directorate-general, a department, corporation or a board. The arrangement and the constitution for the National Tourist Organization vary widely. It depends on factors like political structure of the country, the level of economic development, of potential value of tourism to the economy the level of tourism development and also availability of capital for tourism development including infrastructural developments.

## Tourist Organization in India

Tourism as a separate organization was set up rather late in India. Prior to the formation of a separate organization, tourism was a part of Transport Ministry. The new department was put under the charge of the Director General who had under him one Deputy Director General and four Directors each in charge of administration, publicity, travel relations and planning and development.

The present position of the tourist organizational set up of India is, however, a result of various changes that have been made over the years. By the Presidential Order dated 14th March, 1967, the Department of Aviation and Tourism which was under the ministry of Transport and Civil Aviation was formed into a separate ministry designated as the Ministry of Tourism and Civil Aviation. The Ministry was under the charge of a full time Minister. It was after nearly eighteen years that the subject 'tourism' was accorded a separate entity and thus became independent of transport. With the formation of the new Ministry of Tourism and Civil Aviation, tourism got the importance due to it and thereby achieved all round expansion in its activities.

The Department of Tourism now became an attached non-participating office of the Ministry of Tourism and Civil Aviation headed by a Director General of Tourism. The Director General of Tourism carries an ex-officio status of an Additional Secretary to the Government of India. Although an attached office, the department is both a policy making and an executive organization and corresponds directly with the other ministries and departments of the Central Government and State Governments. The Director General is assisted by one Additional Director General, one Joint Director General, a Deputy Secretary and four Deputy Director Generals.

**Divisions of Department of Tourism (DOT)**

The functions of the Department of Tourism (DOT) are both promotional and organizational which are conducted by the following divisions :

(i) Planning and programming
(ii) Publicity and conference
(iii) Travel trade and hospitality
(iv) Accommodation
(v) Supplementary accommodation and wildlife.
(vi) Market research; and
(vii) Administration.

**Committees and Advisory Boards**

In order to establish liaison with various ministries and co-ordinate various activities pertaining to tourism, the department is represented on the following committees/advisory bodies:

(a) Standing Facilitation Committee of the DGCA.
(b) Civil Aviation Development Fund Committee.
(c) Advisory Committee on the Indian Airlines.
(d) Export Import Advisory Council.
(e) Indian Board for Wildlife.
(f) Central Advisory Board of Archaeology.
(g) Aerodrome Planning Group.
(h) Hotel Industry Study Groups of the Ministry of Labour.
(i) Governing body of the Institute of Hotel Management Catering Technology and Nutrition, New Delhi, Calcutta, Bombay and Madras.
(j) Ad-hoc Committee.
(k) Central Post and Telegraph Advisory Council.
(l) India Tourism Development Corporation. (ITDC).

The Department has a chain of ten tourist information offices established in important cities in India. Remaining sales offices are functioning at focal points of tourist interest. All these offices work in close collaboration with State Governments, travel agencies, excursion agencies, carriers and tour and taxi operators. For overseas promotion the department has eighteen offices located at strategic places abroad. The publicity work of overseas offices is directed in close collaboration with Air India under the schemes known as operation schemes. These offices form a direct link between the Department and the travel trade in foreign countries.

**Organization Chart of DOT – Headquarters**

Minister
↓
Deputy Minister
↓
Secretary
↓
Director General
↓
Additional Director General
↓

| Jt. Director General | Deputy Director General | Deputy Director General | Deputy Director General | Deputy Director General | Director Tourist Adminis-tration | Director Market Research |
|---|---|---|---|---|---|---|
| ↓ | ↓ | ↓ | ↓ | ↓ | ↓ | ↓ |
| Hotels | Publicity Promotion Training Prog., conferences | Travel Trade, Hospita-, lity Prog. | Planning Programme | Supple-mentary Accom-modation, Wild life. | Adminis-tration, Finance, Coordi-nation | Travel, Statistics |

From a small beginning in the year 1949, the tourist organization as it stands now has passed through various facets. In between the year 1949 and today there has been a tremendous amount of work, which has helped in strengthening the organization. The appointment of various expert committees, advisory committees, councils and boards from time to time has helped the organization grow tremendously.

**Organization: Typology**

Men and women and the firms engaged in tourism have come together in a variety of organizations to further their common interests. It is possible to divide these organizations into two main categories in the present content:

(a) Sectoral organizations, which are based on the main groups of providers of tourist services, and

(b) Tourist organizations – There are numerous other bodies with an interest in tourism often governmental or statutory.

*Organization in Sectors*

Sectoral organizations are concerned with particular industries participating in tourism, i.e., the various providers of tourist services such as the hotel and catering services, the transport services and the entertainment services. Following chart gives the structure of sectoral organizations:

**Sectoral Organization**

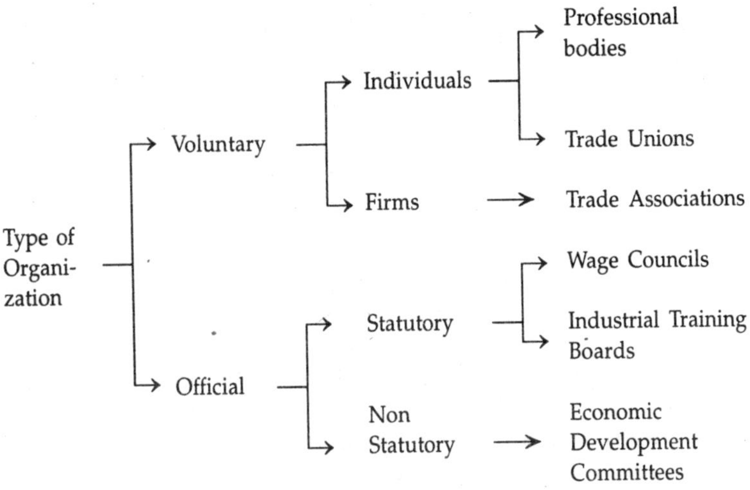


Individual industries engaged in tourism have several types of organizations. Voluntary organizations of individuals range from professional bodies to trade unions. Independent firms form trade associations in a particular industry to protect and advance their common interests.

In countries in which government intervention in industry takes the form of setting up tourism industry, bodies of, statutory or 'official' bodies are also in existence.

*Tourist Organization*

Tourist organization is defined with reference to the interests of a geographical area as a tourist destination, which may be a country, region or an individual town. The tourist organization provides the framework in which tourism operates. Three basic levels of tourist organizations may be distinguished in most countries of any size — national, regional and local—as part of what may be seen as vertical structure.

**Tourist Organization**

National Organization

↓

Regional Tourist Organization

↓ ↓ ↓

Local Tourist organization

↓ ↓ ↓ ↓ ↓ ↓ ↓ ↓ ↓

*National Level:* At the national level, tourism is in the first instance a government responsibility to formulate a tourism policy, which may be translated into a plan. When the role of tourism is defined, the policy provides a statement of the means by which objectives are to be attained; the means cover such matters as the administrative arrangements, the respective roles of the private and public sectors and the fiscal arrangements. The government usually delegates its detailed formulation and its execution to National Tourist Organization, which may be governmental, semi-governmental or non-governmental, with a scope and sphere of influence.

*The Local Level:* In a country of any size they are best performed at the level of each destination and this creates a need for a regional and local tourist organization as the second and third level of tourist organization. Whilst the Central Government does not always retain the National Tourist Organization within a government department, local tourist organization is often based on local government since physical planning is normally the domain of local government. The local organization provides a strong solid basis for the co-ordination of local tourist interests, for the provision of information services to visitors, and for the wider aspects of local promotion and development.

*The Regional Level:* Regional tourist organization is an intermediate level between the national and local levels and represents the latest development in tourist organization. This comprises of government authorities, transport and hotel companies and other providers of tourist services operating in those areas.

The tourist organization does not exist and functions in isolation for development and coordination of the efforts and interests of all involved in tourism, there are many links and cross relationships between the tourist organization and other organization at all levels.

*International Organization*

The increasingly international character of modern tourism and the growing influence of international agencies in many fields are reflected in the growth of international organizations in tourism, which has been stimulated by the need for discussion and co-operation between individuals, firms, associations and governments of individual countries.

Many of the special agencies are not concerned or only indirectly concerned with tourism. Some include tourism and its particular aspects among their responsibilities. Others are concerned with particulars sectors, e.g., the International Civil Aviation Organization. The two main inter-governmental organizations concerned with tourism are the World Tourism Organization (WTO), and through its Tourism Committee, the Organization of Economic Co-operation and Development (OECD).

**Issues and Problems**

The first fundamental question, which arises while one can discuss the issues and problems is that: Is the present structure of the Department of Tourism tuned to meet the needs of present day tourism? With the growth of tourism as a world-wide phenomenon the National Tourist Organization has had to assume new functions which were not envisaged 25 years ago. Hence the problem of setting up the right type of national tourist organization has been debated in many countries.

**Non-statutory Commission on Tourism: Reasons**

However, if the experience of other countries is any guide it will thus be seen that a majority of the countries prefer some sort of an autonomous organization. Hence it can be stipulated that ITDC, which was originally created as an operational arm of Department of Tourism should be placed under the control of a non-statutory commission because of various reasons such as :

1. Tourism permeates so many activities in the public and private sectors that it would be impossible to have a single department with everything with which tourism is evolved;
2. The present organizational set up of the department is not attuned to developing tourism. In India at the moment, development lags behind marketing;
3. A government department in essence may not be discriminatory. In tourism promotion it is necessary to be selective, to build on strength rather than on weakness. In this position, a government department is handicapped by the political and local pressures;
4. Tourism is becoming increasingly a matter of professionals and employment of professionals in government services can give rise to difficulties by the very reason of its nature.

Other than these reasons, it has been observed that over the years the department has grown in size, the structure has become somewhat hierarchical or dysfunctional. An important reason why the department has not functioned as it was intended has been the low salaries fixed initially when tourist branch was created. It is not possible to recruit men and women of necessary caliber on low pay scales. Although pay scales have been gradually upgraded but not in real money terms. Many officers have reached their 'level of incompetence'. Lack of motivation is a result of not having right man at the right job. There are too many Joint Director Generals or Deputy Director Generals. Instead the posts must be filled with technical personnel rather than borrow officers from other services on limited tenures of a few years.

Regardless of whether a new statutory body is established or not, what is immediately needed is a machinery for coordination. It is hardly necessary to restate that tourism can best be promoted by the joint efforts of the government and the industry. Most countries have found it necessary to set up co-ordination machinery. This is a matter of utmost importance in a large country like India, with its semi-federal structure.

*Twelve*

# Growth of Travel Agencies

With the arrival of scheduled airlines, the travel agency business began to change. In the 1930s Pan American World Airways was so small that they could not afford a ticket office, it borrowed three feet of counter space from Thomas Cook and Sons in New York. Following World War-II, the travel urge broke loose, and numbers of people set themselves up in business as travel agents. Teachers, clerks, and housewives worked out of their homes part-time as travel agents. Such an arrangement would be almost impossible today.

The idea of opening a travel agency has natural appeal to many people, who probably think that the business requires only limited capital and a minimum of travel information and will satisfy their desire to meet people and see the world themselves. Experience reveals that being a travel agent is more complicated and expensive than it may seem.

Within the United States and Canada, some 40,000 retailers of travel are in operation, they include clubs, banks, department stores, airlines, and hotels. Each year over 1,000 new agencies are started, and every year several hundreds are closed.

Until the nineteenth century, discretionary travel was limited to a very small percentage of the people. This changed dramatically as the industrial revolution gave millions of people in North America and Europe some discretional income. More importantly, the railroad made travel comparatively cheap and convenient. In response to travel demand, entrepreneurs such as Thomas Cook, Cox and Kings, etc., helped promote and make travel arrangements easier.

**Functions and Activities of Travel Agencies**

The following charts give us a bird-eye view of the various functions and activities of travel agencies.

## FUNCTIONS OF TRAVEL AGENCY

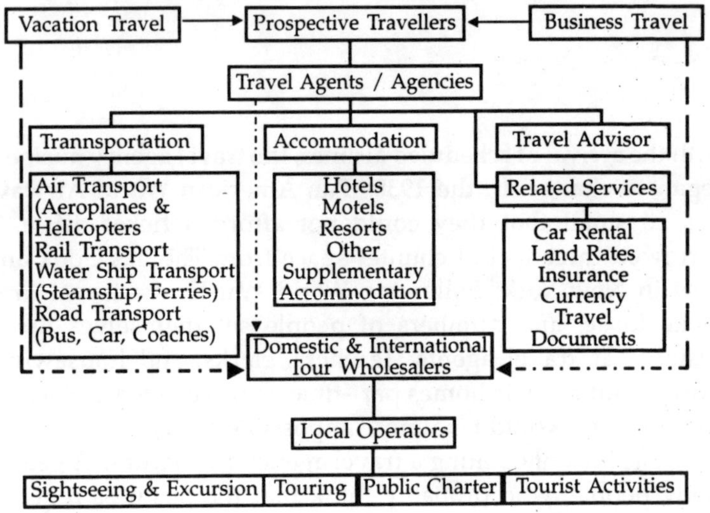


## ACTIVITIES OF TRAVEL AGENCY

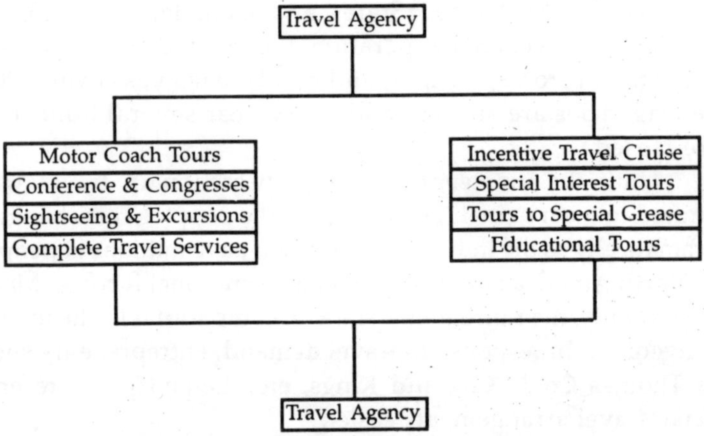

**Attractive Features of the Travel Line**

Thousands of people take up travel courses, with the expectation of going into the business. A number of retirees do it because they want to travel; others study the field because they want an income producing avenue. The attractions are several – free airline passage or a 75 per cent discount on travel, hotel rooms free or discounted by 50 per cent, passage on trans-Atlantic ships for a quarter of the lowest priced accommodation and on cruise ships for half the lowest rates. Agents are also invited on free or heavily discounted familiarization trips by countries, resorts, airlines, and hotel chains.

**Travel Agents as Professionals**

Travel agents are business people selling travel services. A more descriptive term for them would be travel advisors or consultants; perhaps broker is even more apt. Agents are entrepreneurs in the sense that they are usually in business for themselves, and professionals because they have the skill and training to draw on a particular body of knowledge in a meaningful way, in order to help travellers get the pleasure conveniences, and experiences they want.

A good agent is like a personal counsellor, a psychologist, and an expert in the art and science of travel. Agents not only know the advantages and disadvantages of various modes of travel, their costs, and their schedules, but in many cases they also act as counsellors in adjusting travel services to fit the personality of the client. As a professional the agent follows a code of ethics which may not always favour her or him economically.

Travel agents must base their recommendations on the answers to such questions as : How old and energetic is the client? Should the client's travel schedule be arranged for arrival at a destination in the early evening or in the morning. What about the effect of crossing time zones, the effects of altitude in some cities, the dangers of food poisoning in certain areas? The list of considerations stretches on and on.

Agents must learn to keep their cool under pressure – when flights are delayed, tickets lost, clients sent to wrong destinations or ticketed on an expensive flight when a cheaper one was available, and so on.

**THE TRAVEL AGENT : NEXUS IN THE TRAVEL TRANSACTION**

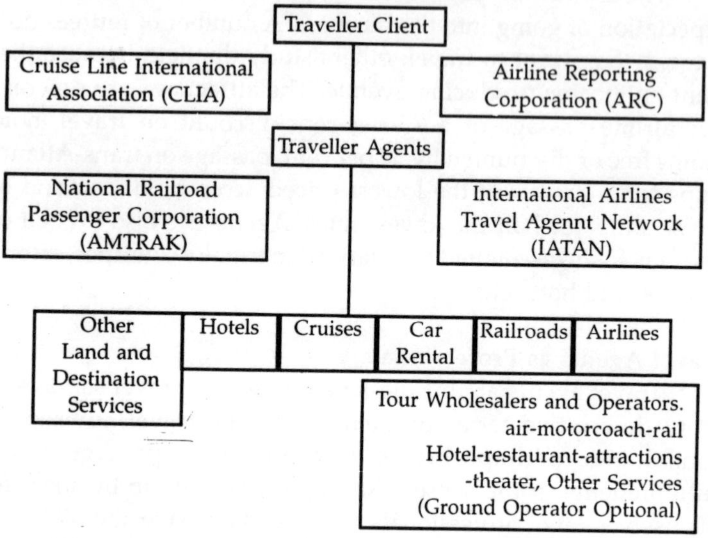


## Job Description of a Travel Agent

The successful travel agent's range of knowledge needs to be large and constantly growing. A job description would include all of the following elements :

(1) Prepares individual preplanned itineraries, personally escorted tours and group tours, sells prepared package tours. Nine of ten agencies plan group travel.

(2) Prepares for hotels, motels, resort accommodations, meals, car rentals, sight seeing, transfers of passengers and message between terminals and hotels, and entrance to special attractions such as music festivals and the theatre.

(3) Handles and advises on the many details involved in modern-day travel, such as travel and baggage insurance, language study material, traveller's cheques, auto garages, foreign currency exchange, document requirements (visas and passports) and health requirements (immunization and other inoculations).

(4) Uses professional know-how and experience, such as schedules of train connections, rates and quality of hotels, whether rooms have baths, whether their rates include local taxes and gratuities. The traveller could spend days or weeks making phone calls and writing letters to secure this information and, even then, it still might not be right.

(5) Arranges reservations for special-interest activities such as religious pilgrimages, conventions and business travel account for half the travel agency business, nine of ten agencies, report handling corporate accounts.

**Evaluating a Travel Agency**

The value of a travel agency brings on its ability to produce profits, now or later. It may also have value as a tax shelter for a person in a high-income tax bracket who wants a tax write-off for several years but expects that the agency will gradually increase in value and eventually be sold at a profit, such profits of course are taxes as capital gains and not as earnings. Usually the buyer is interested in an agency that will produce a livelihood immediately or within a short time. He or she will want a record of its past sales and commissions for at least three years. From such records, the buyer can see whether the trend of sales and profits is up, down, or flat. He or she will also analyse the sales mix to learn what percentage of sales is of minimal profit (point-to-point commercial air sales), and what percentage produces higher profits (tours, hotel reservations, car rentals, and large ticket vacations).

The location is always important. If the agency depends upon volume commercial sales, a street level location is an asset. Is the neighbourhood changing for the better or for the worse? Are the agency's clients moving into the neighbourhood or out of it ? Is the character of the neighbourhood attractive, or at least suitable for the clientele?

A rule of thumb regarding the value of an agency was proposed by Leuence Stevens a travel agency expert, in *The Travel Agent* magazine. His contention is that a retail travel agency is worth somewhere between 4 and 10 per cent of its average annual gross sales. In other words, an agency grossing $ 1,000,000 with a favourable sales mix that produces maximum profits would be worth up to $ 100,000 to the buyer. Some agencies would be liabilities from the date of purchase. Stevens recommends a provision in the contract that permits the buyer to participate in the business during a transition period. The buyer would naturally be interested in retaining customers and building new business while becoming familiar with the agency. Stevens also suggests that the seller may wish to receive payment over a number of years to avoid having to pay very high taxes for the year of the sale.

**Nature of Work**

The main functions of a travel agency are to ensure a smooth, comfortable, and definite travel by taking all the responsibilities of making reservations and assisting the passengers in completing all the formalities involved in the travel.

As a salesman, the travel agent must be able to motivate his client, to take advantage of his services. The salesman studies the interest of his travel customers, learns where they travelled, appraises their financial resources and time available and presents alternative places in the most effective fashion.

As a travel consultant, the agent gives to his client various suggestions regarding travel plans and itineraries, information on transportation alternates and advice on class and rates of hotels and motels. He also helps with passports and visas regulations, foreign currency and exchange, climate and wardrobe, health requirements, customs regulations, baggage and accident , travellers cheques or letters of credit, car rentals, sightseeing welcome or escort services.

Many travel agents only sell tours developed by travel organisation. The most skilled agents, however, organised tours on a wholesale basis. This involves developing an itinerary, arrangement of tour leadership, making tentative reservations for transportation, hotels and even for side trips publishing the tour through descriptive brochures, scheduling reservation tours arranged at the specific requirements of a group to meet a particular need.

In addition to other duties, travel agents may serve as tour guide, leading trips ranging from one week in a local area to six months around the world. Agents often find tour leadership a useful way to gain personal travel experience and to become thoroughly acquainted with persons who may represent potential customer for additional trips. Tour leaders usually receive all their expense. However, most travel agents must arrange for coverage of work during their absence, which often prohibits tour leadership for small, self-employed agents.

The agent serves as a book-keeper to handle the complex pattern of transportation and hotel reservation with characteristics of each trip. He works directly with airlines, steamship, rail road and bus companies. He makes direct contracts with hotels and sightseeing organizations or works indirectly through a correspondent agency in the city involved. These arrangements demand exacting standards of accuracy. After reservations are made, the agents must write or obtain tickets, develop itineraries and send out bills for reservation involved.

In larger agencies, one staff member may become an authority on sea cruises, another on trips to the Far-East and a third may develop an extensive knowledge of their low-budget or luxury trips.

In addition to regular travel business, a number of travel jobs are offered by oil companies, automobiles clubs, and transportation companies. Some jobs in travel are on the staff of state and local governments seeing to encourage and expedite tourism.

Thus, the services of a travel agent consists of advising travellers and bookings on their behalf, transport and accommodation services, etc. Following the great expansion of travel after the development of the railways, the travel agents continue to play a far more fundamental part than merely acting as a go-between a consultant or an advisor. The main agents act as distributors (retailers) and thus relieves transport companies, hoteliers and other manufacturers of travel services from the need to open sales branches over wide areas.

Today, these agencies offer a wide variety of services.

(a) Arranging basic transportation, i.e., air, steamship, cruised, rail, bus, car rentals and other related services.

(b) Preparing individual itineraries personally escorted and group tourism.

(c) Using professional knowledge and experience to interpreting train schedules, airline tariff and hotel rates.

(d) Handling and advising on the many details of modern travel including baggage restrictions, insurance, language, study materials, travellers cheques, auto garaging, foreign currency exchange, documentary requirements (Passport and Visa) and health regulations (immunizations).

The number and variety of jobs of a travel agent are determined by the size of the agency. In a small agency one manager can also be a salesman, a secretary and may keep the books. In a large agency, jobs are more specialized. The travel agents are not providers of tourist facilities like hotels, air, rail or road transport. They merely use and co-ordinate the facilities that exist. Right from the time a tourist sets his foot on our soil, a travel agent takes charge and undertakes to handle the tour throughout the country till his final departure. He has to use the facilities at the airports including those of the customs, as they are available and as they exist. The travel agent has to make the best of given set of circumstances sufficient or insufficient and his skill lies in how best he is able to use and co-ordinate these existing facilities. It is the moral duty of the travel agent to sell his client the best on the airlines, more suitable hotels, more pleasurable destination and more convenient connections. It is in this context that a travel agent assumes great importance. He is the discriminating buyer who helps in making the choice for his client and also determines his needs and protects his interests. In a developing country like our where such facilities are limited, the role of the travel agents becomes all the more difficult and one which requires great ability and hard work.

**Domestic Department**

This department looks after the domestic air travel and thus deals with only the services relating to internal airlines. It is continuously in touch with the passengers and gets the tickets delivered to him. It generally keeps a good stock of tickets of the airlines and issues tickets on behalf of the airlines.

**Booking Procedure**

When a person is interested to travel by domestic airlines, he has to contact the travel agency and ask for an air ticket. He has to supply all the required information to the travel agency—name, place, date and flight, etc. The agency will take out a ticket from its stock and will ask the airlines for reservation on that specific date and flight. If the seat is available, it passes on the name of the passenger and the ticket number to the airlines. In case of onward travel, fax, telex messages or telegrams or the letters are sent to the respective stations for confirmation. When confirmation is received the customer is informed and ticket is delivered to him. In addition to the reservation of ticket the agency makes the necessary reservation of hotel and transport (car, etc.) at various places of his journey, if the client is in need of it. Necessary vouchers are issued and the original copy is given to the client. The client hands over the voucher to the respective hotel or transport unit and signs the bill. He need not to make any payment of hotel accommodation and transportation.

The bills signed by the client are the proof of availing the services. They are forwarded to the concerned travel agency in due course for facilitating the payment. The travel agency makes the payment and receives it from the client when the counterfoil is produced to him. Thus, it is seen that the bother for the purchase of ticket, reservation of seat, hotel accommodation, provision for ground transport and the payment for the services availed are not faced by the passenger. The work for the travel agency simplifies all these time consuming processes.

**Ticketing Procedure**

The different types of clients who book tickets through a travel agency are corporate clients. FIT (Foreign Independent Traveller), independent clients who are offered special credit card services, e.g., Diners' Club Card Holders and walk in clients.

The corporate clients come directly or indirectly in person or through a telephone. Once their bookings are made, they are normally billed in the name of the company itself.

The free individual traveller comes directly to the travel agency and is expected to pay in cash once his bookings are confirmed.

Travel Agencies offer special services to the Diners' Club Card Holders. They book tickets either by coming in person or through the telephone. This service is known as tele-ticketing. Their card number and the card expiry date is taken along with a contact number and address.

Walk-in-clients are just like the FITs. They too are expected to pay in cash.

In India, besides the national carrier, Indian Airlines, many private airlines are also operating. These are Jet Airways, Sahara Airlines, Archana Airways.

Now, a wider choice is open to the domestic market, thus, reducing the waiting list on Indian Airlines and their air traffic pressure.

**Ticketing Procedure**

This is one of the most important activity of the travel agency business. The important point regarding the airline ticketing are as follows:

(a) Preparation and completion of reservation sheet.
(b) Booking the desired tickets with the appropriate carrier/s.
(c) Writing the airline tickets.
(d) Invoicing the sale.

**Reservation Sheet/Cards**

The basic step in airline ticketing is the preparation and completion of reservation sheet. These sheets may differ from one travel agency to another but all of them contain the travel information, i.e., airline codes, airport codes, flight member and type of service, etc. The basic information included in these sheets is concerning the following:

1. Date
2. Name/s
3. Number in Party
4. Home Address

5. Telephone (home and/or office)
6. Ages of Children
7. Billing Information—Credit Card, cash, etc.
8. Travel plan—sectors
9. Carrier
10. Flight number
11. Date of Week
12. Date of Departure
13. Date of Arrival
14. Status (OK or Wait List)
15. The fare and taxes of each flight
16. Other information such as name of airline representation making reservation, date of reservation, person making reservation , hotel, tour, rail, rental car bookings.

Thus, it is clear that the reservation sheet or control sheet contains all the relevant information necessary for the trip of the customer. Each head of information gives a clear picture about itself. Take an example of an item like 'Status'. The different meanings of status may be expressed as follows:

| | |
|---|---|
| OK | Means that this particular segment has been confirmed by the airline. |
| OK/F/WL/Y | Means this particular segment has been confirmed 'first class' and is 'wait listed' on the Y class. |
| RQ | Means this particular segment has been placed on request from another airline. |
| NO-OP | Means this particular leg does not operate as requested by the client. |
| UK | Means this particular leg is unable to confirm either class of service. |

Among the various activities of travel agency, writing the airline ticket is an exciting and interesting work. The interesting part of ticket writing is the very activity which represents the totality of a travel agent's work, i.e., counselling, reservation works and customer satisfaction. All the tickets stock is accountable as unused, issued, void or refunded. The travel agency is responsible for ticket stock received, collection of the correct amounts, written on the issued tickets and remittance of all funds collection in trust for the air carriers. Air passenger tickets are usually issued in sequence by serial number and reported in the same way. The amount of ticket said is also reported in a foreign currency. The passengers coupon forms a standard airline ticket. It has four copies:

(i) Passenger's coupon
(ii) Auditor's coupon
(iii) Agent's coupon
(iv) First Flight's coupon

The auditor's coupon contains such information as the passenger's name, all flight segments of the passages, fare calculation and form of payment collected. This coupon along with the sales report is mailed weekly to the Central Accounts Office. The fare calculated by travel agents are checked by central accounting. Any discrepancies are reported and adjusted.

The flight coupon authorizes passage between the points shown on the light area of the coupon and serves as an evidence that the fares shown on the coupon have been paid. The coupon is an agreement between the airline and the passenger for reserve sheet on the specified flight. The coupon contains all necessary information for handling of the passenger and his luggage, it helps airline agents to guide the passenger on the correct flights. It indicates all conditions, which must be known to a ticket agent in case he has to re-issue or refund the coupon. It also contains information which enables the carrying airline to bill the issuing airline for the fare between the two permits indicted on it, if the issuing airline and carrying airline are not the same. These coupons cannot be honoured individually. The passenger must present the coupon to the carrier to which it is made out, in the order in which it is issued, all unused coupons are presented together.

Most of the scheduled airlines have established standard reservation procedure. Each airline has its own established method of controlling seats on an airplane. These airlines operate on the principle of centralized space control and on a 'First come first Serve basis'. Each system is so designed so as to give the public an immediate 'yes' or 'no' answer in regard to available airplane seats. Every airline has certain basic and uptodate information in order to make a reservation. The first contact between travel agent, his client and airline reservations agent is through the telephone call. In case, the travel agent knows in advance about the desire of the client, he can prepare his information prior to the call and thereby efficiently relaying this information to the airline reservation agent. He should know the items needed by the reservation agent in order to conclude a reservation transaction so that a telephone conversation can be expedited. The reservation agent needs the following for each flight segment with regard to planned reservation :

(a) The flight number
(b) Class of service
(c) Date of departure
(d) The originating point
(e) The destination
(f) The desired number of seats
(g) The passenger's family name and first initials, residence and/or office telephone number
(h) Time as given by which the passenger must secure the confirmed ticket or else suffer loss of the reservation
(i) Travel agent's name and name of individual handling itinerary.

**Discounts**

The airlines offer various discounts and concessions.

*Indian Airlines*

- Child discount ( 2 to 12 years ) – 50 per cent on basic + FS + IATT
  PSF is full
- Infant (below 2 years) – 90 per cent on basic + FS.
  IATT and PSF is not charged.
- Student discount – 50 per cent on basic.
  Rest is charged full.
- Youth Fare – This is only for foreign nationals below 30 years – 25 per cent discount.
- Discover India – Valid for 21 days, one sector to be utilized only once. The package is for US$ 400.

- Wonder Fare – USD 200; and if Port Blaire is included in the itinerary that is for USD 300.
- Sr. Citizen discount – 50 per cent

*All private Airlines offer :*

- Student discount – 25 per cent on basic fare.
- Child discount – 50 per cent on basic and FS.
- Infant discount – 90 per cent on basic fare.

**Refunds and Cancellations**

When a traveller does not want to travel for that itinerary then he can cancel the tickets. He will have to produce the tickets at the travel agency counter in the case of cancellation.

The cancellation charges implied here are as follows :

| | |
|---|---|
| 1. Before 48 hours | Rs. 20 only |
| 2. Less than 48 hours but before 24 hours | 10 per cent of the basic fare. |
| 3. Less than 24 hours but before 1 hour | 25 per cent of the basic fare. |
| 4. Less than 1 hour or now show ticket | 100 per cent of the basic fare |

(All above said timing implies on the time of flight departure, it should be presented on the Indian Airlines office or other private airline office).

For an 'open' ticket the cancellation charges are Rs. 20.

If the ticket is waitlisted then the cancellation charges are NIL.

The refund is being made in form of the M.C.O. by airlines. The MCD is issued in the name of the Travel Agency and after that the travel agency can make the refund to its client in any form.

The domestic department, maintains the cancellation book, which has the account concerned with the cancellation.

In the cancellation we have to write down the passenger name, on agency counter and also the coupon number with the sector, carrier, flight number, class, date of departure and cancellation charge also.

**Hotel Bookings**

A successful travel agent must understand the needs of the individual clients, e.g., commercial and vacation travellers. The best selling tools are the hotel, resort and motel literature/ brochures. They tell about the 'who, what, where, when, why and how much' about a particular destination. In addition the travel agent must visit these properties and personally evaluate the accommodations. FAM trips are very useful in learning more about new destinations.

The grading and classification of tourist accommodation are understood throughout the world by general definitions. It is being frequently difficult to understand whether the hotel is being described accurately and reliably or misleading by a promoter. In many countries there is neither an official nor generally accepted rating system for hotels, if we consult the directories and sometimes evaluate the accommodation. Some of the countries rate their hotels according to international five star (delux) system under which a five star hotel is the best accommodation. This classification is like :

- Five Star Deluxe
- Five Star
- Four Star
- Three Star
- Two Star
- One Star

The Michelin Travel directories refer to hotel under the following terms :

Luxury, Top Class, Very Comfortable, Good Average, Plain but adequate and other recommended accommodations at moderate prices.

Another way of rating the hotel accommodations by their amenities is :

Pleasant hotel; Pleasant restaurant; Particularly attractive feature; Very quite; secluded hail; Quick hotel; Exceptional view; Interesting view.

For purpose of hotel reservation the travel agents usually work with hotel representative. These hotel representatives offer hotel reservations to agents, wholesalers and public and are paid by the hotels represented on a fee basis. A travel agent makes a reservation for the client giving complete information concerning date and time of arrival, rate and plan of accommodation and length of stay. Hotels answer all requests for reservations or information within the shortest time possible by telephone or by fastest mail or by fax or telegram. Most of the overseas hotels may require that funds should be sent in advance.

Reservations when confirmed by the hotel, are usually considered firm without re-confirmations by the agency, unless otherwise specified by the hotel at the time of confirmation. Reservations are held without deposit until 6 pm or some specified time on the date of arrival. All reservations made by telephone or direct conversation should be reconfirmed in writing with specific reference to conversation and name of employee who took reservation. No reservation should be made on long distance telephone calls. Most of the hotel chains like Holiday Inn, Sheraton, Best Western, Howard, Johnson, Raddisson, Ramada, Milton Hyatt, Quality Inns have reservation system s which use central computer reservation banks and nationwide toll-free (800) telephone number reservations. The travel agency should try to use the standard reservation and confirmation forms. When booking a room accommodation, the following hotel reservation information should be provided :

(a) Name and address of the customer
(b) Date and time of arrival
(c) Method of arrival for complementary transportation arrangement
(d) Number in the party
(e) Specific type of hotel room, e.g., SWB, DWR, DDWB, TWB, Suite, etc.
(f) Type of service, e.g., EP, CP, AP, and MAP
(g) Rate confirmation
(h) Duration of Stay number of days/nights between check in and check out.
(i) Method of payment
(j) Special Arrangement: request special requirements for client, e.g., flowers, etc.

*Commission on Hotel Reservation*

The travel agencies are entitled for commission on reservation. The commission is paid on only the room portion of the client's account unless it is made on American Plan. Generally the commission is paid on sojourn not to exceed 60 days or unless specified by the hotel at the time of confirmation. In case a client extends his stay beyond period for which reservation was made by the travel agency, the hotel pays commission for full length of stay. Hotels pay the amount of commission as soon as the client checks out but no later than the 10th of the following month without billing from the travel agency. In case of overseas hotels the payment is paid periodically as per the agreement with the currency control officials. It is the responsibility of the respective hotels to promptly notify to the agencies regarding 'no shows' cancellation by clients or non-payment of hotel bill by client. Commission for booking a hotel accommodation is a principal source of earning of the agency. The rate of commission varies from hotel to hotel. This commission varies between 10 per cent to 20 per cent. In many cases the travel agencies collect from the client for the accommodation in advance of the trip and send the appropriate hotel the collected amount less the commission earned, thus they do not receive any commission from foreign hotels.

*Hotel Vouchers*

Voucher is a document issued by a travel agent or airlines, stating that one has paid for and is entitled to certain accommodation and services. These vouchers are issued for hotels. The vouchers are the record of sale of the travel agent. For client it is the protection on arrival of the hotel. The standard voucher is printed on a paper which cannot be erased. It is like the type of paper which is used for paper currency. It is to eliminate any chances of alternations. This voucher serves both as a reservation confirmation as well as a receipt for the money collected by the travel agent. The voucher contains the following information:

(a) What accommodation has been confirmed in the reservation?
(b) How many days and nights?
(c) What rate they have been confirmed?

(d) What rate of tax?
(e) Date of arrival and departure of passenger.
(f) What special information have been given to the hotel in advance of the guest arrival?
(g) Who confirmed the reservations?
(h) On what date the reservations were confirmed?
(i) Value of coupon based on the money being sent by the agency for the client.

Each hotel voucher can have a face value, as a money order because it is guaranteed by the travel agency. The agent places his name and address as the guarantee. The Travel Agent guarantee is used only when you know your client and also under the following circumstances :

(1) Uses for guests arriving after midnight.
(2) In event the hotel guest does not arrive until after 6 p.m. the room will be held all night.
(3) In the event the guest does not arrive, i.e., 'no show' the hotel then he has the authority to bill the travel agent for that particular night accommodations.

The top part of the hotel voucher is for the client use, and the bottom part is for the hotel's use and sent with the payment from the agency. A voucher can encourage the hotel front desk to think twice before a client who has a confirmed reservation walks in.

Three types of payments are generally sent by the travel agency to the hotel :

(a) A deposit which is one night room rate and no commission is deducted.
(b) A partial payment which is more than the one night's room rate but not the total number of night staying. No commission is deducted.
(c) The full payment, i.e., pre-payment, which covers all the night staying. In this case, the amount of commission is deducted and the hotel tax is inducted with full payment.

## Car Booking

To make a car booking the customer has to call in advance and fill up the particulars, i.e., type of car, make of car, AC/Non-AC, distance to be travelled, time, etc. The travel agent then contacts the car rental services and books a car, which then goes directly to the customer. Any further instructions are passed on directly to the driver or chauffeurs.

The travel agent always calls back to the customer to confirm whether the car reached on time.

**Railway Reservation**

Modern day, rail travel is as attractive as air transportation. Comparatively it is becoming less costly and in some cases it is faster than air service between cities. A reservation is an agreement for travel between railway and customer. A travel agent should give an order to the railway for travel in the name of the client. As a result of contact with the railway reservation, the space requested for the client is set aside from further sale to any one else. A reservation is a conditional request for space and is not a contract for travel with the railways which has been notified that a particular ticket has been issued. Reservations are required for all sleeping (overnight) journeys. Coaches and club car accommodation reservations can be obtained for any reserve train by calling the appropriate Central Reservation Office designated to handle the calls. Reservations are booked in the traveller's name. The name of travel agency, telephone number and address is included. All reservations are subject to hold 'Hold Limit' cancellations. Until appropriate tickets have been issued and reservations have been furnished the reservation accommodations may be automatically cancelled if the hold limit is passed. Agent may wish to advise the customers of the reservation hold limit, if tickets are not issued at the time of booking. Travel agents themselves are ultimately responsible for protection of reserved space by issuing tickets and advising association members to rail reservations before the assigned limit was passed. Reserved accommodations which have not been ticketed and are no longer desired should be cancelled promptly to make the space available to other travellers.

For railway reservations, one form is used for only 6 members if it is a family, and 4 members if it is a group. Following points have to be noted while reserving a seat.

- In the Railway control chart, the journey particulars, age and sex of the passengers has to be filled up.

- Where there is a computer link reservations can be taken, otherwise tickets are used on request message.
- The different classes available in the trains are:
  1st AC
  2nd AC
  First Class
  AC Chair Car (C/C)
  AC 3T
  II 3T (Sleeper)
  II Ordinary Seat
- For ordinary seat reservation, initially we allot the ordinary seat to the passenger, but he can be allotted sleeper at a later stage when there is cancellation or seats are available due to release of quotas.
- When quota is full then they start RAC (Reservation Against Cancellation) in certain trains and certain classes.
- When RAC is full then they start a waiting list which is also limited to some extent after which the booking is closed.

*Discounts*

- Student – 50 per cent on basic fare.
  For a student concession, the form has to be signed by the principal. The concession is offered only while going to ones hometown and for vacations.
- Disabled/Handicapped – 50 per cent
- Senior citizens – 65 years and above for IInd class only and the journey should be beyond 500 KM – 25 per cent concession.
- Escort with blind passengers.
- Defence personnel – 60 per cent warrant.

Reservations are done 45 days in advance, except in a few trains and local trains, where the reservations are done 15 days/ 10 days/1 week or 3 days in advance.

*Indrail Pass*

To provide easy and comfortable journey to the foreign tourists in a planned manner, Indian Railways have introduced the facility of Indrail Passes which offers all budget visitors to travel as they like from any point to any point over the IR without route or train restrictions including Rajdhani and Shatabdi Express Trains within the period of validity. Indrail passes are sold only to foreign nationals and Indians residing abroad holding valid passports against payment in US Dollars or Pounds Sterling. A tourist travelling on Indrail passport is exempted from paying reservation fee, sleeper charges, supplementary charges for travelling by super fast trains or for meals provided in Rajdhani and Shatabdi Express trains.

Indrail pass has to be validated before commencing the first rail journey by getting the columns of 'first day and last day' properly filled in by authorized official. To facilitate Rail tourism the IR have introduced the Indrail Rover Scheme which envisages confirmed train accommodation provided booking is made a minimum of 90 days in advance.

Outside India Indrail passes are sold through General Sales Agents in London, New York, Paris, Sydney, Frankfurt, Tokyo, Toronto, Bangkok, Port Luis, Helsinki, Sharjah, Kaulalumpur, Muscat, Amsterdam and Dhaka.

In India, Indrail passes are available for sale in Railway Offices in New Delhi, Mumbai, Kolkata, Chennai, Agra Cantt., Ahmedabad, Aurangabad, Bangalore City, Chandigarh, Gorakhpur, Secunderabad, Hyderabad,, Vijaywada, Jaipur, Rameshwaram, Trivendrum Central, Vadodara, Varanasi, Vasco-de-gama and Amritsar. Certain recognized travel agents are also authorised to sell these passes in Delhi, Mumbai, Kolkata and Chennai.

*Cancellation and Refunds*

The Railway reservation guide states, "If there is a change in your travel plan, please cancel your reservation promptly as it will help others to secure reservation and also you to save money."

If an unused ticket without reservation is presented up to 3 hours after the departure of the train, full fare after deducting Rs. 5 per passenger will be refunded. Tickets with reservation can be presented within 6 hours after the departure of the train for refund. The scale of deductions in case of reserved tickets is as under :

| Sl. | Time of Return | Class | Amount Deducted (in rupees) |
|---|---|---|---|
| 1. | More than one day in advance, excluding the date of journey. | AC 1st Class 1 Class/<br>AC Sleeper AC C/C<br>Sleeper Class II Class | 30<br>20<br>15 |
| 2. | One day in advance and upto four hours before the scheduled departure of train. | 25% subject to the minimum charges | |
| 3. | Within four hours before the scheduled departure of the train and upto :<br>(a) 3 hours for tickets upto 200 km.<br>(b) 6 hours for tickets more than 200 km. but upto 500 km.<br>(c) 12 hours for tickets more than 500 km. | 50 % subject to the minimum charges. | |

No cancellation charges shall be levied on RAC/Wait Listed tickets unless confirmed reservation has been provided at any time upto the final preparation of reservation charts clerkage charges of Rs. 5 per passenger will, however, be payable.

For night trains leaving between 2100 hours and 0600 hours (actual departure) refund is admissible at the station within the time limit specified above or within first 2 hours after the opening of reservation office, which ever is later.

For obtaining refund after the prescribed time limit or on partially used tickets, or due to failure of a A/C equipment, non-availability of onward reservation dislocation of train services, etc., please contact the station masters.

**International Department**

This department specializes in providing facilities to only those passengers who intend travelling abroad. This department has to do varied jobs, therefore, it is divided into following small sections :

*Documentation Section*

To travel abroad one require number of documents and formalities. This section is conversant with all the formalities, involved in and documents required for all types of foreign travel. Any person wanting to go abroad shall have to come into contact with the documentation section of the travel agency. The agent will ask him the reason for travel abroad. After this he will accordingly advice him about the documents needed for obtaining the approval of Reserve Bank of India for the purpose of the ticket.

The formalities and the documents needed for travel abroad differ according to the purpose of visit. There are various reasons for travelling abroad – for higher education, business, medical treatment, immigration, etc. In each case the formalities and the supporting documents differ in order to seek the permission of the Government of India through the Reserve Bank of India to pay the passage in Indian rupees by giving sound reasons in support of the validity of the purpose of the visit. For example, the Reserve Bank of India will give permission for travelling abroad for further studies when the following documents are submitted :

- Admission letter from the University abroad in his favour.
- Sponsorship declaration duly supported from his blood relation who is already staying in that country, stating that he shall bear all the expenses of his brother/ward during his stay there.
- Employer's certificate or his bankers certificate that he is making enough money to be able to support his brother/ward, etc.

Thus, the travel agency will be authorized to negotiate and deal with the transport offices, Reserve Bank of India and Income Tax Officer on behalf of the passenger and will :

- Make the international passport;
- Obtain the necessary permission of the Reserve Bank of India after producing all relevant documents;
- After obtaining the necessary sanction from the Government for the purpose of ticket and making all documents ready; this section will pass the case on the Reservation Section.

*Reservation Section*

This is another section which deals with the reservation of transport and hotel accommodation. This section is conversant with all the airlines' time tables, air fares for different distances and hotel accommodations and the tariff charged. It notes down all the details of the programme. This information is recorded on a specially printed sheet of paper. Thereafter a suitable travel plan is drawn giving suitable flight connections with arrival/departure timings and places of stay. It also makes an approximation of the cost for staying and the air fare. After the approval of the travel plan, a finally typed copy is given to the passenger for his reference. This is known as itinerary.

The next step is the booking of seat. The reservation section then contacts the concerned airlines and asks for a seat as per itinerary. The concerned airline will get the full programme of the passenger. It will send reservation messages to its concerned officers for the onward flight confirmation as per the programme. On obtaining all the confirmation, the airline informs the agent that all the onward reservations are ready. On receipt of this information the agent issues its voucher drawn on the airlines asking them to issue their tickets in favour of that particular person, as per the details of the flights given in the voucher. This voucher contains the following information :

(a) Name of the passenger
(b) Place to be visited
(c) Date
(d) Flight Number
(e) Time
(f) RBI Permit number
(g) Passport Number
(h) Applicable fare
(i) Agent code number

After receiving this voucher the airline issues the tickets. The ticket is sent to the agent who checks it and after being satisfied hand it over to the passenger. The passenger has to pay the exact amount mentioned in the ticket.

Thus, it is seen that the travel agents provide a number of services to the passenger for which no extra amount is charged.

The passenger gets the benefit of guidance and services from the travel agent. In the absence of travel agency, he would have had to waste a lot of time, energy and money.

*Visa Section*

This section keeps all the information for the formalities involved for obtaining visa for different countries. It deals with all these formalities and obtains the visa for the passengers.

*Reservations on International Airlines*

International airlines or the 'flag carriers' represent their country and normally have their own country's flag painted on the airplane. The majority of the international carriers are owned and sponsored by the government of the country. The international airlines and routes require an agreement between the various governments based on socio-economic consideration as well as the frequency of flight from one nation to another. Therefore, the International Air Transport Authority (IATA) attempts to resolve policies and fares applicable to the participating international air carriers.

As a travel agent, it is necessary to use several airlines to complete a trip since no airline services every city, it becomes essential to know the major route structure and remember the general geographical regions serviced. Airlines and travel agencies must have a complete copy of all tariffs at all offices where air tickets are being sold in order to obtain the correct fares. As soon as the latest revision in tariffs are recieved, it is essential to review and revise them promptly. To maintain a tariff properly, the agents should compare each revision transmittal number with the list on the cover sheet to be sure that each revision is in sequence and complete. He should check the correct number on the pages published in the front of each tariff. He should know each effective date and any information on the transmittal that is specially important and then collate and insert in the tariff all effective pages.

The local and joint passenger rules tariff provides the individual and group airlines policies governing the transportation of passengers and their luggage. There are airline rules for handicapped passengers, children under five years of age travelling alone, carrying fire arms abroad, a commercial flight, food service abroad flight, excess baggage charges and regulation in the tariff rules governing all aspects of airline and passenger relations. Recently the use of plastic cutlery on board has been made standard on all flights as a result of the September 11 attack on the World Trade Centre. Once the new tariffs rules are approved and regulations passed these become official dealing for passenger handling. Each travel agent and airline employee must follow the rules published in the tariff otherwise the agent or the company will be liable. Similarly, the local passenger fares tariff contain different regular fares of each participating carrier. A careful study, will make the understanding of these fares quite easy and simple. The joint one way and round-trip fares and rules are published to cover transportation in two different airlines. In other words, a joint fare becomes one fare covering transportation over two different carriers with the stipulation that the passenger must charge airplanes in a certain specified city. The joint fare is available as a single amount to cover transportation over two different airlines. It becomes a lesser amount than the sum of two one way fares would be over the same route.

**Guidelines for International Tariff Rules**

While reading and finding the international tariff rules the following points must be observed :

(a) Refer the latest edition of air tariff including the most recent supplements.
(b) Check the airline tariff fare schedule for the applicable rule.
(c) Consult the tariff index for the rule numbers.
(d) Check the rule for the conditions governing normal and special fares. Identify the section of the rules most applicable. Make sure that there are no recent changes in fares.
(e) The various conditions governing normal and special fares are explained under the subject heading. These headings are :
    - Application
    - Record of Application

- Fares
- Validity
- Group size
- Stopovers
- Advertising and sales
- Affirmity and own use provisions
- Baggage
- Cancellations and refunds
- Combinations
- Commission
- Discount available for different categories like children/infant, tour conductors, sales agent
- Documentation
- Eligibility
- Minimum tour price
- Modification of inclusive tour
- Name change and additions
- Passenger Expenses
- Payment
- Reservation
- Revonting
- Ticketing
- Tour Features
- Tour Literature
- Travel Together

(f) Refer and read the concern rules................Read the entire rule thoroughly.

(g) Read the portions of the rule which are applicable to the carriers.

(h) Check the rules regarding the carriers in question.

(i) Make a study of the portions specially which begin with 'applicable to' and 'not applicable to' to see, if the carrier is mentioned.

**International Airline Ticket**

In case of an international airline the procedure is slightly different from the domestic ticket. The step by step procedure is as follows :

When the client approaches the travel agency, the following information may be acquired :

(i) Nature of client.

(ii) Type of flight.

(iii) Place of departure.

(iv) Place of destination.

(v) Date of journey/departure.

(vi) Date of return.

(vii) Refer the worldwide edition of OAG and look upto the place of departure from the place of destination.

(viii) Write the date, clients, name and residential phone contact on reservation pad.

(ix) Write the flight you have selected and date for customer's flight.

(x) Again refer the OAG to select return flight of the client. Look up to the place of destination from place of departure. See the date of return.

(xi) Transfer all this information to the itinerary pad.

(xii) Contact the concern airline and book the flights.

(xiii) If the flights are available circle 'OK'.

(xiv) Make a note of the airline reservationist's name and date on which the booking was made.

(xv) Convey the passenger's name, residential telephone contact and travel agency phone number to the airline reservationist.

(xvi) Double the fare for round trip and add the international tax.

(xvii) Re-verify the fare. Refer to the Air Traffic Worldwide Book-I (Latest Edition, Yellow Pages). Check the fare. Check the fare from place of departure to the place of destination. Note the fare.

(xviii) If you find that the fare given by the airline is correct, the reservationist should be ready for ticketing.

Similarly, in case of stop-over in some other city for a day in route to the place of destination there will be a different itinerary, check the mileage. In the same way, in the tariff listing. Thereafter, refer to the 'Routing..........non-stop sector mileage's section of the tariff to check the non-stop sector mileages. By looking up the mileage under the stop-over place, we may get the sector mileage listings for both the segments. Now one can complete the sector mileage by comparing both the mileages: the allowed mileage/and the computed mileage. If the computed mileage is well within the allowed mileage, it is not necessary to increase the fare. In case of complicated fare itineraries, verification should be made with the airline rate desk. They will give the rate number. This rate number should be written on the fare construction portion of the ticket.

**ABC – World Airways Guide**

ABC – World Airways guide has compiled from information updated from over 700 airlines. It includes :

- Worldwide city to city schedules
- Travel planning information Airline features
- Car Hire (North American Promotional Fares)
- Fares Supplement
  How to use the fares information :
  English, Frangain, Deutsch, Espand, Italiano, Japnese
- Currency Conversations
- Guide to fares construction
- Ticket and sales taxes
- Airport taxes
- Ticketed point mileages
- Excess mileage percentage told
- Validity indicator for special fares
- City-to-City fares
- IATA traffic conference Area Map
- Fares Notes
- Stop Press Information

Geographical routing codes :

EH - Eastern Hemisphere routing
AP - Atlantic Pacific routing
AT - Atlantic routing
Di - direct routing
NP - North Pacific routing
Pa - Pacific routing
Po - Polar routing
Ts - Sibarian routing

**Guide to Fares Construction**

*The Currency System*

The Airline Industry introduced a new currency system on 1st July, 1989. The system is based on local currency fares. To enable fares to be combined a unit for currency construction has been established called the Neutral Unit of Construction (NUC).

NUC conversion factors are specified to convert local currency amounts to NUC amounts and to convert the total NUC amount back to the currency of sale. These conversion factors will change four times a year (1 Jan., 1 April, 1 July, 1 Oct.), or more frequently of a particular currency has a significant change in its value between these months. These factors will be published in the ABC World Airways Guide Fares Supplement every month and it is important that users use the factors quoted in the current edition for all rates, i.e., for sales made in July, use the July edition of the fares supplement. This rule also applies to advance sales, so that for a journey commencing in September, but sold in July, use the conversion factors published in the July edition.

Where D is shown in the IATA exchange rate column fares are sold in US Dollars (Refer to country USA for factors).

Local currency amounts will not be affected by changes in the NUC conversion factors, except where the fare is constructed, using an add-on which is specified in another currency. They will only be affected by normal periodic fare changes.

An example: A fare from Vancouver to Paris, quoted in Canadian Dollars, is actually made-up of an add-on from Vancouver to Montreal in Canadian Dollars. As these amounts are both in the same local currency, they can be added together, and they are unaffected by conversion factor charges.

However, a fare from Paris to Vancouver quoted in French francs is actually made up of a fare from Paris to Montreal in French francs and on add-on from Montreal to Vancouver in Canadian dollars. As these two amounts are in different local currencies, they are first converted to NUCs, and then the total NUC value is converted to French francs and therefore the total in French francs will be affected by changes in the relationship between the NUC and the Canadian Dollar/French Franc.

*How to use NUCs to calculate fares*

To combine fares which have different local currencies the following procedure must be followed : Firstly, take the fares in the relevant local currency and convert the amount to NUCs by dividing the conversion factors, and taking the answer to two decimal places with no rounding-off. Add the NUC amounts together and multiply the total by the conversion factor from NUC to the currency of departure country.

*For example:*

A journey from London to Rome, Rome to Stockholm and Stockholm to London. Find the quoted fares :-

| | |
|---|---|
| London to Rome | GBP 406.00 |
| Rome to Stockholm | ITL 13350.00 |
| Stockholm to London | GBP 444.00 |

*Convert to NUC*

London to Rome GBP 406.00 divided by NUC conversion 0.58 NUC 700.00; Rome to Stockhohm ITL 13350.00 divided by NUC conversion 1374 = NUC 971.61; Stockholm to London GBP 444.00 divided by NUC conversion 0.58 = NUC 765.51

| | | |
|---|---|---|
| Total NUC amounts | : | 700.00 |
| | | 971.61 |
| | | 765.51 |
| | | 2437.12 |

Convert to currency of departure country : Currency of departure country GBP Multiply NUC 2437.12 by IATA exchange rate to GBP 0.58 = GBP 1413.52

The result is then rounded off to give a total of GBP 1414.00.

**Note:** The figures quoted above are examples only.

If the last sector leads back to the country of origin, use the local currency fare from the country of origin. In the above example, the last sector Stockholm to London takes you back to the UK which is the country of commencement, therefore, the fare is GBP from London is used.

**Ticket and Sales Tax**

These taxes are collected in addition to the fare when a ticket is issued. Other documents as Excess Baggage Tickets and MCO are also subject to tax in some countries.

*Airport Taxes*

These taxes are normally paid in local currency upon departure. In many countries diplomats, transit passengers, and infants are exempted. Taxes for children and innumerable conferences, assemblies and national symposiums which are held every year within different countries vary. Local, state-national and international conventions are continually being held. Yearly meetings are held by national associations, union groups, fraternities and societies, educational associations, professional groups, educational advertisers and corporations of all types. These conferences and meetings sometimes outnumber hundreds and thousands of participants. These participants stay several days in the city of the host country. Many countries are aware of the serious economic aspect of conferences. They have to prepare appropriate premises and build necessary infrastructure to ensure their satisfactory operation.

The tourists visit India with varied aims. They visit India with the purpose to get into the heart of a country, eat the traditional food, drink the local beverages and live as near to the natives as possible. Many of them prefer to survey strange lands from familiar surroundings. India has pleasures and facilities for all types of tourists. It is a colourful and picturesque nation. Its monuments, and buildings, its customs, its festivals, religions, philosophy and art, testify to one of the oldest and richest civilizations. The forests, mountains, valleys, plains or desert walls all are of great interest to the naturalist, the botanist and the lover of nature.

The following abbreviations are commonly used in the travel and tourism community and are not necessarily used in the accompanying text.

**Abbreviations**

| | |
|---|---|
| AP | American Plan |
| MAP | Modified American Plan |

| | |
|---|---|
| EP | European Plan |
| CP | Continental Plan |
| F | First Class |
| J | Business Class |
| Y | Economy Class |
| PATA | Pacific Area Travel Association |
| UFTAA | Universal Federation of Travel Agents Association |
| IATA | International Air Transport Association |
| IATO | Indian Association of Tour Operators |
| WTO | World Tourism Organization |
| OW | One Way |
| RT | Round Trip |
| WL | Wait List |
| CT | Circle Trip |
| OK | Confirmed |
| FIT | Foreign Independent Traveller |
| GIT | Group Incentive Tour |
| IBT | In Bound Tours |
| OBT | Out Bound Tours |
| GSA | General Sales Agent |
| ATO | Air Taxi Operators |
| CMS | Conference Management Services |
| IAAI | International Airport Authority of India |
| DGCA | Director General of Civil Aviation |
| WATA | World Association of Travel Agencies |
| ITDC | Indian Tourism Development Corporation |
| THEX | Travel House Explorations |
| XX | Cancel |
| CTO | City Ticket Office |
| ARR | Arrival |
| DEP | Departure |
| DOT | Department of Tourism |
| FCU | Fare Construction Unit |
| FHIL | First Class Hotel |
| GMT | Greenwich Mean Time |
| IST | Indian Standard Time |
| Ra | Request |
| ICAO | International Civil Aviation Organization |

| | |
|---|---|
| IHA | International Hotel Association |
| MPM | Maximum Permitted Mileage |
| OAG | Official Airline Guide |
| OTC | Non-stop Inclusive Tour Charter |
| PAX | Passenger |
| PSGR | Passenger |
| SST | Supersonic Transport |
| SUR | Surface Travel |
| TGC | Travel Group Charter |
| THTL | Tourist Class Hotel |
| XO | Surcharge Order |
| XS | Access |

# *Part II*

# Automation in the Tourism Industry

*Thirteen*

# Providing E-Commerce Facilities in the Travel Industry

## The Computerized Reservation System (CRS) and Amadeus

The travel industry of today wears a different look. It is automated and high-tech, thanks to Computerized Reservation System (CRS) technology. A computer reservation system (CRS) functions through a network of global telecommunication channels that distribute a huge database of travel-related information and provide reservation kits. These are also, therefore, referred to a Global Distribution system that serves the information and reservation related needs of the travel agent.

Amadeus is the world's foremost and most advanced CRS company operating from 132 countries around the world. It provides a worldwide neutral booking system of travel professionals on airlines, hotels, car rental companies, and other travel service providers. Amadeus extends its booking capacity and extensive information on the world's travel services and offers powerful travel management tools. The company develops and markets software that helps travel agents and others working in travel-related fields to access flight schedules of 751 airlines, reserve in 506 airlines over 51,300 hotel properties and 300 hotel chains, access car rentals at over 48,462 travel agency locations through 48 car rental companies around the world.

Amadeus are significant providers of information technology and an enabler of e-commerce for the travel industry. Amadeus also delivers the powerful booking engine behind the web pages of more than 3,000 travel agencies and some 81-websites serving 28 airlines. Additionally, it provides similar e-commerce solutions for partners ranging from Wal-Mart (USA) to Gruppo I Espresso (Italy).

The Amadeus group has three central work centres at Madrid (Spain), Nice (France) and Erding, Munich (Germany) that handle corporate affairs, céntral administration and marketing, product/service development and data base development respectively. The company has almost 3,000 employees worldwide.

Having a unique approach to partnership that gives it the competitive edge for a strong market presence both globally and locally, it functions through various National Marketing Companies throughout the world that are responsible for sales and marketing, local product definition and front line training and support. Amadeus, thus, continues to strengthen its position as a global leader among the GDSs of the world.

Amadeus GES was first introduced in the Indian subcontinent in September 1994. Amadues India is a National Marketing Company (NMC) with sole distribution rights for the Amadeus GDS in the Indian subcontinent. It began its operations in India with offices in New Delhi and Mumbai. Since the NMC has strategically expanded its network to cover 23 offiçes in the Indian subcontinent including an office each in Nepal, Sri Lanka and Bangladesh. In less than five years, Amadeus has managed to gain a market share of over 70 per cent in the Indian subcontinent. Today, more that 2,249 travel agencies are on-line with Amadeus with over 3646 terminal installations in 64 cities.

Amadeus India has indigenously developed new products keeping in mind the specific needs of the Indian travel agent. IHRES (Indian Hotel Reservation System) is one example of customization for the Indian market by Amadeus India. This enables travel agents to access not only hotel chains, but also local hotels, and single hotels. Amadeus India has also introduces Power Office a locally developed comprehensive travel agency specific product that enables quick inventory-creation and invoicing by automatically connecting with the Amadeus Central System to collect and details directly for the PNR. The Indian Railways, for the first time, have an exclusive affiliation with Amadeus India to display detailed information pertaining to its commercial, marketing and operational aspects for the travel agents. The Indian NMC also initiated an innovative solution for travel agents while they wait for a full-time telecommunication link with our data centre at Erding, Germany called Dial-up. As a short-term provision the agent just has to connect a telephone to the computer terminal to begin work on the Amadeus system. The Dial-up has attracted an overwhelming response not only from agents but has also proved to be extremely beneficial as a corporate implant and at locations which otherwise may not justify a leased connection. Amadeus India is also the only CRS in the country to have introduced a 24 hour Help Desk service that is, at present, functional at the New Delhi and Mumbai offices. It also has a well-equipped and modular training centres at New Delhi, Mumbai, Chennai, Bangalore, Kathmandu and Colombo. It has also introduced the Training Manual Floppy that contains concise and easy-to-read chapters on various topics dealing with information and reservation on the Amadeus system. The various sections in the Floppy concentrate on each of the application on the system and explain the use of features with examples.

The constant endeavour of Amadeus is to bring to the Indian travel operator the very latest in travel automation technology. In keeping with its policy of providing Global Power Solutions, connectivity to the Amadeus GDS provides you with a distinctive service advantage also. To ensure that every member of the Amadeus team gets the best, Amadeus India focuses on consistent and competent services.

**Training Facility**

Training on Amadeus GDS is also provided on-site to assist its users in understanding the system and the powerful tools available for quick and easy solutions. In addition, Amadeus India has state-of-the-art training facilities in New Delhi, Mumbai, Chennai, Bangalore and Kathmandu that cater to the ongoing training needs of the travel agents from all regions. An innovation of the Indian NMC, the Training Manual Floppy has become a handy reference tool for the gent who is new to the Amadeus concept. In addition, the Company also conducts special 'Train the Trainer' programmes to enable in-house staff to stay abreast with all global developments at Amadeus, thereby maintaining high global quality standards of service and training.

**24 Hour Help Desk**

The Amadeus Help Desk staff at our offices ensures that they are able to provide timely assistance to all Amadeus agencies. The Help Desk extends its support by providing the agent with on-line support in case of a breakdown, facilitating the agency in making reservations, and also aiding the staff of an agency with queries and doubts related to reservations. In an effort to provide agents with exemplary service, Amadeus has a 24 hours round-the-clock Help Desk operational seven days a week at its New Delhi and Mumbai offices. An agent based anywhere in the Indian subcontinent can seek the assistance of this desk through a simple phone call at any time of the day to change, rebook, reschedule or make fresh reservations through the Amadeus system.

**Technical Support**

Amadeus technology brings varied and vital benefits to their customers, such as reliability, productivity, advanced products, connectivity solutions, improved automation and technical integration. Amadeus India's technical teams are based at each of the nineteen offices dotting the Indian subcontinent to ensure that in case of any breakdown they are always present on site to assist in rectifying the error. It has a fare display and a pricing function that is fully integrated with the automated ticketing process. These special fares are visible only to authorised agents. The database of this product allows you to store all your fares. 76 airlines are using their special fares through the Amadeus Negotiated Fares in over 20 markets.

**Ticket Writer**

The Ticket Writer is a windows-based software application designed to interface with the Central Reservation System. It is a key strategic product for the non-BSP (Billing and Settlement Plan) markets of Amadeus. It automatically picks up data from the front-office system and creates and processes tickets thereby reducing the risk of manual errors.

It helps save the travel consultant's valuable time to be able to focus better on sales efforts and customer services. The Ticket Writer is an efficient tool that handles group ticketing with commendable ease and speed. The distinct advantage of this is the export feature that allows the agent to export the ticket date to another application and produce reports while also managing information statistics. Tickets on the system can be saved, retrieved, modified and printed by virtue of this feature. This product is successfully being used in 20 markets worldwide. Amadeus provides constant technical support besides the standard training to all users of the Ticket Writer.

**Value Pricer**

To help keep pace with stiff competition and manage the price sensitive customer, Amadeus introduces Value Pricer—a fully integrated and powerful low fare search tool. The Value Pricer automatically matches the four-desired routes. This is a handy product that saves quality time with the convenience of a single entry and the user gets the best available deal in a few seconds. Another plus point with this user-friendly product is that fare can be found for any sector without a PNR also. You do not require any specialized knowledge of the complex subject of fares and pricing. At a time, it can price fares for up to 9 passengers and maximum of 6 requested segments for 4 cities. It sells at the highest level of access including direct access and last seat availability. The Value Pricer works in tandem with negotiated fares and provides the best choice on the current option along with three alternate flight and fare options.

## THE NEW PRODUCTS

**Amedeus Pro Tempo 2.3**

The upgraded version of the Amadeus Pro Tempo 2.2, called the Amadeus Pro Tempo 2.3, comes with new coherent enhancements and user-friendly features to help you save more time and effort. It provides a graphical Interface to the seat maps—a bright and colourful graphic of the inside of the aircraft simplifies the seat identification and allocation process. An all-inclusive travel information guide gives details about visa, health, weather, currency, airport taxes/customs and other related subjects that are often a cause of concern for the traveller. Additional facilities like Fax and E-mail, a complete car access besides others are part of this latest version. Pro Tempo 2.3 works through an expert mode that can be activated with the keyboard. The speed mode faction of this version functions with the click of the mouse.

**+Scripts**

This is a fully integrated, add-on module of the Pro Tempo 2.3 that works through graphical user interface with a set of guided windows. It uses dialogue boxes to perform tasks specific to the working environment while providing functions and templates for agents. The unique benefit that the +scripts offer is the convenience of not remembering entries for activation of various functions on the system. It prompts the user for relevant commands and then leads one to the desired result after the option is chosen. +Scripts help in improving efficiency and thereby increase productivity, especially at the point-of-sale. This can be helpful to guide novice users through a transition on the Central system. Scripts are already included in the Amadues Pro software for Air, Hotels, Cars and PNR and can be used as designed in the system or customized to suit particular needs.

**Negotiated Fares**

Understanding the need to provide customers with the lowest and most updated fares available, Amadeus has introduced Negotiated Fares—the solution to online distribution of lowest fares in a confidential manner. Amadeus is the only CRS that provide this product free of cost and in a safe and secure medium. It is a product created specifically for tour operators. It offers an on-line database of destination information of over 1,00,000 recreation, adventure and travel opportunities offered by local providers around the world. This includes information on tour offices, operators, brochures and booking functions for four packages, attractions, museums, accommodation, conference facilities, and sporting activities like golf, fishing, etc.

**Power Office**

This is a back office system that facilitates inventory creation and invoicing through an automatic link with the Amadeus Central

System to collect details directly from the Passenger Name Record (PNR). This is aimed at making the operations of a travel agent more efficient and thus cost-effective. Power Office defines and customizes to the travel agencies Management Information System (MIS) formats. It possesses a comprehensive financial accounting application including the ability to generate balance sheets, one of the core functions of Power Office. The System, thus, avoids duplication of data entry that can be tedious process. It organizes customer profiles, outstanding invoices, BSP reporting, passenger sales reports and daily sales record.

**BSP Automated Ticketing**

This software enhances the utility of the BSP (Billing and Settlement Plan). It not only enables the travel agents and their clients to benefit from instant ticket issue on behalf of carriers throughout the world but also automates it. This further helps in not only simplifying work out also result in saving costs. It offers various other functions like India specific software that includes a comprehensive Ticket Quota System. An alert function gets activated as and when ticket stocks need replenishment. All levels of staff in an agency can operate Amadeus Automated Ticketing, equipped with world-class ticket printers.

**Galileo**

*The Company*

Galileo's global connections are unmatched, they provide travel agents at more than 38,000 locations the ability to access schedule and fare information, book reservations and issue airline tickets in more than 80 countries on six continents. It has relationships with over 500 airlines, more than 39,000 hotels, all major car hire companies, and numerous tour and cruise operators around the world. Galileo operates one of the world's biggest commercial data centres, handling over 30 billion transactions a year—up to 5,000 messages per second—with an uptime performance record of better than 99 per cent. And we are constantly developing state-of-the-art travel automation products that enhance travel agents' services and productivity. A high level of technology is very important but people and service are equally important. Travel is one of the fastest moving industries in a fast moving world. Yet what has been true in the past remains true even today: enduring relationships succeed. At Galileo, value is given to the relationships. Every travel agency is important to Galileo, commitment to working in partnership, delivering the products to help the agency to compete in an increasingly complex business environment to succeed.

*Galileo's Services*

Global fares TM is the world's premier fares system, used by 38,000 travel agencies and chosen by more than 100 airlines as their in-house system. Global Fares calculates complicated rates in seconds, and validated all rules appropriate to the itinerary. It allows agents to quote fares that contain all applicable rules and taxes for each segment of the trip, providing travellers with true consistent — and no experience - hidden surprises later. Global Fares has a powerful feature that allows your agents to save time. Best Buy automatically finds the best available price for every segment. Fare Quote Planner provides a unique shopping tool for unbooked itineraries. By combining several extraordinary powerful tools in one, Global fares TM gives the agents the confidence that they are quoting the best fares available. Each fare quoted includes all applicable taxes fees, free baggage allowances and other expenses for each segment of the journey. In a few seconds, an agent can utilise the power of Fare Quote, Best Buy, Private Fares and Fare Quote Planner to provide a client with timely fares that meet every single personal and business requirement. Best by automatically searches available booking classes and applicable fares to respond with a quote lower than that for which the traveller is booked. A private fare maintains a database of negotiated fares and displays them along with the public fares for comparison. And Fare Quote Planner makes multiple fare quotes automatically up to ten at a time. The global fares comprehensive database consist of millions of fares that are updated several times a day to ensure that the agents always have the very latest information at their fingertips. In addition, all fare rules, routes footnotes and applicable fare construction principles are validated in the fare quote process. With global fares, manually intensive and time-consuming operations are accomplished quickly, accurately and automatically, allowing the agents to spend more time assisting other clients.

*Private Fares* TM allows the agency to create and maintain a database of fares that have been specially negotiated for the clients assuring them applicable fares that are the most accurate, timely and best available.

*Airline Bookings:* Galileo maintains relationship with over 500 airlines worldwide, and has direct access to the internal scheduling and fare databases of over 200. As a result, the airline booking of Galileo are the most powerful and flexible in the industry, allowing airlines to offer customers an unmatched level of options and services. The Galileo Availability Display is an unbiased display of all participating carriers, giving the customers choices from virtually every published schedule in the world. In addition, Galileo's offers airlines several business tools to ensure synchronization of schedules in their system with the Galileo system. There are also dynamic tools available to obtain schedules and status data in real time, so the customers can always be assured they are receiving the very latest schedule and seating information. Travellers want not only the lowest fare, but a seat that is guaranteed. Galileo Sell gives agents accurate and comprehensive flight information that's quickly and easily accessible, and reservations that can be guaranteed. For Travellers who have special request, Galileo Enhanced Booking File Service eliminates the complex and lengthy process usually involved in including special requests in a Booking File. All information is delivered in the correct format for each carrier. And Galileo Advance Seat Reservation allows agents to reserve a particular seat on an aircraft with visual seat layout.

**Hotel and Tour Bookings**

*Car Master* TM *and Room Master* TM are considered by many to be the easiest and most flexible car hire and hotel booking tools in the industry. Car Master allows your agents access to the reservation system of the major car hire companies worldwide. It provides instant confirmations, and can be customized to check rules, availability and prices to show only those care that meet a customer's requirements. Car Master is the most accurate, efficient and convenient way to book hire cars with confidence anywhere in the world. And its easy enough so that novice agents using it can become immediately productive with minimal training. Room Master is the most completes and uptodate hotel reservation system in the industry. With it, your agents have instant access to more detailed hotel information than all the hotel books, directories and reference books combined. Room Master provides access to book more than 200 hotel vendors and over 39,000 properties worldwide. Room Master simplifies the booking process to such a degree that, as with Car Master, novice agents can learn to use its power right away. Galileo even provides an extremely easy-to-use graphical interface that makes it easy for anyone—even novices—to book cars and hotels through Car Master and Room Master. The agent is guided through the process with menu-based options and on-line help-there is no need to know industry codes.

**Leisure Shoppers**

Because Leisure Travel is growing — and can become a significant part of your business—Galileo provides real-time availability and accurate pricing to the leading tour cruise vendors. Leisure Shopper gives the agency an instant access to the reservation systems of cruise operations and global tour wholesalers, making it more profitable without increasing its overhead. The powerful capabilities of Leisure Shopper allows the agents to quickly research and compare packages from different vendors, and give instant confirmation at time of booking. Leisure Shopper ensures that the Galileo reservation system and the system of the tour operator or wholesaler are always in prefect synchronization, so agents can obtain instant confirmation of bookings. The agents can also control the agency's special rates, group inventory and commissions. While being extraordinarily powerful, Leisure Shopper is easy to learn. Agents are guided through the process, so accuracy is ensured. Leisure Shopper allows the agency to enter — or get further into — the money-making leisure business, without increasing the overhead.

**One-Size-Fits-All**

Galileo offers a complete suite of self-booking solutions. So it offers three different solutions to meet the needs the customers who want to book their own travel:

**Travelpoint.com or Travelpoint TM**

All the Travelpoint solutions provide the customers with access to the Galileo Systems. All reservations made with any Travelpoint product are ticketed by the sponsoring agency, thereby keeping the customer in touch.

**Focalpoint**

The powerful productivity tools offered by Galileo are easy to learn. Agents can become more productive with Focalpoint a sophisticated reservation, business management and support system that combines the ease-of-use of Microsoft Windows with the power of the Galileo central system. Focalpoint provides the agents with up to nine separate display areas or windows on the screen. Different functions can then be carried out in each window so that the agents save time and are more productive. Workstations can be personalized for the agents and customized to the business process. It allows the agents to integrate vital business management tools with the most-efficient way of making travel bookings.

**Focalpoint Relay TM**

Focalpoint Relay productivity tools build on the power of Focalpoint to make complex, time-consuming tasks easier. Relay provides the agents with the time-saving applications that can automatically capture data, manage queues, create booking files, edit client files, simplify ticket exchange, facilitate print recovery and make changing or editing Custom Check TM Rules a very easy process.

**Travel Document Solutions**

Tickets and oth travel documents demand accuracy and timely delivery. The Galileo systems enables the agents to provide customers with all the relevant documents and uptodate information quickly and easily. Galileo's ticketing product complies with all industry regulations, and it allows to enter variable information including carrier selections, commission percentage, form of payment, and more.

*Electronic Ticketing*

Today's travellers appreciate anything that makes travelling easier. Electronic Ticketing—with no paper ticket to lose—is the latest improvement to the ticketing process and Galileo was at the forefront of its development. In markets that support it, Electronic Ticketing lets the agency give freedom to its customers to travel without paper tickets. In many cases customers merely provide identification at the gate, then board the aircraft.

*Satellite Ticket Printing*

When a client needs a ticket immediately, or when Electronic Ticketing is not available, Satellite Ticket Printing enables the ticket to be printed at the corporate customer's location. With both Electronic Ticketing and Satellite Ticket Printing, delivery costs are reduced, helping the agency maximize its resources while providing state-of-the-art service to its customers.

*Itinerary/Invoice*

Galileo Enhanced Itinerary Invoice is a comprehensive and powerful tool that combines all relevant information regarding customer's travel schedule. Enhanced Itinerary Invoice gives the agency the ability to customize the itinerary and invoice which helps the agents to supply their clients with comprehensive, structured documents that contain all the information they require. For automating repetitive ticketing tasks, Focal point Relay TM productivity tools are unparalleled. Print Recovery lets agents easylink and de-link printers and Response Capture faithfully captures Galileo system information using a choice of text editing methods. The ticketing process is further automated with Queue Ticketing. Using this feature, ticketing for all transactions on the Queue Ticketing can be processed with one input. Multiple ticketing lets agents issue tickets for multiple stored fares with one simple command. For keeping track of all the tickets issued and voided by the agency, the ticket Invoice Number System report is indispensable. Up to thirty day's worth of ticketing information is always instantly available. Ticket Exchange automatically provides information from previous files.

**Business Management Solutions**

Many of the tasks travel agents perform involve repetition. Capturing data, editing Client Files, managing Queues, changing printer status—these are time-consuming jobs that can benefit from automation. Focalpoint Relay productivity tools are a series of point-and-click applications that let the agents use the power of Focalpoint and Windows to automate the complex, repetitive, time-consuming tasks. Very simply, the agents can manage Queues and Client Tiles as well as capture, read and interpret data from the Galileo system. They can easily accomplish ticket exchange and handle the recovery of documents from the printers. With Focal point Relay, there's no memorizing of complex Galileo formats, and the productivity of your agency is immediately increased.

*Past Date Quick™*

When a customer requests information about a booking that is days or weeks in the past, retrieving that information has been difficult and time-consuming. But no more. Galileo provides its agency's with the ability to retrieve it quickly with Past Date QuickTM. Past Date Quick allows agents timely access to past date information. Information up to 60 days old can be accessed instantly. Within 24 hours, information from 61 days to 13 months old can be retrieved, giving you the ability to provide another value service to the clients.

*Queues Manager™*

In order to distribute workload efficiently, in the travel agency, Galileo provides Queues. Queues help to manage business process more efficiently by providing the agents with electronic filing areas within the system that will sort and hold any records requiring follow-up activity. These can include lists of clients to advise vendors to contact, or tickets to issue. Queues can be even more easily managed with Queues Managers TM. Another one of the Focal Point Relay productivity tools. Working with Queues allows agents to distribute the workload, making your agency more efficient and productive.

*Learning Tools from CDs*

Keeping the working staff uptodate on the latest software products and features is important for the business. Galileo offers a variety of learning tools that focus on improving agents' skills in key business areas. Whether training is delivered in a classroom or on a CD, our goal is to ensure to the agents the expertise needed deliver exceptional customer service. In addition to training, Galileo provides a comprehensive database of on-line help, airline information, consulate information and country information as well as customer services and Galileo product overviews. When agents sign on to the system, they are presented with new vendor and pricing information. These information tools mean better informed and more productive and skilled agents.

*Report Generating*

Producing proper reports is often the most time-consuming activity agents are involved in. Galileo provides several products that make report-generation easy and accurate. BSP Handoff automates and streamlines the time-consuming process of creating weekly reports and travel documents enabling your agents to spend more time on customers and less time on reporting. Machineable Interface Record is the Galileo system's data hand-off record that includes all the booking and financial data necessary to drive agency management systems.

*Global Access TM*

Galileo makes it easy to coordinate information with other Galileo and Apollo customers

Global Access TM fets the agents view files on our systems anywhere in the world. Selective Access allows the sharing of data—and updating of files—with other Galileo subscribers thus enabling the agency to form new worldwide business relationships. If you need to work with data from the Galileo system while using your own computer platform, Galileo provides Application Programmable Interfaces. These allow the agency to connect to the Galileo system and work with its database on matter what type of computer platform you operate.

**Control and Productivity Solutions**

Galileo's quality control and productivity solutions help the agencies and their agents to manage large amount of travel data easily, and provide a high level of control that lets agents make the best use of their time. With Galileo's travel solutions, keeping track of customer information, preferences, company policies, restrictions and requirements is made simple-so more time with customers. Complex processes are easily automated, and products can be combined to create customized solutions, assuring the agency the highest level of productivity.

*Travel Screen TM*

Travel Screen TM — a Galileo exclusive-working in conjunction with Client Files, instantly and consistently integrates personal and business travel preferences into all air, car and hotel bookings. It presents only the options that meet your customer requirements so your agents can be responsive to customer needs on the spot. Researching business customers' personal data and preferences and giving them options involving those preferences can be time-consuming. Travel Screen TM makes that task easy. Travel Screen—another Galileo exclusive—stores travellers' personal and corporate preferences, then incorporates them automatically in searching for itineraries. The only travel options displayed on-screen will be the correct ones that meet those preferences, thus saving time for both, customers and agents. Custom Check saves the agents time and gives them point-of-sale quality control, making sure all relevant requirements are met.

*Scriptwriter Plus TM*

Scriptwriter Plus TM is a unique and flexible tool that allows complete customization of the reservation processes. Using Focal-point scripts developed with Scriptwriter Plus, necessary data can be collected automatically, reducing re-entry of information after the booking. Because they can be customized to the needs, the Galileo system's powerful yet easy-to-learn tools help to differentiate the agency from the competition in terms of accuracy, attention to detail, and sheer efficiency.

**Airline Products**

Today's business traveller is more demanding than ever requesting special meals, specific seating or guaranteed seating on specific types of aircraft. Fortunately, Galielo's array of specialized air booking products can handle any request—or demand—with ease.

Galileo Availability guarantees the most uptodate availability from over 500 airline—more than any other GRS—giving the clients the greatest choice of flight options and schedules. The Schedule database contains virtually every published match client's including specific connection points and specific carriers. With Galileo Availability, the agency has the competitive advantage of superior customer service.

Enhanced Booking Files Servicing (EBTS) eliminates the complex and lengthy process involved in sending special requests to airlines in a Booking file. With EBTS, non-standard requests like Ticket on Departure can be accomplished with minimum effort. Agents no longer need to learn special formats or to queue the requests to airlines. EBTS guarantees that the request will be delivered to the airline in the expected format.

With Galileo links to more airlines, Galileo gives agents the ability to offer higher quality service. They can display and sell from seat availability in real time and take advantage of "insider" tools like seat maps.

**The Plastic Money**

*American Express Credit Cards*

Amex comes in three categories.

1. American Express Global credit card
2. American Express Global green card
3. American Express Global gold card

*Master/Visa Cards*

Master card has different categories due to their tie-ups with Indian Banks such as:

Allahabad Bank (Master and Visa)

Citibank Master Cards (Having three categories) (Master and Visa)

SBI credit cards (Master Visa)

Visa power.

*H.S.B.C Credit Cards*
(Having three categories)

*ANZ Grindlays, ANZ Star TV Global Card:*
(Having three categories)
Accreditation by visa and master

*CITIBANK Credit Cards*
Diners' club
Citibank visa gold card
Citibank master card

Are some reputed names in the Travel Business, all these major cards not only provide financial support but also help in travel business. Today the traveller doesn't need to think of how he/she can travel, they need only to dial a number or just enter a travel site and every these cards give a kind of freedom to purchase any thing at any time.

The basic services given by these Credit Cards:

1. Booking of Airlines tickets/Railway Tickets/Car on hire
2. Reward point (earning on spending of the money that can be used for anything such as Entertainment, purchasing gifts, travelling, etc.)
3. Hotel bookings/Medical services
4. Dining lunch/breakfast, etc.
5. Global validity.

To conclude, we can say that today travel management industry is constantly changing, requiring new solutions and new ways of thinking. In just the last few years, the Internet has become a new area of opportunity. Business travel is becoming more far-ranging and complex, and travellers are demanding more services and expecting many relevant choices instantly. Now the travel industry has come up with the solutions in terms of websites opening a diverse nature of information to its users.

1. The SN Expedia
2. Travelcity com
3. Travel and Tourism (ASTA)

4. Travel and Tourism (EUROP)
5. Travel and Tourism (Italy)
6. Travel and Tourism (U.S.A.)
7. Travel and Tourism (CANADA)
8. Travel and Tourism (AUSTALIA)
9. Travel and Tourism (MAGASTA)
10. Travel and Tourism (STNGAPORE)

**References**

Amedius
Galileo
Mr. Mahesh (Asstt. Manager)
Web Site
www.Travel tourism (Mantraonline com).

## *Fourteen*

# Automating the Hospitality Industry

Hotel and Restaurant Systems (HRS) has developed a network of cutting-edge information technology solutions to automate the hospitality industry. By partnering with Micros/Fidelio leading innovators in technology solutions (hardware, software and peripherals) for the hospitality field, HRS is able to facilitate property and point-of-sale management to increase bottom line performance and enhance daily operations, as well as define services offered. In addition, to provide hospitality paging systems, performance door locking systems, mini-bar systems, print production of consumables, a back office management system and an electronic reservation gateway for hotels to access travel agents worldwide.

Support for information technology fosters efficiency and greater knowledge for streamlining operations. The HRS team of highly skilled, industry consultants is available twenty-four hours, seven days a week. Additionally they offer remote modem support, extended on-site maintenance, consultation, project management, training, network configuration and installation services.

Over a period of eight years, HRS has focussed its efforts in the CIS and Baltics, often working with the Russian government and regional administrations to bring international standards and automation systems to restaurant and hotel properties. They are currently supporting over 700 restaurant workstations and 7000 hotel rooms. HRS is represented with major offices in Moscow, St. Petersburg, Kiev, Tallinn and Riga. Beyond a growing reputation in the CIS and Baltics, HRS counts as its clients such leading international chains as Kempinski, Hilton, Marriott, Colony, Hyatt, Marco Polo, Radisson, Inter Continental, Sheraton and Best Western.

They approach the application of technology as an advancement towards hospitality management, committed in partnership and support.

**Front Office Management Software**

To achieve the best possible performance from a hotel's front office, Fidelio's Front Office Management software is an invaluable asset to the company already implementing this software. This is one of the world's best selling front office systems, and it's the system of choice for Hilton International, InterContinental Mandarin Oriental, Forte, CIGA and many other chains and independents around the globe.

Fidelio Front Office is an integrated family of property management software modules that work together to maximize the efficiency of the entire organization. Front Office includes features that speed and simplify all of the functions needed to serve guests, manage hotel operations, and maintain an efficiently run enterprise. All Front Office features are designed to be easy to learn and use.

Front Office offers interfaces to a host of third-party systems. In addition, Front Office can be combined with other Fidelio products such as Sales and Catering, Food and Beverage, Engineering Management, Accounts Receivable, Travel Agent Processing, and Frequent Flyer. Front Office can also be integrated with the MICROS-Fidelio Central Systems, the Customer Information System, and the Central Reservations System for comprehensive central management of guest profiles, memberships, rates, and reservations.

*System Architecture*

- Network: Windows NT Server 4.0 or Novell IntraNetware 4.1 are supported.
- Database: xBase running under DOS 6.22/Windows 3.11.
- Client: Windows NT 4.0 Workstation or Windows 95.

*Hardware Configuration*

- Application Server: Scalable to support any size property, from 100 rooms on up. Basic system is 166 MHz Pentium, 128M RAM, with 4G hard drive.

- Database Server: 133MHz Pentium, 16M RAM, standard hard drive.
- Standard Client Workstation: 166MHz Pentium, 32M RAM, standard hard drive.
- Other Hardware Requirements: Backup workstation, Night Audit workstation, interface PC, printers.

***Software Features***

Following is a brief list of some of the main features offered by Front Office.

*Reservations*

Front Office features handle all aspects of the reservation process from setting up rates and booking the reservation to change management, shares, and profiles.

- Multiple Reservation Types: Individual, company, travel agent, source and group.
- Easy setup: defaulted values, automatic calculations, pick-lists.
- Room rate/type availability can be linked to hotel sales strategy.
- Availability display can show important events.
- Waitlisted reservations.
- Create and break shares.
- Guest loyalty awards and memberships handling.
- Profiles for guests, companies, travel agents, sources and groups may be attached to reservations.
- Suite handling.
- Unlimited rate codes. Automatic or manual rate assignment.
- Rate projections in multiple currencies.
- User-definable Confirmation letters automatically generated via fax, e-mail.
- Routing instructions for billing.
- Supports reservation queries by over 30 characteristics (e.g., name, partial name, arrival or departure date/time, source, confirmation number, travel agency, membership number, etc.).

- Reservation modifications, cancellations (including mass cancellations), reactivations.
- Copy feature supports add-on reservations.
- Easy automatic room assignment by arrival date, group order, rate code, market code, room type, room features, etc.
- Guest message management including support for multiple languages.
- Multiple traces handling. Action traces may be assigned to specific departments. Certain types of traces can be handled automatically on due date.
- Package elements may be added to the reservation "on the fly".

*Groups and Blocks*

Front Office efficiently manages group reservations for tours, conventions, social affairs, and business meetings.

- Ability to set up group room blocks and allocations. Blocks may be set up to allow overbooking (elastic blocks) or not.
- Special group rates.
- Integrates with Fidelio Sales and Catering.
- Multiple cutoff dates supported.
- Automatic release of unsold rooms by cutoff date.
- Tour series (recurring blocks).
- Create rooming lists.
- Automatic room assignment, optionally based on room type, room features.
- Group or individual check-in and check-out.
- Group generation of keys.
- Group or individual action traces and messages.
- Individual billing or group master folio.
- Group statistics and reports.

*Rates and Availability*

Front Office includes sales strategy tools to maximise occupancy and revenue.

- Unlimited rate codes supported.
- Rate availability can be based on rate code or category.

- Change availability of rate code, rate category, or room type globally or based on dates, day of week, or on day-to-day basis.
- Room status can include: Open, closed, closed to arrival, minimum length of stay, minimum stay through, etc.
- Rate grid allows selection of available rates based on reservation data.
- Set overbooking level for hotel per day and per room type.
- VIP override of overbooking parameter.

*Packages*

Front Office can handle even the most complex package requirements.

- Package prices can be added to rates or included in the rate.
- Package elements can be printed on separate folio lines.
- Package prices may be per adult, per child, per person, or flat rate.
- Variety of posting rhythms supported.
- Integrates with POS to simplify handling of inclusive meals.

*Front Desk (Check-In, In-House)*

A complete selection of features to expedite front desk responsibilities.

- Query arrivals and in-house guests by over 30 reservation characteristics.
- Quick location of guest information for check-in, viewing, modification.
- Display available rooms by type, any combination of features, or status.
- Optional automatic room assignment.
- Walk-in handling.
- Modification of any reservation details.
- Option to print registration card.
- Up to four folios per guest.
- EFT interface for obtaining automatic credit card authorization.

- Credit authorization may be set up to include or not include room rate.
- Multiple guest messages in user-defined languages. Send messages to individuals or to groups (based on VIP status, arrival or departure status, group, etc.).
- Sort, display, print messages.
- Supports virtual DID numbers for voice, modem, fax, pager, etc.
- Maintains room history.
- Easy room moves.

*Profiles and Guest History*

Front Office gathers and manages information that can make the reservation process more efficient, increase guest satisfaction and augment revenues.

- Create profiles for individual guests, companies, agents and sources.
- More than 20 standard information fields, plus user definable fields.
- Master Account numbers, Frequent Flyer and Frequent Guest memberships.
- Guest room preferences that become default when reservation is booked.
- Cashlist and restricted list.
- VIP override of overbooking parameter.
- Commissions for agents, source, clients.
- Multiple credit cards per profile.
- Match and merge duplicate profiles.
- Revenue and statistics displays for up to 3 years.
- Purge program removes inactive profiles.
- Create mailings by user-definable selection criteria.
- Statistical reports include revenues, stays, nights, no-shows, cancellations, etc. by guest, company, travel agents and sources.

*Guest Accounting Features*

Front Office accounting features allow detailed tracking of deposits, payments, taxes, and may other specifics related to billing and revenues.

- Up to 799 user definable department codes and 9999 articles.
- 50 paid out and 50 non-revenue accounts.
- 80 payment accounts (credit cards, currencies, bank transfers, etc.).
- Routing instructions for automatic posting of specific charges, with or without date limits.
- Modify and split postings.
- Manual adjustments to room and tax postings.
- City ledger accounts.
- Postings after check-out.
- Display and print folios for checked out guests.
- Interfaces to POS, PBX, minibar, etc.
- Reservation deposit accounting features.

*Check-out, Folio and Cashiering*

Front Office Cashiering features assist in guest check-out, folio preparation.

- User definable folio format in up to five languages.
- In addition to regular folios, print advance, interim, and information folios and pro-forma invoices.
- Detailed folios, expense folios, daily group summaries, and over 20 other folio styles.
- Remote check-out interface.
- Quick check-out without folio printing.
- Early departure with pre-posting of room and tax.
- Automatic detection of late departures.
- Unlimited payment combinations (e.g., credit card, cash, direct bill).
- Batch folios can be printed using numerous customizing options.
- Group check-out.
- 99 cashier numbers.
- Check and currency exchange.
- Supports triangular Euro exchange requirements.
- Complete cashier journal. Cashier closeout with automatic balance calculation.
- Fixed starting balances and blind drop.

*Night Audit*

Balance the day's activity and complete the hotel's accounting functions for the day.

- Post room and tax charges, other fixed charges.
- Process guaranteed no-shows, change status of non-guaranteed no-shows.
- Display open cashiers, departures not paid, no-shows.
- Prepare unlimited management reports and statistics.
- Perform block control (respond to cutoff dates).
- Create system backups.
- User-definable Night Audit sequence, management report selection.

*Reporting*

Front Office report generator provides a full range of standard and custom reports.

- Report menus for Guests in House, Reservations, Financial and A/R, Night Audit, Housekeeping, Profiles, Statistics, and other features.
- User-definable printer setup files.
- Comparison with previous year (day, month, year) and budget.
- Mailing module (mail merge, labels, confirmation letters, etc.)
- Fax interface.

*Housekeeping and Rooms Management*

Front Office features assist with details of housekeeping and maintaining room inventory.

- Housekeeping status by room type.
- Room assignment and allocation reports.
- Attendent worksheets.
- Room attendent productivity reports.
- Room discrepancy reports.
- Change room status via telephone interface.
- Function key room status display.
- Linen management features.
- Quick cleaning options.
- Out of order and out of service statuses.

*Leisure Management*

Easy control of unlimited activities that are reserved by time slots, such as tennis courts, golf tee-times, massages, horseback riding, hairdresser, etc.

- Graphical reservation booking screen.
- User definable time slots.
- Seasonal and time-sensitive pricing.
- Bookings for guests, staff, members, walk-ins.
- Leisure activities may be supported through service outlets.

*Setup and Configuration*

These Front Office features make it easy to get the system on-line and to customize and modify the system to meet the needs of the hotel.

- 32 flexible room type definitions.
- Unlimited number of rooms supported.
- 10 reservation types supported.
- Unlimited rate codes.
- User definable guest award system.
- Multiple language support.
- Multiple currency support with foreign currency exchange rate support.
- Market codes, source codes, region codes.
- Over 100 parameter "switches" to customize Front Office for country, tax handling, etc.
- Unlimited number of users.
- External programs (DOS) can be called from Fidelio main menu.
- User-defined standard texts (in multiple languages) for registration cards, confirmation letters, folios, etc. Custom fonts and page layout.
- Customized general hotel data (decimal points, default country, default currency, VATs, commission percentages).
- User-definable Night Audit sequence, management report selection.

*Security*

Non-intrusive security features protect against misuse and unauthorized access.

- User ID and password uniquely identify each system user.

- User activity log audits all system activity.
- User rights control access to system features.
- Special cashier identification.
- Passwords may be set to expire at regular intervals, with or without a grace period.
- Individual user IDs may be suspended to disallow logon without deleting user information.

*Interfaces*

Front Office may be integrated with a host of MICROS-Fidelio and third-party systems.

- MICROS-Fidelio CIS and CRS (Customer Information System and Central Reservation System).
- Fidelio and third-party Sales and Catering Systems.
- Fidelio and third-party Back Office systems.
- Telephone and Call Accounting systems.
- MICROS-Fidelio and third-party Point of Sale systems.
- Key Service systems.
- Electronic Funds Transfer systems.
- Energy and Engineering Management systems.
- Voice Mail systems.
- Paging system.
- Remote Check-in and Check-out systems.
- Yield Management systems.
- Minibar and Vending systems.

*Customizability and Ease of Use Features*

The design of Front Office includes a variety of features that make it user friendly and easy to learn.

- Immediate access to the most used features from anywhere in the system via function keys.
- Screen painter lets you create user definable screens for guest address, company address, guest history, reservation, check-in, check-out, etc.
- User definable colours for screens, pick boxes, help text, input fields, etc.
- Pull-down menus.
- Configuration context-sensitive help.

- Hotel floor plan.
- Built in tools such as a currency exchange calculator and text editor.

**The IDeaL Solution**

Today's business environment creates ever greater challenges to hotel leaders to choose their most profitable business mix. Correctly managing this complex issue can have a tremendous impact on a hotel's profits and increase property value. The IDeaL Solution from Integrated Decisions And Systems (IDEAS), delivers significant and measurable results, increasing room revenues guaranteed for 4 per cent, and typically much more.

There are 5 key elements that comprise this state-of-the-art solution for hotels and resorts.

The IDeaL/YIELD system optimizes the sale of the hotel's room inventory by managing length-of-stay available rates, and overbooking levels. The system's Full Precision Forecast is based on a mathematical model of a hotel's business patterns, management experience and business strategy.

IDeaL/CARE sets the industry standard in supporting a hotel's revenue management operations. Providing seven day a week, twenty-four hour a day access to IDeaS Yield Specialists, IDeaL/CARE includes daily automatic remote monitoring and periodic quality audits to enable the best decisions even in rapidly changing market conditions.

IDeaL/RESULTS is a benefit measurement system which accurately determines the true impact of IDeaL/YIELD for a client. This unique and conservative approach has been accepted by hoteliers and their financial auditors around the world.

Hotel Management plays a critical role in the solution, determining the pricing, business, and risk strategies which are incorporated in the IDeaL Solution. Management is equipped with hotel-specific IDeaL training, detailed reports, and exception alerts to assist in making strategic decisions and directing attention to areas requiring hotel management's expertise.

Finally, Decision Integration brings it all together, ensuring that better decisions actually deliver a more profitable business mix to the hotel's owners and stockholders.

*Fifteen*

# IT-Enabled Services in Tourism: Their Role and Future

## Services

IT-enabled service providers help their partner airlines are in process of providing high quality customer service while maintaining cost efficiency by applying best business practices through automation and using IT-enabled services effectively.

They offer a wide range of IT enabled services to support the airlines and help them enhance customer experience, efficiently and effectively. Their Portfolio includes :

•Loyalty Programs •Revenue Accounting •Yield Realization •CRS Management •Web Customer Care.

## Loyalty Program Support Services

They provide data processing services for airline loyalty programs. They understand the demands of the high-volume and competitive airline business. They know that customer care is absolutely indispensable for retaining their customer. They have the expertise in airline systems and management to deliver customer satisfaction through cost effective service modules.

They offer their services on a worldwide basis or for a region as their operation is scaleable and flexible while delivering to agreed service levels. Their loyalty program support work processes are designed to :

- Ensure effective and secure transfer of both physical and electronic data;
- Provide accurate and time bound manual data entry services;
- Review data capture for any non systemic update; and
- Provide personalized responses to passengers as per agreed standards.

They have an effective training process for its team of executives and highly skilled, professional administrators. Their processes have in-built quality checks to assure high standards of delivery across their range of services. This allows the airlines to concentrate on what they do best – serving their passengers—secure in the knowledge that they partner the best in the business.

Security, for them, is an absolute must. For this :

- They maintain stringent standards of data and document security.
- All database application software files are baked up off-site.
- Firewalls are in place for the safe and secure transfer of data, both from clients to us and in between our locations.
- There is restricted access to the area of operation.
- There is video camera monitoring by on site security personnel at all points of entry and exit.

**Revenue Accounting — Passenger and Cargo**

Revenue accounting for airlines is a complex activity, that involves large sums of money, and, therefore, accuracy, efficiency and prompt processing are the cornerstones in optimizing revenue and management information. The most critical areas are the probation and the interline billing where inaccuracies and inconsistencies can have a serious monetary impact.

They have extensive domain knowledge of the airline accounting processes, supported by a team of highly trained and experienced fare and tariff experts, and can handle :

- *Passenger Sales Accounting*: This includes ticket stock control, uploading of BSP data, consolidation of agency sales returns, generation of accounts receivables, preparation of sale and refund reports and handling remittances.
- *Airport uplift and processing*: This captures the ticket data from uplifted coupons and is used for multiple location processing, pro-rations, as well as to generate MIS reports and to estimate flown revenue streams from first coupon data capture.

- *Interline Billing*: For incoming invoice audit, the services include registering, checking and processing of invoices from other carriers. The exact coupon values are calculated; using IATA rules and interline SPAs to ensure correct pay-out. For outgoing invoice handling is, prorate and client flights charge, exchanges and refunds. Evaluations are based on Multilateral Prorate Agreements (MPAs), including Provisos or Special Prorate Agreements (SPAs). Financials are supported by all information necessary to charge the airline directly or through the IATA Clearing House. The outward sampling and non-sampling bills are generated for OAL documents with documentation in accordance with ICH rules.
- *Pro-ration*: The system has a high degree of automation that allows the bulk of the ticket coupons to be processed for revenue realization with accuracy, efficiency and minimal human intervention, using the SPAs and IATA rules applicable.
- *Cargo Sales Accounting for the Region or Country*: This encompasses, AWB stock management, sales returns processing, generating accounts receivables from agency sales reports and AWB data capture, interline billing, rate audits, and debit note generation in case of under-collections.

**Yield Realization**

Airlines have sophisticate yield management system to optimize their revenues, and correct revenue realization is a key objective for the airline's success. Correct revenue realization is based on the following premises:

- The value of the coupon correctly corresponds to the class of service that was booked.
- The rules of the fare applied have been observed and followed, for example, class of service, stopovers, etc.
- Taxes specific to the routing have been correctly collected.

These redeemed ticket coupons constitute the airline's realized earnings, and any compromise on the revenues realized, results in direct reduction from the airline's profits. Airlines have two constraints that limit the possibility of auditing for each ticket coupon for accuracy of fares:

- The sheer volume of data processing to be done.
- The requirement to send physical tickets with interline bills.

As a result the normal accounting and billing system generates invoices, based on the fare and taxes stated on the coupon.

The unrealized earnings are revenues that are rightfully due to the airline, but lost as leakage because of manipulations on account of class of service, fares, fare rules, and seasonality. These leakages cost airlines large sums of money, which normally range between 0.5 per cent to 2 per cent of gross revenue with a direct impact at the bottom line.

They have processes to help the airline recover its due earnings through,

- Pre-Ticketing Audit
- Post-Facto Audit

*Pre-Ticketing Audit*

They work with airlines to audit their information database, to help them realize their due/expected revenue. Their revenue realization support service works on a holistic system, and the process commences even before the sale of the tickets.

They provide support, based on data sourced from CRS's, MIDT tapes, and the airline's own reservation system. This data is evaluated for reservation class conformity with the various fare rules and other factors to highlight wrong bookings and minimize leakage before erroneous tickets are actually issued.

The system has the ability to incorporate and recognize bilateral and multilateral fares as well as Standard and Special Prorate agreements and thus identify PNR's with incorrect reservation classes.

In the pre-ticketing stage, PNRs are scanned using an intelligent system, to identify reservations with incorrect class of bookings. Based on this list, the reports are generated for follow up and corrective action.

Detailed reports are also generated with an analysis of discrepancies by travel agency, regional, or sales office thus helping the management to put an accurate figure to the cost of sales for each market segment.

An intelligent feedback system ensures that in case of above average incidence of errors from any segment, e.g., by region, or by agency, the bookings originating from that segment will be under greater scrutiny.

*Post Ticketing Audit*

They work with airlines to audit the ticketed sales data from BSP, and Data captured from flight departure ticket coupons, which are matched against flight reservations to ensure that correct booking rules have been adhered to.

The system incorporates and recognizes bilateral and multilateral fares as well as Standard and Special Prorate agreements and thus identifies tickets with incorrect reservation classes. We have a team of reservations, tariff and ticketing experts, who have extensive knowledge spanning over a decade, to handle exceptions to the automated processes.

In the post-facto audit there is a 100 per cent match and audit of ticketed fare-data against the class of bookings as per the PNR's. The objective is to detect losses as soon as possible once the ticketing and fare-data is available, and to recoup any short collections. Cases of short collection are rechecked for accuracy, before necessary reporting and issuance of debit notes for recovery of dues.

Detailed reports are also generated with an analysis of discrepancies by travel agency, region, or sales office. This helps the management to put an accurate figure to the cost of sales for each market segment.

They thus, provides the airline with multiple levels of control to protect their revenue and profit, by integrating various modules of IT enabled services. With technology and software evolving very rapidly, most airlines are hesitant to commit large resources for manpower, training, hardware, and software for auditing solutions. On the other hand, they are able to provide the required solutions cost effectively as their cost of operations are defrayed over a larger base.

## CRS Management

To improve the capabilities of their distribution channel, airlines helped provide Travel Agencies with CRSs and real time access to their very expensive and highly perishable inventory of services. The accessibility has now become even wider with passengers making airline reservations directly over the Internet. This wider access requires airlines to continuously monitor and action booking requests to ensure effective utilization of business opportunities, and to provide effective customer support.

*Areas Requiring Attention*

The actions required to be taken, to achieve the above, are in the areas of:

(a) Queues for groups, fares, booking assistance, and special handling requests.
(b) Non-routine messages/ requests and special services such as meal and accommodation requests.
(c) Correct utilization of capacity. Often agents and passengers make multiple bookings to cover various eventualities. These duplicate bookings need to be captured and purged to ensure non-wastage of inventory.

Processing of STPC requests, advising passengers of re-scheduling flights and re-booking and advising for cancelled flights, etc. In these areas, airlines require a system and process that ensures data capture, action on, and processing of the information requested, and feedback to the passengers and agents. The system needs to service all non-automated action requests promptly, and resolve errors that may be made by untrained personnel, feeding garbage data or making entries in incorrect fields.

*Support Services Provided*

They provide efficient back-office support for these non-systemic services at a regional as well as global level. Their highly trained executives have an in-depth knowledge of the reservation procedures and systems to provide the following support services on 24X7 day basis :

(a) Action the special handling requests.

(b) Manually correct the fields/abbreviations for most of the rejected PNRs.
(c) Queue and follow up garbled requests with originating agents.
(d) Bridge the gap between the web based requests and the reservation systems.

Their efficient and cost effective CRS support services are provided by a team of experienced executives drawn from the air transport industry, trained to international standards. This team has clear and defined objectives, and functions with strict quality control norms, which add value to the airline's operations and profitability.

**Web Customer Care**

The World Wide Web has very rapidly evolved as a crucial and effective mode for distribution of company information and more importantly as an effective channel of distribution for various products. Specifically, today the travel industry gets 2 per cent of its booking from the web, and trends indicate that by 2004 the web will account for 25 per cent of all travel bookings. The travel business like any other, is racing to build an online presence and capture its share of the market—viewing it as a key to success in the new economic age. The web site as a 24X7 day E-commerce platform raises some crucial support issues.

*Reasons for Non-effective Service*

A leading survey has shown that many top websites could not provide effective customer service—they took over five days to respond to customers' e-mails when accessible on e-mail, i.e., Customers are looking for an immediate response to make a buying decision or solve a problem, and lack of support will prompt the customer to move elsewhere. There are three factors that result in non-responsive websites:

(a) Lack of understanding by the manager of the desired "Net Experience", which results in overlooking the need to provision content and support mechanisms that meet the demands and expectations of the visitors.
(b) The prohibitive cost of employing and training

adequate support staff to respond online and offline, track frequently asked questions, and develop and modify the content/pages appropriately.

(c) Lack of appropriate tools for tracking and servicing the customer needs hampers the managers ability to understand trends issues and requirements, adversely effecting the responsiveness.

They recognizes that the web media has tremendous scope and Airline-clients will need to be serviced at various levels and with different tools to deliver the ideal responses. The benefits of an effective Web Customer Support System are manifold. It generates customer satisfaction, which translates to retention of existing customers and development of new customers, reduction of a manual e-mail response support, and direct cost savings in terms of reduced load for telephone customer-support.

**Web Support Services**

They use the 'best of class technologies and back that with a strong team, built, using world class recruitment and training systems to deliver the web service support that delights the customer. Their web customer care service centre is structured using platform independent software and technologies, that collect the caller's ID and account number, access and match it with legacy call-context data available, and route the request to the most appropriate agent with all supporting information for action. The system allows scripting capability, to refine the pre-routing selection, based on agent scheduling and capabilities, with scope for management over-ride. Each media of our web support services is explained below:

(a) E-mail based Support Services
(b) Online Support Services

*E-mail Support Services*

1. *E-mail servicing*: The e-mail solutions allows them to route and respond to the customer's inbound e-mail messages automatically. A sophisticated routing engine examines the content of each message and, based on which it responds automatically or routes the message to the most appropriate

servicing agent while generating automated solutions, using standardized text/phrases that allow best practices to be implemented across the entire operation.

2. *Automated responses to structured queries*: An intelligent engine, sorts e-mail messages, which are organized into pre-determined categories based on their content. Our system then responds automatically with modular replies, for these pre-determined categories of e-mail. This avoids the involvement of customer care representatives altogether. Being a dynamic system, the list of pre-determined responses continually grows to include standardized and routine queries.
3. *Hybrid Responses for form generated queries*: This is done by using modular blocks of pre-written response text, that allows a customer care representative to select, move, delete and insert these blocks into an appropriate message for your customers with a simple click of a mouse. With effective routing management, and the ability to append web pages, legacy data, or tables and files, effective responses can be generated very rapidly.
4. *Intelligent responses for free field queries*: Here again modular paragraphs in individually written notes and attached files allow rapid response time. For this segment pre-routing categorization ensures that the message is routed to the right skilled agent who prepares the ideal response using standardized text and modular attachments. The system can be configured to include private notes that are retained and are accessible only on the host for record. Systematic quality controls, with supervisory inspection capability at the processing stage helps ensure high quality responses. The timeframes for responses are defined and monitored by the supervisors. As a rule, all e-mail responses returned for clarification, are responded to, only by a supervisor.

This results in an e-mail being handled with 99.9 per cent accuracy and efficiency. The passenger's issues are resolved—and their questions are answered—quickly, thoroughly and economically.

*Online Support Services*

1. *Chat Mode*: For a visitor/buyer it is very inconvenient to access the net, face a problem, and then disconnect to call a toll free number to seek information or clarification. Chat response provides live, on-line and real time text based support, with 24X7 day accessibility that allows the customer to get immediate responses to his queries while viewing the airline web site.With Voice Chat, the customer can speak with our help desk over the net without disconnecting and thus get online support conveniently. The intelligent call management system captures the clients' ID, and client entered data, along with the web page last viewed to route the query to the agent with required expertise and skills for support using multimedia tools. The online service executives are recruited from the airline industry, are highly trained with in-depth knowledge of, and to the standards of, the airline they represent, which ensures high quality and effective online support.
2. *Screen Synchronized Support*: This support system, using industry standard 'customer collaborative software' allows the support executive to view the customers screen and cursor as seen by the customer. As a result, it is possible for the support executive to advise the customer on the correct method of navigating the web site through Chat or VoIP; making their web experience more satisfying.
3. *FAQ and Knowledge Base Updates*: All queries and online viewing patterns of the site content by visitors is monitored by a sophisticated page and mail tracking system. This information is systematically analyzed, based on which the content and FAQ areas are dynamically updated to address the information needs being accessed most frequently. The knowledge base and site content is dynamically updated to make the experience more responsive and friendly for the customer. As a result he feels he is in dialogue with an individual, while in reality he is in a self-service mode, answering his own questions, based on a tree and branch series of queries and responses.

All these media of communication are effectively supervised and monitored using tools that allow supervisors to join (invisibly) and if necessary over-ride an executive during the session on a real time basis. E-mail, communications of a trainee, could be queued for inspection before despatch, and transcripts of all outward mail are retained for post facto review. Multiple level of reports and effective quality checks covering various aspects help ensure ideal response times, and minimum errors and effective service recovery systems.

With the knowledge of the software and hardware industry, and as the best of breed integrator, they bring together the ideal mix of technology tools available in the market to provide comprehensive Internet customer care solutions, that include multiple customer care touch points for our airline clients.

With in-depth knowledge of the airline industry, complemented by the teams of software, communications, and web enabled servicing professionals allows InterGlobe to provide comprehensive Web Customer Support to the Airlines, and allows them to leverage the potential of the web for an effective E-commerce strategy to achieve their business goals.

**Conclusion**

We can say that in a developing country like India, the role of private sector in the area of tourism is that of complementing the public sector, but at no point can its contribution be underestimated.

Private sector, can play a significant role in tourism development in a country like India. They have a pivotal role to play in the development of technology as per international standards, delivery of better services, more organized customer care and more value added customer care services for repeat business. This can be clearly noticed from the list of their esteemed patronized clients.

These solution providers maintain database and deliver IT-Enabled services for international airlines for whom it also serves as the GSA and their head office in India. These airlines have their counter and general customer care services being successfully provided by the company. Also, they benefit from the vast online technology being used by the company in looking after their operations and web-related services.

Thus, we can see, how the private sector can play a considerable role in the development of tourism in developing countries. Also, it gives competition to similar kind service industries in other parts of the world with not only its updated technology, but also more dedicated, hardworking and cheap manpower. IT-Enabled airline and tourism services have a bright future in India, with its high and more able manpower and appropiate training facilities in the area of both tourism and IT.

*Part 3*

# Tourism Management: Community Approach

# Sixteen

# Role of Management in Tourism

For any industry to develop management is essential as it plays a vital role in coordinating the whole structure of that particular industry which leads to planning, development and growth. Management consists of all the individuals whose primary role is the achievement of the objectives for which it has been set up. It helps to direct the personnel, control and other techniques related to operation of the organization. The aim of the management is to arrange people into groups associated with similar functions or purpose in order to work efficiently to obtain desired results from their combined actions without wastage of available resources, i.e., to make optimal use of the available resources. It relates thus to the structure of the industry and is concerned with the issues involved in, and the approach to it. This need of management has given birth to so many management institutes in the country itself. Since management is a skill "to manage the man with tact", its need has been felt in all industries including the tourism industry. Being a service-based industry the need of management has become a basic determinant of success in tourism industry where management has become a tool in success of the tourist destinations. The proper management thus leading to definite success or one can say decreasing the level of risk or failure.

The management of tourism may fall into two parts. Firstly, there are sectors of tourism, i.e., the various providers of tourist services—the hotel, transport and entertainment services. Secondly, there are the levels of tourists management—national, regional and local. The management of tourism can therefore be horizontal as well as vertical. The management of tourist industry in any country varies widely as there are a number of considerations, which influence the nature of management set up.

With the rapid growth of civilization, almost all the countries have realized the strong and important relationship of tourism with management. Off-late there has been a rapidly growing awareness of economic, financial and social advantages of tourism development, together with the recognition that such advantages can best be achieved through systematic efforts to expand tourism. This has lead many states especially after the World War II to extend and enlarge their direct interests in tourism through management.

With the development of major civilization people began to manage tourism on scientific lines, many nations set up organizations dealing specially with the subject of tourism on the lines of management. However, the pattern and nature of these management differ widely from one country to another.

**History of Travel**

Travel, the very essential component of tourism is an ancient phenomenon. Travel has had a fascination for man. Due to lack of accessibility it is witnessed that travelling was very hard in older days. Men of ancient civilizations travelled as merchants, for example, traders in the age of Mauryas used to move from the main city of Pataliputra to other cities of that kingdom using punch marked coins as the currency which they carried with themselves while travelling. Another reason for travelling was pilgrimage. The Buddhist priests and even Jain priests moved from one city to another for spreading their religions. The great travellers of that time like Huen-Tsang gave the concrete proof of people travelling from one place to another. These people were monks. Due to the development of these religions new places like Bodhgaya and various Buddhist monasteries around Nalanda began to gain identity and importance in the eyes of common man. So, people started travelling due to this reason also.

However, trade and commerce was the strongest force for travelling in the ancient times. It made people travel to distant lands. As large volume of people began to move from distant places and as civilizations developed, conscious travel in order to explore and see the world began. The invention of money by the

Sumerians (Babylonia) was a significant step towards the proper management in travelling as it led to commercial dealings. The people began to manage their dealings in trade and commerce on the basis of proper scale. Many traders could pay for transportation as well as accommodation either with money or by the exchange of goods.

The rulers realized the importance of travellers specially in the field of trade and commerce. One such ruler was the ruler of Babylonia who ordered for the construction of proper roads and rest houses for traders. These halt houses became the ideal place for rest for the traders travelling to distant areas. These rest houses were also used by travellers who travelled with the religious and cultural motives, i.e., the purpose was other than trade and commerce. In the places like China and India the trade and commerce was resting on the shoulders of the travellers.

These travellers and expeditioners returned home with new ideas and beautiful pictures of these lands which inspired the people of their civilisation to travel to those places. The other effect was that these travellers carried fabulous rich treasures of highly advanced civilizations of one country to the other country of the world. Hence the travel/tourism began to metamorphisise and began to take up a proper shape. The transport/communication systems in those times as we know was very hard. But people still used to manage it. The land migrations were done by foot and on horse back, elephant, camel and water ways in Europe, Asia/Africa.

The development of a full scale urban movement brought the idea of grand tours into being. These grand tours followed a shift in the focus of culture and of economic and political power. Slowly and steadily these grand tours covered the target group of local people also. Thus, these grand tours managed to draw popularity for tourism in the 19th and 20th century.

In 18th century the origin of the concept of annual holidays brought a wave of change in the European society. The need of utilizing these holidays, made the Europeans to travel in much more volume with the motive of recreation. The other wave of change was brought by the appearance of industrial revolution in the societies of West Europe/North America. It brought about changes in economic and social systems. It gave birth to factory towns both big and,small. Due to rapid industrialization there was massive increase in material wealth and noticeable improvement in management in transport and communications during the second half of the 19th and eatly 20th century.

The introduction of railways led to better management in the field of travel. It helped to stimulate travel and to manage the system in a more efficient and improved way. In addition to this, the cars managed to make the journeys more comfortable. Hence the railways can be considered as one of the most powerful forces which developed and managed mass travel in 19th and 20th century. The steamships, on the other hand, managed to cross the boundaries and made studs in intercontinental travel. This led to developments which provided opportunities and fortunes for people of those times. Transport by water made a significant contribution to the proper development of travel. The two world wars necessitated innovations in the fields of motor transportation for the sole purpose of using them in war. However, after the wars were over, the technologies developed during pre-war periods were further employed to bring innovations in the areas of air transport, jets and high speed trains. This was supported to a great extent by the rising standards of living of the working and middle-classes in the post war period which created demand for such developments.

Though tourism suffered a setback at the time of war but after the Second World War the growth and development of modern tourism occurred with more specialized management skills. The growth was rapid due to social and technological reasons. Since there was boom in tourism people also began to gain opportunities in areas of employment, income, better education and international understanding due to the development of this industry. So people began to take this industry as a serious source of money earning. Even the governments of various countries began to realize its' importance. On the stage of World big international organizations related to tourism like IATA, WTO, PATA, ASTA, etc. were formed so that proper management could be done to provide support for the efficiency of the travel Industry.

This increase in industrial activities, in turn gave rise to new settlements, towns and cities. This was a sign of rise in prosperity which also gave a boost to the tourism industry as people began to seek relaxation through tourism.

The importance of tourism industry was not only recognized by the Asian or European countries but by India also. The first step towards the development of the tourist industry in India was initiated in the year 1945, when the Sir John Sargant Committee was appointed. It was set up with the intention to develop tourism in the metropolitan cities of Mumbai, Delhi, Kolkata and Chennai so that with the proper management the tourism could be promoted for India. In this direction another effective step that was taken by the Government of India was on 1st March, 1958 when a separate tourism department was created in the Ministry of Tourism. This gave birth to two constituent departments :

(i) Department of Tourism;
(ii) Department of Civil Aviation.

The present scenario is that the Government of India has formed an Organization called ITDC (India Tourism Development Corporation) whose different outlets are looking towards the better development and management of tourism in India. This is the result of need of better management of accommodation for tourists.

Tourism is found as a highly complex phenomenon. The various developments in the field of tourism are the result of contribution of various socio-political as well as technical developments over generations. However, these have been headed under the new disciplines of management and marketing. In addition, management techniques such as planning, statistics and market research are also involved and used extensively in day to day time of tourism enterprises to reach their heights of success and this has resulted in development of a proper management framework in which tourism can fit through proper planning, organizing, developing and promoting researching work.

The crux of it is that the prosperity of Mankind in the last generation motivated him for leisure, pleasure and recreation that gave boost to the tourism industry. As mass movement developed the man started putting efforts to manage the tourism industry in a more coordinated and organized manner to make its management more productive and efficient.

Thus, each generation of man's civilization has made contributions to make this industry successful through the waves of technology and efforts. So it would not be wrong to say that the relation of tourism with management is as old as the day when one started travelling from one place to another.

# Seventeen

# Sustainable Eco-Tourism Values and Principle Modes

The need for this subject has arisen because in the Indian Tourism planning process, the need to be environment-friendly has not yet been fully appreciated. Sustainable development, according to World Commission on Environment and Development (1987) is "It is development that meets the needs of the present without comprising the ability of future generations to meet their own needs." In other words, sustainable development is the process which allows development to take place without degrading or depleting the resources which make that development possible.

Tourism is a major development sector whose resources are mostly derived from the natural and cultural environment. It was in 1988 that for the first time a spectrum of tourism resources and opportunities in the context of sustainability were discussed involving a spectrum of programmes, services and accommodation facilities, located appropriate to the natural environment and responding to the range of opportunities and activities sought by the markets.

## Spectrum of Programmes and Services in Eco Tourism

1. *Social Goals*
   (a) Community Involvement
   (b) Sharing of Responsibilities and Benefits
2. *Economic Goals*
   Economically viable industry
3. *Policy Goals*
   (a) Extent of hosting mega events.
   (b) Preparation – pre/post
4. *Environmental Goals*
   (a) Resource benefits

(b) No degradation of resources.
(c) Demand vs. supply oriented.

This spectrum demonstrates a great deal of confusion regarding "Nature of Eco-Tourism" because it comprises of a varying mix of so many different activities and experiences. Rather than trying to define Eco-tourism by product it would be more valuable to comprehend the Environment-Tourism Relationship because as rightly stated by Hunter and Green (1995).

> "Sustainable development is conserving, maintaining and enhancing environment resources, the quality of life of local people and quality of tourist experiences."

**Lessons Learnt from Hunter and Green**

There are two clear perspectives of Hunter and Green that :

(i) Tourism if it is properly planned and managed on help conserve the environment and in some places even enhance it because of the characteristics and quality of natural and cultural environment which provide the attractions for tourist.

(ii) If tourism is not carefully controlled it can degrade the natural environment of the tourism area, thus leading to loss of cultural character and identity of the area's people. Although as a result of growth globally many eco-tourism organizations have sprung up world over: like the Eco-Tourism Society (TES) in the US, the Eco-Tourism Association of Australia, Institute of Eco-Tourism, Srinakharinwirot University Bangkok, the World Travel and Tourism Research Centre (WTTRC) in Oxford, the International Centre for Eco-Tourism Research (ICER) Australia, and Centre for Eco-Tourism at University of Pretoria South Africa but India is far behind its competitors like Malaysia, Indonesia and Thailand.

**Sustainable Tourism**

If we look at the situation related to other types of development, much has been studied about the relationship between environment and tourism during the past three decades of the globally rapid growth in this sector. The approach now to planning and managing tourism should also be that of sustainable development. This sustainable tourism development should be viewed as meeting the needs of present tourists and the host regions while at the same time protecting and enhancing tourism development resources and opportunities for the future. This rightly justifies what Bramwell (1993) feels about sustainable tourism development "It is working for long term viability and quality of both natural and human resources with the aim to increase visitor's satisfaction". In other words the environment and cultural integrity of tourism area is indefinitely maintained for both the benefits of tourist and residents.

How is sustainable tourism development achieved? According to Young (1992) three broad policy goals of sustainable development are – "eco-efficiency; social equity and environmental integrity".

These, in other words, can also be referred to as policy goals to assess the impact of hosting an activity in an area, Eco-efficiency will indicate at new jobs created in construction, hospitality, catering, etc. or construction of fast tracks to faster movements. Social equity refers to sustaining local social system or ways of life as well as social equity between people at the present and between generation environmental integrity talks about use and degradation of environmental resources as a result of developmental activities.

According to Edward Inskeep: the key sequential elements for achieving sustainable development are proper development planning; effective implementation of planning and continuing management of tourism development and visitor use. From this point of view it would be more valuable to recognize that there is a spectrum of experiences in eco-tourism which may be supplied or demanded. The spectrum may vary from:

Supply factors which include (i) nature and resilience of the resource; (ii) type of accommodation and facilities.

Demand factors which include (i) types of activities, (ii) degree of interest in natural or cultural resources, and (iii) degree of physical efforts.

Before carrying out any exercise on proper development planning, it becomes imperative to sum up factors which are key part of the spectrum of sustainable Eco-Tourism. According to

Ruschmann (1992) "The spectrum of sustainable Eco-tourism can be summed up in two :

(a) Accommodation spectrum; and
(b) Market Spectrum.

*Accommodation Spectrum can be:*

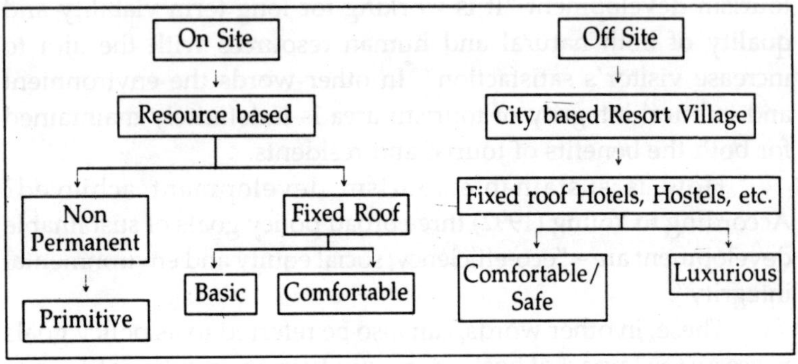


*Market Spectrum can be:*

| Primary Market/ directly related | Secondary Market/ indirectly related |
|---|---|

Studies the demand pattern and decides on what kind of accommodation/product should be provided combining supply and demand factors related to environmental, social, economic and policy goals including factors like perceived market preferences, appropriateness of site, resilience of the resource, cultural or local community preferences, etc. Essentially these factors have to be observed for proper product-market matching. Too often, in eco-tourism examples are found where luxurious accommodation are offered where there is market for budget/ economy class accommodation. Therefore, there comes the need for taking into consideration of 'Carrying Capacity' as a vital ingredient for successful achievement of sustainable tourism development. Carrying capacity can be viewed as an essential technique in planning for sustainable tourism development. This technique is now being applied widely in recreation planning to determine systematically the upper limits of development and visitor use of an area without degrading it and to help establish the optimum use to tourism resources. In other words, the carrying capacity of an area is the maximum level of development and number of people who can use a site without generating an unacceptable alteration in the physical environment and adverse impact on the society, economy and culture and without leading to an unacceptable decline in the quality of experience gained by visitors. By maintaining this carrying limits or by remaining within carrying limits, sustained tourism development can be achieved and resources can be maintained for continuous future use.

**Principles of Eco-Tourism**

If we try to underline key principles fundamental to eco-tourism these can be listed as eco-tourism is:

(a) Nature based;
(b) Ecologically sustainable;
(c) Environmentally educative;
(d) Locally beneficial; and
(e) Generates tourist satisfaction.

Eco-tourism is rightly characterized to be holistic combining both nature based and adventure tourism. It is also educative and with conservation supporting activities. For instance, Ranthambore foundation takes their visitors to their foundation to buy handicrafts and paintings made by local people, contributing to local community. Many states are also considering setting up of "ecology parks" to increase awareness.

The PATA sub-committee on Environment and Heritage has estimated that within the developing countries, eco-tourism is estimated to earn US $ 12 billion from an overall US $ 55 billion in tourism earnings. PATA has also developed an environmental ethic agenda, adopted by 182 governments, providing blueprint for securing the sustainable future in 21st century.

**Problems of Eco-Tourism**

This committee has also listed some of the problems associated with the advancement of eco-tourism which are :

(a) lack of infrastructure development;
(b) the need for and adequacy of personnel training;
(c) the implementation of plans and political instability;
(d) Changing habits and attitudes of millions.

To select an example from India, Manali provides best illustration of environmental pressures which can be assoicated with the unplanned and uncontrolled growth of tourism. The destination has been aggressively promoted as a major destination by both private agencies and state tourism authorities. Out of 500 hotels in the valley 400 falls in Manali area with the result, the environment is under increasing pressure viz. damage to river at large because large volumes of untreated effluents which are discharged in to the river. Another dimension of the pressure is that this unplanned development has marred the distinct rural charm of scenic beauty of the valley. To add to the pressure there is illegal mining and tree cutting. From the river bed valley has become prone to natural hazards like landslides, etc. Keeping this example in mind it is necessary to act within the framework of appropriate overall policy and planning. The specific facility planning and design standards, environmental controls, visitor use programmes and community relationship mechanisms applied, will largely determine the lasting success or failure of any type of development in term of its sustainability.

To conclude through a system of integrated planning and effective management sustainable tourism development can be achieved. Important implementation technique would be indispensable through zoning. At national and regional level it refers to designation of tourism regions and development areas such as resorts. At local level zoning refers to detailed plan specifying most suitable specific location for various types of development and conservation. It is through zoning regulations that the upper limits of development intensity within each land use category such as number of hotel rooms and maximum building heights are established so that sites are not overdeveloped like that of Manali and Mussorie resulting in environmental problems. Besides, implementation also requires enlightened and committed political leadership backed by strong public supports in addition to technical capabilities. Lastly, it would be an exaggeration to say that national and international conferences would help in providing the vision and means to achieve environmental sustainability in all development efforts including tourism.

# *Eighteen*

# The Need for Public-Private Sector Cooperation in Tourism

The need for the Public-Private Sector cooperation in Tourism is not merely desirable; it is a necessity as is the case with all important industrial sectors. And yet at the national and regional level one can witness an ongoing public-private sector antipathy and even hostility which has blunted our competitive edge and has led to under-achievements of our professed goals.

If we analyse the reasons which have necessitated this study we find at the core of situation lies mutual suspicions and mutual disrespect. This mutual suspicion has arisen from divisions borne out of our historical past. These traditional divisions put businessmen (private sector) on one side and bureaucrats and politicians on the other. It has become very difficult to break hundreds of years of established traditional perceptions barring few exceptions in different situations. Both the sides advocate their own agenda in order to seek the right and wrong from their perceptions. When this extremism exists it leads to mutual disrespect. There is a natural tendency among people in private sector to express the view that people in the government are both unprofessional at what they do and are ignorant of how business is really done at the ground level. A private operator can point to the governments onerous policies or a National Tourist office workers are burdened by obliging political favourites rather than experienced, trained and hard-nosed professionals to examine why we are not able to meet our target goal of five million tourist arrivals a year.

It is true that there is some element of truth on both sides but the position becomes worse when we see lack of communication and failure to perceive the community of interests. We cannot think of any industry than tourism when interests of public and private sector are so common. Because in each case it is our country and her resources, is the product that is offered by them. However, beautiful and attractive a destination it may be to offer a carefree and relaxed holidays, for it to work well the physical offer of the destination must be complemented by (a) the country's infrastructure, public services and utilities, (b) the attitudes of front line staff of private sector at destination must be implemented by cooperative attitude of their counterparts at arriving gates or any other point of entry (POE), or for that matter custom and other public services. Only then several hundreds of thousands of people can be persuaded to travel many thousand miles away.

Given the small size and limited financial resources of the majority of small private tour-hotel operator only few have resources to market themselves worldwide or to monitor world trends. As a result, this majority is dependent on government/ public sector for information related to changing patterns in demand as well as for worldwide marketing of product, i.e, country and her attractions.

An introspection of the existing situation will reveal that this adversial position is due to the failure of both sides to understand and appreciate each other's role. In a free market economy, like ours, the entrepreneur has a duty to himself, his stakeholders, and even to the country to make a profit. It is he who earns the foreign exchange for the government's balance of payments exercise; it is he who generates employment and fulfil/achieve social responsibility of government to provide livelihood to all its citizens; it is he who creates the government revenue needed to finance public services. The government, therefore, in its own interest must create the conditions and business environment within which private business can make reasonable profits. Unnecessary bureaucratic bottlenecks and poorly throughout fiscal measures are not only likely to deny profit to private sector but will also make government loose its revenue.

On the other hand, private sector fails to realize that services they expect the government to provide for their profit making business are/shall be paid for or else what will be the source of earning for the government. The government has no money except what it raises from taxing the private sector or from local or foreign loans. The less money it borrow the better it will be for all of us. The money it collects from taxing public servants ultimately does not count, once we realize that salaries are paid for from the money raised by taxes or loans. For all these reasons when private sector/businessmen make reasonable profit but do not pay their share of taxes whatever the short term benefits he earns to himself but in broad economic term he as creating conditions in the country which will haunt him for the end. In return, government will not be able to maintain high level of public services required for a successful tourism industry especially in a country, which is in process of unleashing its potential like India.

**Government's Role in Tourism Development**

This clearly indicates that the government has realized the socio-economic significance of tourism development. Therefore, apart from providing public services for all sections of society, the government has another important role to play; the role of referee or regulator between conflicting interests of society. This of course is a difficult role but if not played will result in social chaos. Government's regulatory role can be examined in some of the relevant areas like environment, security, technological advances, etc.

*Provision of Pollution Regulations*

It has been increasingly noticed that quality travel is and will be equated with 'green travel'. In other words travel will also be concerned with quality of environment beyond the boundaries of place of their stay. It is government's overall responsibility to handle/regulate air, water and noise pollution making activities. These activities may range from aircraft noise to deforestation due to urban spread through erosion of beaches, coral, river banks and mountain sides as well as degradation of eco-system with threatened flora and fauna. It is a tough task for government to address these extremes clashes of interest of people; between residents who do not want aircraft noise and airline who want more and more convenient airport infrastructure; between those who wish to use land for building houses and those who would prefer to use the same site as event/exhibition site; between the residents who wish to walk on seaside and hotelier who wish to construct hotel on sea-beach to provide sea facing rooms for guests.

*Provision of Security*

Another important area where government is expected to play a key role is to ensure safe condition for the travellers both en-route and at the destination. For instance, we have been witnessing activities of terrorists by hijacking aircraft, using them for terrorism (Sept 11, 2001, US case) as well as kidnapping of foreign tourists. It also calls for protection from criminals and narcotics, which try to harass both locals and tourists. Thus, it is the government's responsibility to protect the rights of those vendors who wish to make a legitimate living from tourism.

*Deregulation and Privatization*

In developing countries like India, today deregulation and privatization are new buzz words. It means on the one hand that the government is expected to solve all problems and on the other hand it is expected to deregulate and privatize. We have experienced it in the case of Civil Aviation Board (CAB) in Washington and Open Ski Policy of Director General of Civil Aviation (India). In both the cases, Boards ceased to regulate fares and route which led initially to more airlines with competing fares increased services and bonanza of other activities but as a result of this price war airlines were declared bankrupt. We saw national, regional and global contraction in the number of airlines and creation of near monopolies of mega carriers resulting in lack of competition, higher prices of services (average increase of 8 to 10 per cent in fares). Government, therefore, must realize that the most blessings are mixed and that some regulations are required in best interest of all technological advances.

During the earlier days the government's responsibility was to protect the travelling mass in less technologically developed age at the national and international level. But, today the increasing use of technological tools not only at the product formulation but also at product distribution/product serviced stage has forced the government to play a serious regulatory role to ensure forced exit of unethical and unwanted practices in use of technology as a mean as well as an end.

In a nutshell, the private sector should see itself as providing the locomotive and public sector laying the tracks on which the train runs. Private sector providing the hotels, public sector provides roads, electricity, sewage and other infrastructural and superstructural facilities required for providing best value product to guest. If rails are correctly laid and hotels are located at convenient locations, nothing can protect tourism from increasing in India at the same place with that of developed countries. But private sector always complains that government does very little in tourism. In fact the government is said to have taken it for granted a great deal that the private sector will solely develop tourism at destination. It is unfortunate that there are cases where government is neglecting the role of providing basic infrastructural and superstructural services but is showing an unnatural fascination for occupying the drivers seat. It must be understood that our future lies not only in cooperation and doing things collectively but also in determining what we can do best, i.e., Private Sector shall take up what ever it can do best and government sector must assume roles it can do best with available resources and expertise.

**Case of Uttaranchal**

The newly formed State of Uttaranchal, which has tremendous potential for tourism related activities evolved a strategy for public-private sector cooperation for promotion of tourism and growth of tourism industry in the State. The Government of Uttaranchal does not agree with the common belief that the central government has given an apathetic treatment to tourism. Because, central budget has given sufficient allocation of funds for development of roads, aviation services and other infrastructural apparatus which will ultimately contribute to the growth of tourism.

The Government of Uttaranchal has adopted a four point programme to eliminate or at least reduce the clash of interest between public-private sector in the State. This may be seen, for every State government for the beginning of process of cooperation and communication. The government in fact has taken the following steps :

1. First of all, government has adopted an investment friendly tourism policy where private sector would play a role of importance. The public sector should concentrate on building good means of accessibility such as airstrips, roads, providing uninterrupted supply of power and sufficient water as well as recreation. The rest shall be left for private sector with sufficient support from the State. This will broadly cover accommodation, recreational facilities, resorts, and other facilities. State government has earmarked for private sector two proposed sites for promotion.

   (a) 55 km. fruit belt from Mussoorie – Chamba.

   (b) Lake studded stretch from Nainital to Naukuchital.

   Government of Uttaranchal has also assumed the responsibility of ensuring business to grow in a friendly land of law. It would also be the responsibility of public sector to improve upon the accessibility of State due to uphill terrain. For this government has already initiated the task of developing airstrips of Dehradun and Pantnagar to meet the requirements of larger aircrafts. To cater to medium sized aircrafts, new airports have been planned at Gauchar, Pithoragarh and Chinyalisaur.

   For the smooth functioning of private sector in the State the highway connecting Delhi-Badrinath has been declared as national highway, which would facilitate two way traffic. In the same manner roads connecting other resorts are in developing stage.

2. Second, the government has been consulting the private sector a great deal more. Private sector is even involved in negotiations where its vital interests are involved when decisions were taken on initiating development along above given two sectors or for converting existing medium sized aircrafts suitable for long sized aircraft private sector was also involved in discussions.

3. Third, the state department of Tourism in line with National Tourist Organization, is so structured as to make

public-private sector communication and cooperation inevitable. Uttaranchal has participated in Singapore Travel Mart as well as Travel Jakarta with the objective of providing private sector an opportunity to sell their tours or to familiarize delegates with Uttaranchal.

4. Fourth, State Tourism department and private sector sit together to consider all the dynamic and dramatic changes currently taking place in world of tourism and review how their existing policies, mechanism and ways of doing businesses are generally in line with these developments. For instance, it was felt all over the world that "community involvement" is a top priority. In Uttaranchal public-private sector in a joint effort started movement on "people's participation in development of tourism". It is a success story of Kerala that peoples participation in the development of tourism is the key to success. Uttaranchal has already initiated this in direction of religious and leisure tourism components.

To conclude, as a result of mutual cooperation and communication between private-public sector at different stages of development has achieved the disappearing of distrust, which existed between them at large. This has not only enhanced the cause of tourism but has earned us the trust of external private sector entities who now feel that investment in tourism will reap good dividends since tourism in India is a golden goose which is yet to be nurtured. It is time we shall start to treat it as such.

# Nineteen

# Tourism Development: Sectorial - Regional Planning

Tourism is a tricky business since it involves isolation of motives for travel. Man's motive for travelling has always been mixed. No single factor can explain the total motivational pattern although one can pinpoint the predominant motive.

In any policy management regarding tourism the consumer must first be separated from total existing and possible sets of consumers in order to determine the actual size, the facilities of measurement of intended results and unintended consequences. They should be conceived in terms of objective outlined. Further, the results and consequences are to be made compatible with the input to the enterprise. Each set of question must be viewed in its historical context before it is viewed contemporarily.

The prospective visitor to India is endowed with a given mental framework having cognitive, emotive and affective aspects. This mental framework only reflects the attitudes but it also determines the type of message, which are permitted to flow through the selector system and the likely outcome of various stimulus situations.

From a managerial angle tourist system is concerned with meeting the demands with the available resources with a view to maximize the return. Input is the wants and the general resources. System is concerned with converting these inputs into tourist plants in terms of goals and objectives. The output is the services and information available.

Input $\rightarrow$ System $\rightarrow$ Output

The important aspects in tourism development is the management of sector and land. Before doing sectorial planning we should consider the regional planning as well. The regional management for tourism development should not result in the deterioration of the fragile environment and attractive landscapes through overbuilding and excessive number of visitors.

The quantum of tourist traffic is directly proportionale to the number of people with a sufficient discretionary income. In designing a strategy for growth of tourism in India the policy makers have to bear in mind the place of tourism in the overall pattern of political and economic growth. The development plans will have to be dovetailed so that there is a minimum loss which while shifting priorities from the immediate of short term objective of earning foreign exchange to a long term one of general expansion.

Within these constraints alternate mixes of ideal types can be isolated to indicate the levels of return in the long and short run of operation. In fixing the target for return one has to bear in mind the character of the local traffic and its compatibility with the foreign markets.

**Sectorial Management**

In Sectorial Management we try to study the main sector where tourism is prospering and flourishing. It includes the perfect management of a sector. Any country whether it already has an active tourist industry or it is thinking of developing a tourist sector has many problems to face and resolve :

1. The government has to decide upon the rate of growth of tourism sector whether indeed it wishes to encourage mass tourism or develop it more slowly and selectively. Such a decision may of course be taken for it by circumstances that already exist. For instance, a country with an incipient industry simply can not cope with a vast influx of tourists. Since it does not possess the tourist plane capable of dealing with large numbers.
2. It must make a decision as to the importance which tourism is to have in the national economy and how its development and growth is to fit in with the plans for national and regional development.

3. It must decide what are to be the respective roles of the public and the private sector in the development of the industry. The Public Sector as we have seen will almost certainly have to provide the necessary costly infrastructure before the private sector can begin to operate.
4. It has to determine the roles to be played by domestic and foreign capital.
5. It has to decide whether the decision needs to be made as to whether the tourist industry should be treated in the same way as other industries. Or whether the tourist industry should be considered peculiar. The character of the industry warrants it being given special administrative and financial arrangements.

Tourism planning and general plan should be coordinated globally. The coordinated approach has a direct bearing on the success of tourism industry. As it involves many industries and a whole range of complex processes. The sectorial planning should be done in such a way that it can achieve an optimum level of expansion without creating serious imbalances of various kinds.

If a country, region or an area possess attraction and provides some hospitality for prospective tourists, tourism will probably develop. If this tourism development is to benefit the host area, formal forward looking planning is essential. If tourism planning is to happen in a specific area some entity must stimulate the original idea. This basic inspiration must be shared by some entity, which holds controlling interest and responsibility for the resources to be utilized by tourism industry.

Before selecting the sector we should keep the area or place also in our mind. The disadvantage of haphazard and unplanned management of tourism development germinates special economic problems not encountered in other type of economic activity. The great increase in the number of visitors to these areas resulted in rapid unplanned construction of hotels and dwellings for tourists and migratory service employees. This expansion threatened to destroy the very environment that is tourist attraction. The environmental amenities, which attract tourists, have tended to be taken for granted. The quality of the tourism product depends upon a high quality natural environment.

*Factors to be kept in Mind*

The sectorial management should be done by taking care of following things :

(a) Which is the state, in which tourism can be developed, which type of tourism is it natural attraction or artificial.
(b) The resource available and potential of that sector.
(c) What are the available facilities. What other things are required to be created to attract tourist.
(d) What should be the funds. We have to depend upon domestic or foreign capital. What is the rate of interest.
(e) What is the volume of tourist.
(f) The area people are involved in that specific tourism activity or not. If not then what are the reasons. How can they be motivated.
(g) What is the attitude of the tourist. What are the special facilities they are demanding for.
(h) What will the strategy adopted for the marketing and promotion.
(i) The environment is also taken care of. We should do proper research that whether the environment is harming the monument or the tourism activity is harming the environment and what are the remedies and precautionary measures.
(j) The carrying capacity concept should be taken full care of.
(k) The decision making in the various areas of tourism is spread over a large number of structures with differing and sometimes competing priorities. So, the planning and policy making becomes difficult and arise as organization problems and specially in mixed economy.
(l) The cost shared by different department should also be taken care of.

**Land Management**

Underdeveloped societies are characterized by asymmetrical, uncoordinated and often times rapid changes in values, goals and political framework. The basic variables of social life in these countries are in a state of constant disequilibrium. The element of instability and uncertainty has serious repercussions on planning. The planner has to operate virtually in areas of the unknown and unpredictable. There is always a lurking suspicion in the mind of the entrepreneur that things may not remain the same for a definite length of time.

So, land management is also an important factor taken care of. If a country region or an area possesses attraction and provides some hospitality for prospective tourists, tourism will probably develop.

Developing societies are interested in telescoping the changes at all levels—economic, social and political. Centralized guidance is essential for conscious effort of directing the changes. The land is the foremost element, which is a type of base for all tourism activity. So, the selection of land should be done by a perfect planning process.

- We should see whether the land available is fertile in nature or industrially important. Whether the artificial attraction has to be made to attract the tourist or not. If the land is historically important then before developing that land as a tourist place we should keep many things in mind. The various precautionary measures should be taken care of. For example, Taj special care is being taken for protecting it from the pollution created by the factories.
- What type of tourism the land is suitable for should also be taken care of and accordingly the various facilities should be made available. The resort planning should be done carefully. In accounting for the setting of many seaside towns the existence of an earlier nucleus of settlement to which the modern town is attached must be recognized.
- Various approaches to that land area should be kept into consideration. Transport has been the cause and an effect of the growth of tourism. Improved transport facilities have stimulated tourism, the expansion of tourism has stimulated transport. The degree of access to a particular place in terms of distance, time or cost. The number of opportunities available for a given travel cost, and reflects the quality of transport network, i.e., the availability and quality of service provided. Accessibility has been a very

important factor affecting the rise and growth of many individual resorts and tourist areas.

- The total area (geographically) which can be developed. What should be the perfect planning of the various facilities, like hotels, resorts should be done properly in very organized form. What part of land is used as residential area. How the people living near the tourist developed land are reacting.
- What are the basic infrastructure and superstructural facilities should be made available to attract more and more tourists in that land.
- The carrying capacity of that land area should be taken care of. This varies with the fragility of the area concerned and the nature of the tourist activity contemplated, e.g., an island rain forest is a fragile environment, which could be endangered by excessive number of people.
- Of all modern industries tourism has the greatest need to protect the environment of the places of natural and cultural importance—be it a monument, a beach resort or a wildlife sanctuary. The planners must consider the environmental process wherever large investments are made in tourism development. Destination noted for their particular character and beauty should not be reduced to innocuous urban jungles in order to keep pace with the visitor inflow, wildlife which is deteriorating and vanishing so rapidly can be safeguarded.
- To avoid excessive concentration in one land area the territorial planning is also very important. It must be reconciled with the limits in place of industrialization and urbanization which even though complementary to tourism, and can constitute a serious danger to it.
- Specific infratructure areas are power, water, communication, sewage and drainage, roads and highway and parks, recreation and health care facilities should also be taken care while doing the land management.

This approach would recommend development to accommodate maximum possible number of projected visitors and to design facilities to generate the maximum possible spending by the tourists.

**Hierarchy in Tourism and its Development in India**

India being a vast and diverse country has something to offer to everyone. The beauty of its ancient monuments, the beat and rhythm of its folk and classical dances that have come down the ages almost unchanged, its colourful crawled bazaars contrasting with the peace and grandeur of the snowcapped mountain tops, the quiet backwaters of Kerala and their beautiful beaches, and above all its well-meaning, charming people—these are a few of the countless facets of India which are timeless in their appeal. Tourism Development in India more than Fifty Year Back started.

In 1945 an expert committee under Dr. John Sargent was formed to review the nature and extent of tourist and pilgrim traffic in India both from within the country and overseas. In the year 1951, the government started paying attention to giving an impetus to the development of tourism particularly attracting foreign tourists. The broad objective is to organise publicity in foreign countries and to ensure that visitors from abroad are provided comfortable facilities during their sojourn in this country.

In the year 1952-53 the objectives were repeated again. The domestic travel was given importance in Ministry of Transport and Communications resolution on 27th February, 1958. On 1st July 1966—the need to boost tourist traffic mostly foreign tourism was felt. Two major steps required to be taken for this :

1. Traditional role of promotion of international cooperation.
2. India should present an image abroad of a country full of tourist attraction.

In 1967, the goals of tourism were reiterated by our Ministry of Tourism and Civil Aviation.

In Fourth Five Year Plan the target figure of 500,000 tourists by 1971 was changed to 600,000 tourists in 1973. In 1969, the figure was again changed to 400,000 tourists by 1974. The tourist arrivals have increased nearly seven fold from 188,820 in the year 1968 to 13,29,950 in 1990.

A proper organized and conscious planning has helped tourism industry to develop a lot. It is necessary to develop any area with respect to its attraction and funds availability. A perfect department was made in the Ministry of Tourism to see the proper planning for hotel travel agencies, wildlife, etc. The appointment of various experts committees advisory committees councils and boards from time to time has helped the organisation grow tremendously.

### Organisational Chart of the Department of Tourism — Headquarters

Minister
↓
Deputy Minister
↓
Secretary
↓
Director General
↓
Additional Director General
↓

| Jt. Director General | Deputy Director General | Deputy Director General | Deputy Director General | Deputy Director General | Director Tourist Adminis-tration | Director Market Research |
|---|---|---|---|---|---|---|
| ↓ | ↓ | ↓ | ↓ | ↓ | ↓ | ↓ |
| Hotels | Publicity Promotion Training Prog., conferences | Travel Trade, Hospita-, lity Prog. | Planning Programme | Supple-mentary Accom-modation, Wildlife. | Adminis-tration, Finance, Coordi-nation | Travel, Statistics. |

Due to historical reasons, India started taking interest in the modern concept of tourism. The economic and social advantages of tourism which were being exploited by many countries especially in west, recognized India in early sixties. Although considerable time and attention were devoted to the development of tourist traffic immediately after independence.

The history of India contributed for the development of tourist traffic. Throughout ages, many races and people who came either temporarily into contact with India or settled permanently within its borders have contributed to it.

India's glorious traditions and rich cultural heritage are linked with the development of tourism. Its magnificent monuments attract large number of tourists from all over the world.

India also occupies a unique geographical position. The climatology is quite varied. The wealth of cultural traditions, extending over thousands of years, the natural surroundings, the architectural masterpiece, the music, dance, paintings, customs and languages all these together make India a tourist paradise. We can not think of any other country having all the features of tourist attraction found like we have in India.

History has been equally generous in bequeathing a treasure of monuments. There is the immortal Taj, the Dravidian temples of South especially those of Madurai and the world famous frescoes of Ajanta and Ellora. There is also no dearth of cities that create an impression on the tourist.

According to Mark Twain, "India is the one country under the sun that is endowed with an impression interest for alien prince and alien peasant for lettered and ignorant, wise and fool, rich and poor, bonded and free and on land that all men desire to have seen and having seen only by even a glimpse would not give that glimpse for the shows of all the globe combined."

This sums up the relationships of history with tourism and how these two put together contribute towards the development of the country's economy.

For the best results in the development field of tourism various plans were laid down like Sargent Committee. The Central Tourist Organization with various separate Tourist Traffic branch in 1949 was set up that whole time attention was paid to the development of tourist traffic in India.

Various recommendations were made and were also implemented in 1949-56 due to the increase in tourist traffic. The Headquarters branches were increased to four (1) Tourist Traffic Section, (2) Tourist Administration Section, (3) Tourist Publicity Section, and (4) Distribution Section.

These branches were fully developed and started functioning under one Deputy Secretary and two Under Secretaries. At this stage the Directorate General of Tourism was made. It was on 1st March 1958 that a separate tourism department was created in the Ministry of Transport to deal with all the matters concerning tourism.

By the Presidential Order dated 14 March 1967, the Department of Transport and Civil Aviation was formed into a separate Ministry designated as the Ministry of Tourism and Civil Aviation.

It was after nearly eighteen years that the subject of tourism was accorded a separate entity and became independent of transport. It had achieved all round expansion in its activity.

Tourism in India is developing since independence. And it will go on developing more and more with the passage of time.

**The Planning Process**

With the carefree planning the tourism developing programmes are gaining success. Tourism is a source of eco-development. It brings foreign exchange and employment. IUOTO seminar held in Prague in 1964, examined in great detail the many problems involved in the development of a tourist industry and concluded that planning whether at national, regional or local level was indispensable. The planning process involves five things fundamentally:

(i) It must make an inventory of all the facilities available and of the potential facilities.
(ii) It must assess the tourism markets and attempt a projection of future tourist flaws.
(iii) It must look for area's where the demand is greater than the supply.
(iv) It must investigate investment possibilities both domestic and foreign, for the financial commitment in tourism development is likely to be substantial.
(v) It must attempt to conserve and promote the natural endowment, cultural legacy and social amenities.

Planning after all is really about supply and demand, the planning process requires an assessment of the supply of resources and the potential demand upon them.

So, with the help of planning the Tourism Development programme can be increased and developed with a tremendous speed. It will be able to achieve the complexities of tourist activity the manifold resources and facilities required to meet the demand of the market. The coordinated development of the various inter-depended sectors can be achieved properly.

# *Twenty*

# Tourism as an Industry

Tourism industry if broadly interpreted depicts that the dominant sectors are seen to be accommodation related activities, transport in its different modes, and leisure and recreation services. There are also specialized forms of services in both the generating market and at the destination guiding and events. Some of these activities involve the public sector as a direct provider or as a coordinator. The components of the tourism industry in a developing country may be relatively simple to identify as compared to the components of the tourism industry in an industrialised nation where sophisticated segmentation techniques result in adverse range of market niches. Consequently, the industry is much more complex and there are many hundreds of operations which are influenced by the tourism industry but which may not be obviously associated with tourism. With the tourism industry cutting across so many sectors and impinging upon such a wide range of operations, educators are faced with a bewildering choice of markets at which their products should be launched. The workforce in tourism has traditionally been poorly rewarded by employers in terms of training, education and financial rewards and, as a result the perception of tourism as an undesirable sector in which to be employed is perpetuated.

It is quite surprising that tourism had not been accorded the status of an industry by the central government till very late. To be very precise, not before the commencement of Sixth Five Year Plan. It was only during the mid 1980s that such a late decision was taken during Seventh Five Year Plan. That might be because of the fact that our country has been receiving a large number of tourists as well as good amount of foreign exchange earnings from tourism. However, before the Seventh Five Year Plan only one serious effort by the Government of India can be traced, i.e., during the Second Five Year Plan that our special budget of Rs. 3 crores was assigned for the promotion of tourism. Other than this, few other minor steps were also taken up by central government like in 1945 a committee was set up to examine the efforts and steps taken for the promotion of tourism, as a result of the recommendations of this committee, Indian Tourism Development Corporation was formed and a hotel loan development fund was created. Till the early 1970's all other efforts towards the promotion of Indian Tourism were made by Air India Corporation. It is primarily because of this that in the field of tourism our contribution in the total global tourist arrivals is still below one per cent, as compared to smaller countries with less diversity or less diversified products like Singapore, Malaysia, Thailand, Indonesia, etc. Thus very late the need was felt to give tourism the status of an industry although during the Sixth Five Year Plan, there was much of debate on whether to grant the status of an industry or not. If yes, then what will be the advantages and disadvantages of such a step to the central exchequer. If not, what all sectors of Indian Tourism Industry should be awarded with this status and which should not be.

The question whether tourism constitutes an industry or not is debatable. Industries are made up of firms which produce the same product or groups of products so that the consumers regards them as ideal substitute for one another even though the products may differ slightly. However, Medlik in 1972 argued that a firm may consist of more than one establishment and operate in more than one industry. Here, the problem is to recognise first as to how establishments as well as firms make up an industry and thereafter as to how there can be some overlap between different industries. Wahab (1971) writes, "For the country concerned, tourism is an industry whose products are consumed on the spot forming invisible exports." Again in 1975 in his later work, he opposed that any product whether tangible or intangible that serves to gratify certain human needs should be considered as an industry or industrial product and that if a bond of products unity exists between various firms and organizations in a way that characterise their overall function and determines their place in economic life, they should be considered as an industry. Other experts, Lundberg (1976) and Mcintosh (1977) often referred to tourism as a business or industry. It is due mainly to its broad nature that we find some confusion in accepting it as an industry.

Tourism envelops various other industries such as the airline, rail, accommodation and food service industries. It also involves wholesalers, retailers and attractions as well as a range of public services. This is supported by Young (1973) when he opines that it is a heterogeneous group embracing a large variety of trade and industries which have the supplying travellers' need as their common function. As tourism does not produce a distinct product, some of the exports such as Chadwiek (1981) argue that it can not exist as an industry. Further Papadopilis (1986) opines that tourism in the conventional sense is not a market since it does not sell simply one product and there is no single sector involved. Smith (1988) implicitly agrees with the notion of a tourism industry and like Medlik (1988) has formulated an operational measurement for tourism industry activity based upon providing a weighting for standard industrial classfication.

**Sectors of the Industry**

*I. Travel Related*

(i) Travel agents
(ii) Tour operators
(iii) Airlines
(iv) Cruise companies
(v) Bus and coach companies
(vi) Railways
(vii) Taxi operators
(viii) Courier services
(ix) Reservation consultants
(x) Marketing and Technical Consultants

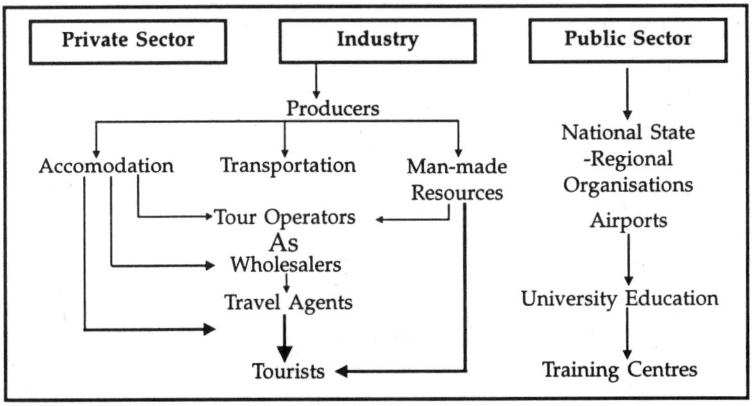

*II. Leisure and Entertainment*

Hotels, Guest Houses, Camping Sites, Hostels, Restaurants, Cafetaria and Bar.

- Art Galleries, Museums, Theme Parks, Zoos, Sport Centres, Gardens, Country Parks, Cinemas, Amusement Arcades.
- Other Organizations

National and Regional Tourist Offices. Tourist Guides, Advertising Agencies, Copywriting Agencies, Marketing Companies and Training Institutions.

**Indirectly Related Sectors**

This includes construction, insurance, ship building, road building, car manufacturing, food processing, manufacturers of tents and outdoor sports equipment. Technically the term industry can be defined as a group of firms producing similar or identical products. This definition can also be applied to tourism, wherein the term product is replaced by services.

Two criterias are commonly used for defining industry.

(a) The product being produced.
(b) The process of manufacturing.

**Product, Price, Promotion and Place**

According to the first criteria the firms are grouped as an industry. If their products are similar or they are close substitutes whereas in the second criteria, the emphasis is on the similarity of raw material going in the production of a product. Only variation can be the quantity. If we apply this definition or these criterias, we find, that tourism fulfils all the criterias and proves to be the most deserving sector to be granted the status of an industry. Factors present in Tourism which justify all the four features of an industry are :

1. The effect on income
2. Employment generation
3. Effect on Balance of Payment
4. Balance between investment and development. An industry provides jobs so does tourism rather it provides more jobs than any other industry because here one man is served by two and half men.

Tourism industry provides jobs to unskilled. In view of the aforesaid facts it is clear that it is difficult to define clearly the tourism due to the expensive spread of activities it covers. It is not proper that tourism does not produce a distinct product and so, it cannot exist as an industry. Tourism businesses constitute some of the largest single economic groups to be found throughout the world. This industry is defined for the central services of airlines, wholesalers, hotels, etc. but not for those providing peripheral services. It is important here to mention that the largest tourism companies making available central services embark upon vertical or horizontal integration which strengthen the area of tourism as an industry. Here, it is clear that if major companies create a stronger bond which helps product unity, this will create more need for tourism industry terminology. In his so called supply side view of defining tourism Smith (1988) identifies two-tier tourism business. The first tier is seen to be composed of business which serves tourists exclusively while the second ties is seen to serve a mix of tourists and local residents. We agree with his approaches and arguments for a definition, if tourism which at the first stage is identified as an industry and at the second stage allow it to confirm to existing definitional standards and conventions used in other fields. An economic or operational approach gives tourism academies greater status in the eyes of industry and government. Despite a number of comments and arguments and frequent debates on the problem, it is right to say that tourism can be included as an industry. Of course, it is not a single industry. Indeed, it is a multi segment industry. We consider it an industry whose products are consumed on the spot forming invisible exports. It is also a fragmented industry with high complexity due to the price sensitive nature of demand and the intangibility, perishability and inseparability or say, it is an industry with no clear boundaries or a hodge-podge of different component parts.

**Characteristics of Tourism vis-a-vis Industry**

- Products tangible or intangible serving certain human needs should be considered an industrial product.
- An amalgam of products characterising their overall function and determining their place in economic life should be considered as industry.

- Tourism envelops various other industries and so, we call it a multi-segment industry or a composite industry.
- It is an industry with no clear boundaries.
- In the Indian context, the recognition of this sector as an industrial activity came on the recommendation of National Development Council.
- The declaration of this sector as an industry envisages a package of incentives and support services to the sector.
- The structure of the industry is a hodge-podge of different component parts.

In India tourism generates jobs for more than six million people with the direct opportunity to work in travel trade. And it provides an opportunity to 8 million people to associate themselves indirectly with the travel trade. The economic significance of tourism could not be realised till late 70s when late Prime Minister Smt. Indira Gandhi decided to set up a separate Ministry of Tourism and Civil Aviation under a Cabinet Minister.

Tourism now in India has been given the status of an export industry by the Ministry of Tourism and Planning Commission. This means that tourism related activities will be entitled to incentives and concessions given to other exports industries, but this message does not seem to have percolated in other states and Union Territories for instance, the manufacturing industries pay a concessional rate for power consumed by them in the manufacturing process whereas Tourism Industry still cannot avail this concession by respective governments. Several years ago a study was carried out to reveal the contribution of tourism in the multiplier effects. The conclusions of this study were that Rs. 3.50 were generated for every one rupee invested in tourism. Therefore, the Seventh Five Year Plan is considered as a watershed in the development of tourism in India, because it was for the first time, the vast potential of tourism as a foreign exchange earner and generator of employment opportunities was recognized. And several new policy initiatives were taken up to develop tourism sector on an accelerated growth path. By 1997 March, 16 states and three Union Territories have declared tourism as an industry. In addition to this, four states have accorded the hotel and catering sector the status of an industry. It was only after this that the first time foreign collaboration in hotels and convention industry got permitted on Franchise basis and Management contract basis.

Equity participation in Foreign Exchange has also been permitted upto 51 per cent of the total equity for the proposed company. The advancements in this field have gone to such a height that GATT has given birth to GATS (General Agreement on Tourism Services) under the recent liberalized economic scenario. India has become the member of GATS not only to win but to woo the investors from private sectors in India but also from other parts of world, more particularly NRIs settled in different locations to make investment in infrastructural development which offers attractive returns. This was possible only by giving tourism the status of an industry with all the incentives and concessions which are given to other industrial sectors in India. (Reduce power tariff; gas lines; telephones, 50 per cent concessions on items that they import).

Globalization of development programmes has raised the foreign exchange requirements of developed as well as the non-developing countries. A number of manufacturing and non-manufacturing, traditional and non-traditional industries, no doubt, have helped them in their stupendous task of industrial transformation but at the same time the harmful side-effects have resulted in atmospheric pollution. In addition, the inadequacy of financial resources has also been an important barrier in speeding up the process of economic transformation. The magnitude of completion is found at peak which necessitates world class excellence for excelling competition. Amidst all these constraints, the development of tourism industry appears to be an important solution. An analysis of positive effects makes it clear that to be more specific the developing countries like ours should change their priority order and should assign due weightage to the development of tourism industry.

Widening of social opportunities, setting up of the nation's social life, promotion of inter-regional and intra-regional understanding, creation of national identity and national integration are some of the important positive effects of tourism industry on social transformation. Tourism is a sensitive device to speed up the process of social transformation. An expansion in the social opportunities is found to have been generated, generating since the general masses have had an intercourse with the people of different places and regions. This helps in narrowing the thoughts and ideas. The creation of national identity is possible. There is national integration of people of any culture and religion when they meet together and evince interests in subserving national interests. Tourism is basically a social activity which in addition to creating a national understanding paves ways for international understanding and projection of a fair national image abroad.

Recognizing the tourism industry as one of great potentials, the Government of India has drawn up ambitious plans to develop it with the partial implementation of the tourism action plan. India hopes to earn foreign exchange worth Rs. 10,000 crore by the beginning of the 21st century, while the foreign tourists arrivals are expected to be 1 per cent of the total movement of tourists all over the world within the next five years. Under the action plan, steps are being taken to improve the tourism infrastructure. The Tourism Ministry is also evolving suitable policy for increasing foreign tourist arrivals and foreign exchange earnings besides restructuring and strengthening the institutions for the development of human resources.

The total budgetary allocation for the Tourism Department is Rs. 109.28 crore, although tourism industry is one of the major foreign exchange earners and there is a tremendous scope for its further growth. Over 5.5 million persons are directly employed in the industry and another 8 million are involved indirectly in addition to the domestic publicity abroad through Air India. The need to increase the outlay for publicity abroad has been stressed by the Parliament Committee on Transport and Tourism. Actually only 1 per cent of the Foreign Exchange Earnings by the country are being spent on overseas publicity. This should be increased to 2 or 3 per cent of the Foreign Exchange Earnings, the Committee has recommended.

However, the committee has pointed out that the India Tourism Development Corporation, which is given a budgetary support of Rs. 5 crores by the Government, should be asked to generate its own resources and in future, it should not depend on the government. It was suggested that there should be special allocation of funds for promotion of tourism in the economically backward areas of the country. It was further pointed out that the decrease in expenditure on development of tourism infrastructure from Rs. 11.10 crore in the Budget estimate of 1991-92 to Rs. 13.60 crore in 1993-94 was not commensurate with government policy of attracting more tourists. The actual expenditure in this regard during 1991-92 was Rs. 18.64 crore and for 1992-93 it was only Rs. 14.82 crore.

The Committee felt that the targets of tourist inflow into the country could not be achieved by merely increasing the expenditure on tourist information and publicity. The actual expenditure on publicity during the current year would be Rs. 48.40 crore. The Committee is of the view that increase in expenditure on publicity was no substitute for reduction in the expenditure on development of tourist infrastructure, which may have an adverse effect on tourist inflow.

Meanwhile, the department of tourism has proposed a plan outlay of Rs. 990 crore for the Eighth Five Year Plan but the Planning Commission had proved it to Rs. 272 crores only, with a Budgetary support of Rs. 240 crore. The balance of Rs. 32 crore is expected to be generated by the ITDC from its internal resources and market borrowing.

The Committee has felt that the Budget allocation for the Tourism Department is too low as compared to the foreign exchange earning and the potential to generate employment in this sector. Today, tourism can create jobs in far-flung areas where other industries would feel shy to go.

It can also open up backward and remote areas by providing not only jobs but also creating better and sustained economic growth. The committee has however, come down heavy on the ITDC and has said it had not been functioning properly due to mismanagement and inefficiency as performance of the ITDC hotels were running into losses. Accumulated losses were of great magnitude and unless drastic steps were taken, the situation was likely to become unmanageable. The government should sign a MoU with the ITDC and it should also mobilise private capital. ITDC should recover its dues from the State Governments, it was urged.

Destination India is suddenly the password to a magical mystery tours. Buyers and sellers from Israel to South Africa descended on India recently to foster an industry which is today, one of the fastest growing industries in the world. Tourism Ministry reports confirm these facts. Between January 1992 and 1993, foreign tourists inflow dropped by 15.50 per cent from 1,80,000 to 1,50,000. And to add insult to injury, the US government issued a travel advisory warning its citizens against travelling to India, particularly New Delhi.

Tourism industry may bring disastrous results, if not planned properly and found inconsistent with the social norms. The large influx of tourists from affluent to poor countries may result in social problems such as dishonesty, cheating, violence, crimes and development of inferiority complex. The development of tourism industry instrumentalises the process of cultural transformation but the aggressive development of active tourism introduces an element of cultural damage. It is very natural since the old forms are transformed with the influx of large number of tourists. No doubt, there are a number of positive effects of tourism on the protection of environment but at the same time, we find possibilities of environment pollution due to a large influx of tourists to relatively small areas.

Even as industry representatives tried to impress on the ministry that tourism was an intangible product and there needed to be an interface between the buyer and the seller. Jena, the Tourism Minister maintained that the technology available in today's world obviated the need for tourism marketing when flabbergasted industry leaders who included hoteliers and travel industry representatives persisted in convincing Jena that Marketing was the major area to be focussed upon and it was suggested that the task should be entrusted on the Indian Embassies. There is no real agreement between government, industry and academies as to what actually constitute the tourism industry. They agree only on the fact that tourism is enormously diverse in terms of the range of sectors it encompasses and the variety of organizations it incorporates.

Tourism spans several industrial sectors and there are

therefore differing interpretations of the categories of employment at various levels of skills, and thus the specific needs of each sub-sector of the industry are significantly different. There are also specialized forms of services in both the generating market and at the destination of guiding and events. Some of these activities involve the Public Sector as a direct provider or as a coordinator.

**Conclusion**

Tourism arises from the movement of people from their homes towards various destinations and their stay over there for sometime. During this activity, they indulge themselves in various pleasure activities like sports, sight seeing, shopping and relaxing in their own ways. In this activity of tourism, people spend money on transportation, accommodation, shopping and sight seeing. This is the money which they earn in their normal domicile. Thus, this money spent is earned by various people involved in the transport business, hotel business, handicraft business, etc. All these businesses are solely based on the travel and tourism phenomenon whatever the reason of travel may be.

According to the definition of an industry, an industry refers to a group of firms producing identical goods, that is, which the consumer regards as being perfect substitutes for one another although they may be physically different. If a bond of product unity exists between various firms and organizations in a way that characterizes their overall function and determines their place in the economic life, they should be considered as an industry.

Tourism fits in exactly in the definition of industry hence it can very well be called an industry as such. As the tourism products are intangible and the services are offered to the customer instead of goods, it can be called a service industry.

Thus, tourism should be given the status of an industry which implies that such business activities would in future be entitled to the same incentives and concessions as are applicable to the industrial and export sector of India. It is already an industry of the 21st century. *Times* magazine recently had a cover story on the dawn of a new golden age of travel—an age of voyaging on a truly global mass scale.

It is a complex industry of many parts, ranging from a giant airlines and a giant hotel to a husband and wife guide service of only 2 employees. The tourism industry is expected to double in the next decade heralding an unprecedented explosion—this explosion however being peaceful and non-destructive.

# Twenty One

# Community Attitude in Tourism Planning

The product and image that intermediaries package and sell is a destination experience and as such creates an industry that is highly dependant on the goodwill and cooperation of host communities. Many destination area attractions are public property or public goods and the hospitality needed for memorable visit must come from members of the public as well as employee of the industry. Increasingly, development of new facilities requires public investment in infrastructure and shared facilities and many festivals or events that evolved to fill local needs are being commercialised and promote as tourist events. It is the citizen who must live with the cumulative outcome of such developments and needs to have greater input in to how his community is packaged and sold as a tourist product on the world market.

**Community Approach**

Community response to the opportunities and challenges of tourism management depends to a large extent on its attitude to the industry. Attitudes are personal and complex variables but in terms of community attitudes to tourist, three determinants can be identified:

1. The type of contact which exists between resident and a visitor can have a bearing or impact on the resident reaction to add support to the industry.
2. The relative importance of the industry to the prosperity of individual and community will be a factor. Inconvenience become more tolerable if some compensation is evident.
3. A tolerance threshold in resident receptivity can be accepted in terms of the volume of business a destination can handle.

**Social Interaction at Tourist Destination**

The three contact situations have been identified by a German research scholar 'Dikadt' each having its own influence on local values and attitudes. These contact situations are.

1. When the tourist purchases a good or service from the resident.
2. When the tourist and resident finds himself side-by-side at an attraction such as a 'Beach ' or a 'Golf-Course' or at a local activity such as a festival or a 'Night-Club'.
3. When two parties come face to face with the objective of exchanging information and ideas.

But according to 'Dikadt' the first two situations are more common than the third one which means transiting and commercials exchanges taking precedence in most cases over the opportunities to increase mutual understanding.

In industrial nations when domestic tourism is predominant it is often difficult to distinguish or differentiate tourists from residents, during such transitory or commercial meetings which results in a low profile of the industry in many communities. Another British research scholar 'Mac Farland' has carried out a comparative survey of social interaction in several tourist destinations which reveals that the level of personal contact is moderate in nature. He found approximately half of the residents surveyed, reported little or no personal contact with the tourist.

This fact has also been established by another survey carried out by British Tourism Authority. This survey had gone further ahead to note that people most affected in their everyday life work by tourist activity.

1. People living and working in the centre of the tourist destination.
2. People living in small tourist towns where there is no place to hide from tourists.
3. Students and old age pensioners who are dependant on cheap accommodation and are unable to meet the inflated prices in popular destinations.

These observations would indicate that the type and level of contact between the visitor and the resident is partially selective. Those who live close to tourism activity will be aware of the industry and feel the full impact of its traffic and sales disruption. Those in the suburbs meanwhile will be largely unaware of the industry and will seldom come into contact with visitors.

**Levels of Tourism Development**

Another British scholar 'Smith' has illustrated a spatial-attitude link in her model of tourism and regional development.

*Level 1*

Contains all those attractions and facilities that make a community a tourist destination.

*Level 2*

Direct support zone contains houses and various functions required by the community these consist of stores, recreation and government offices and municipalities serving the people in addition to support services for the tourism industry.

*Level 3*

Indirect support zone consists of Hinterland which incorporated the area affected by the multiplier effect and involves the investment opportunities of the host states.

Through this model, Smith contends that if visitors expectations and needs can be met in a core zone, then the tourist will seldom need to leave the area to penetrate into adjacent neighbourhood and thus preventing the privacy and separate living cultures of local residents. Therefore, her model also suggests that those who live far from the core zone will be able to avoid personal contact with the industry though they may be induced by earnings from visitors.

Hence, due to different types of contacts, certain residents can be expected to develop much stronger attitude to tourism than others. Those residents with the commercial stake in the business whether they are employers or employees are likely to have more definite or positive attitude towards tourism than those with little or no direct involvement.

**Community Attitudes to Tourism**

How a community responds to the opportunities and challenges of tourism depends to a large extent on its attitude to the industry. Attitudes are personal and complex variables, but in terms of community attitudes to tourism, three determinants can be identified. First, the type of contact which exists between resident and visitor can have a bearing on a resident's reaction to, and support of, the industry. Second, the relative importance of the industry to individual and community prosperity will be a factor. Inconvenience becomes more tolerable if some compensation is evident. Third, a tolerance threshold in resident receptiveness can be expected, in terms of volume of business a destination can handle.

It was Pizam's contention that "entrepreneurs saw tourism as having many more positive impacts on the quality of life on Cape Cod, Massachusetts and these impacts were not restricted to the economic type only. Entrepreneurs also attributed better police and fire protection, plus more recreational facilities, to the presence of tourism. Murphy's cross-sectional analysis of decision-making groups in three English tourist centres found a similar disparity. He found that the decision-making groups, represented by the business sector and local administration, had a more positive attitude to tourism that the residents. Interestingly, however, it was the local administration, represented by councilors, planners, and other senior administrative personnel who appeared more enthusiastic about the industry and its potential for the community. They were the strongest advocates of tourism's economic advantages and had a higher attitude profile than the industry representatives.

One reason why residents have consistently lower attitude ratings for local tourism, compared to other groups, is because they are often unaware of its economic significance and overall contribution to their community. The British Tourist Authority observed "many residents are unaware of just how tourism benefits an individual who is not directly employed in the tourism industry". Its survey found the public was largely ill-informed concerning tourism's contribution both to the national and local economies. This is a common problem, demonstrating a general weakness in the industry's public relations, when it fails to explain its role and contribution to those local people whose cooperation and goodwill are essential.

When Murphy analyzed his data from a different perspective, another social-spatial dimension emerged in community attitudes. His discriminant analysis of the three English tourist centres found a strong link between the relative importance of tourism to the community and resident attitudes. For example, Torquay's dependence on tourism and the distinct seasonal profile of this resort generated strong reactions. While the majority of respondents were positively disposed toward the industry, some were highly critical. One resident went so far as to state "Torquay and the tourist industry make sure I keep my place, and that I and many more like me are kept in reserve for low-paid jobs". Here the seasonal nature of a resort created either "seasonal employment" or "seasonal unemployment" depending on one's point of view and economic circumstances. In contrast the more balanced economies of York and Windsor provided a less conspicuous industry, which generated less emotional responses and more moderate attitudes. While many of the residents of York and Windsor were favourably disposed to tourists, some still had reservations about the industry itself. They noted that those engaged in tourism seemed to be prospering but questioned how much benefit the community at large was receiving, which reveals again how the degree of involvement affects attitudes to the industry.

The third determinant of community attitudes is linked to the scale of the industry and its associated volume of business. As the industry grows, not only does the quality of social interaction change, but residents come under increasing stress as they begin to compete for space and resources within their own home communities. Some degree of stress is inevitable in an industry which asks residents to share their environment and culture with strangers, but research has revealed there are some constant irritants which commonly mould attitudes.

The most frequently quoted irritant for residents is congestion, particularly with respect to traffic and parking, but also in terms of longer shopping lines and the loss of a favourite spot in the local restaurant or pub. In some cases the problem of congestion outweighed all other perceived disadvantages, particularly in the smaller and more popular destinations. Second to congestion is a concern that as tourism grows in importance local councils begin to give it preferential treatment. Here some residents felt that the character of their community was being changed for the convenience of visitors rather than for local people. The growth of motel strips and the advent of fast-food chains have been linked to tourism demand, and some residents felt they were losing control over the form and function of their own community. Another worry associated with tourism development is that property values will be inflated, particularly those in or adjacent to Smith's core zone, and taxes will be raised as local councils invest in additional infrastructure. Residents are concerned also about the growth of litter and vandalism, commonly associated with tourism development. Residents of Britain appear to be particularly sensitive to this problem, and the industry should perhaps take more responsibility for the refuse and anti-social behaviour it sometimes generates.

In the surveys referred to above, the overall attitudes toward tourism ranged from slightly negative (Cape Cod), through neutral (Torquay), to slightly favourable (Strafore, York, Lake District). From this somewhat limited sample it is apparent that no tourist destination widely enthusiastic about the industry, and in some cases the residents appear to be disillusioned with this activity.

If the industry is to improve its community relations it must find ways to maximize the positive features of its development and minimize the problems. An obvious place to start is reducing the social stress and irritants associated with increasing business volumes, by separating functions and placing limits on development. But much more can be done by demonstrate that.

**Tourism as a Community Industry**

Planning for tourism has changed and evolved along with the industry since the Second World War. It has developed from a site oriented and physical emphasis into a more regional and systems approach. Part of the systems approach includes a management concept in recognition of visitor and resident perceptions and their bearing on a successful travel experience.

This process of evolution will continue as tourism enters a new phase, with different demands and priorities.

The tourism industry is entering a stage of maturity after its 40 years of rapid expansion and development. There has been evidence of a slowdown in growth rates during the 1970s, part of which may be attributed to the recession, but part of which can be linked to changing demographic profiles and consumer preferences. The days of novelty and naivety on the part of the tourists have disappeared. Tourists now expect and demand more because they are experienced travellers. They will be satisfied no longer with second-rate attractions and accommodation, nor with poor service and rudeness. It is a buyer's market and there are many destinations and alternative experiences from which to choose. Increasingly one hears the call for quality, hospitality and value for money—and all of these require careful planning and management.

It is not only the industry which is facing maturity, for the mass tourism experience has taught destination areas many hard lessons. In this competitive business changing circumstances or fashions can quickly erode an established market. A destination needs to protect the integrity and attraction of its own product, plus guard against the action and rivalry of competitors. This is forcing destinations to look beyond their own situation and consider joint ventures with other destinations in order to create a more coordinated and appealing product. The key lessons emerging from the past 40 years are quality, flexibility, and coordination.

The residents of destination areas have received their instruction as to the benefits and problems associated with the industry. This activity, like all others, has its costs to society and the environment. In economic terms, it brings low-paid and seasonal employment, with most of the benefits traditionally flowing to a limited number of businesses. The environmental and cultural conservation interests of the industry have not prevented over-exploitation and destruction of the physical and cultural landscape. Socially, the number of visitors can exceed the capacity of local communities to absorb and benefit from the interaction.

The evidence suggests that tourism is an established part of our lives and is unlikely to retreat into its past as the exclusive pursuit of a privileged few. The maturity of the industry and destination communities will require more comprehensive and balanced planning, that can take into account both the issues and options which have emerged since the Second World War. One possible direction for such planning would be to view tourism as part of a destination area.

**Public Participation**

The community emphasis of the ecological community model indicates that as the scale of planning decreases, more public participation should be expected and encouraged. Planning experience in other fields reveals that informed and able citizens are willing to participate in decisions regarding the development and future of their communities. The same public has considerable tourism experience both as hosts and visitors, providing a reservoir of information and enthusiasm, if properly tapped. Runyan and Wu believe that:

> "The inclusion of complex impact considerations in a tourism planning process, strongly implies relatively wide community involvement in impact assessment. Increased involvement in estimating complex impacts, contributes to the reliability of the estimates. Such involvement also serves as a constructive vehicle for appraisal of impacts by individuals and groups other that those which are expert, a body of interests most planners feel should be included in a planning process."

The strength of professionals lies in forecasting relatively simple and quantitatively definable impacts, the wide involvement allows a look at more complex impacts, their comparison with those that are relatively simple, and a appraisal of the combination. Although resident involvement can significantly increase the time and effort required by professional to complete a project, the pay-off is impact information of increased reliability and usefulness.

The call for participatory planning is a criticism of the business and physical orientation of past tourism planning and its failure to keep abreast with developments in urban and environment planning. Goodman describes the move towards community planning as:

> "A system of community socialism, in which the economic institutions would grow from the smaller government units in society, is a model which would allow social outputs to be determined by the people most immediately affected by them."

Input from concerned community groups could provide a balance to the short-term objectives of the business sector, and possibly encourage greater variation and local flavour in future projects which would be a welcome change from the growing homogenisation of present development. Past experience with public participation in other planning areas indicates participation on a mass scale is an idealistic dream. In a representative democracy, it is impractical and unnecessary, in a political culture with a tradition of elitism it is out of the question. Thus, in many instances, it has been found that the process has been institutionalised or even conservative in approach, representing a middle class and environmentally conscious involvement, rather than a radical fringe as had first been expected.

Public participation experience on both sides of the Atlantic, indicates the process is predominantly issue-oriented, and is able to operate most effectively when these issues are local and can be approached at an early stage in the planning process before commitments are made and battle lines drawn. The Skeffington Committee report argued persuasively for wider public participation in British Planning, and many of its recommendations were subsequently adopted in the structure planning process of the late 1970s. In the US, the wave of citizen participation has spread from the model city programme of the inner cities to include interest group participation in the preparation of environmental impact statements as outlined in the National Environment Policy Act of 1969.

**Conclusion**

The community concept has been presented in its system form as a means by which to develop and assess the tourism industry. Although none of the ideas or techniques suggested are original in themselves, their combination and orientation toward a tourism goal is new and reflects the growing importance of environmental and political decision making. The industry's attitude toward the environment needs to progress from economic exploitation to one of stewardship if attractive landscapes and amenities are to be preserved or developed. Public opinion and political power must be courted and won if the industry is to continue to rely on government support and community assets for its survival and success. By stressing the community and systems aspects of tourism it becomes apparent that this activity is now interwoven into the social, economic, land environmental aspects of all communities, whether or not they are major destinations. Under these circumstances, tourism can be integrated into the general planning procedures of all communities and become coordinated with facility developments in the physical and social, fabric of destinations areas.

The economic problems of the late 1970s and early 1980s have led many communities to consider embracing this growth industry of the post-industrial era. To do so, however, without careful analysis and consideration of the consequences can lead these same communities into a quicksand of false expectations. This book has attempted to pull together the various threads of modern tourism, to reveal its interrelated nature, land two-edged capabilities, so that communities and individuals may approach the industry in a more judicious manner.

# *Twenty Two*

# Consumer Behaviour in Tourism

Can we ever define what it is of our culture, what it is of our tradition that gives the serene, calm feeling of joy, ecstasy and even relief? Perhaps no. It is the intermixing of so many feelings, sentiments and emotions that have to be expressed, that may be expressed and those that are waiting to surge out of our souls so that they can become self-expressions.

## Motivations of Tourists

Historically tourists have travelled as a major life event. The pilgrimage grand tour or health cure visit may have been a major experience in the life of individuals from the time of Romans until the present day. We could embark on a number of generations regarding the needs which may have been associated with these trips but it may be impossible to judge earlier motivations utilizing current ideas of what constitutes contemporary motivations.

Although dimensions of concept of motivations in the context of tourist behaviour are not easy to map out yet it seems to include:

(A) Idea that travel is need related and that this manifests itself in terms of wants and strengths of motivation. In his work John Crompton 'Why people go on pleasure vacation' in *Annals of Tourism Research,* Vol. 6, p. 4) believes that essence of a vacation as being a break from routine but it does neither necessarily mean an escape because it does not explain how travel would occur when someone wanted to escape nor necessarily meant doing different things or change in lifestyle. Indeed it may mean doing the same kind of things but in different physical or social context.

To him travellers are motivated by general ability of destination to meet their psychological needs and support their values. Crompton further categorises psychological needs as :

(a) Self-exploration
(b) Social interaction
(c) Excitement
(d) Ego-enhancements

(B) Motivation is grounded in sociological and psychological aspects of acquired norms, attitudes, cultural perception, etc., leading to person specific forms of motivation.

According to McIntosh and Goeldner we can incorporate four categories in this context of tourist behaviour :

*(i) Physical Motivators*

Broadly include physical rest, participation in sports, beach recreation, relaxation, entertainment and health related suggested motivations.

*(ii) Interpersonal Motivators*

Broadly include desire to meet new people, visiting friends and relatives (VFR), escape from routine life, neighbours and even from family to interact with new people or to make new friendships.

*(iii) Status and Prestige*

Broadly covers desire of people to travel to different places not for the sake of enjoyment but to discuss about various travels to different people as a mark of gaining status and prestige among friends, employees, relatives or colleagues.

*(iv) Need to Compensate*

This broadly covers basic need among people to compensate for regular work routine one follows. In other words, accomplishment of every assignment calls for a recreation or rejuvenation of energy and for which change is required. Survey in Britain reveals that 43 per cent of travel is due to change in weather. 38 per cent is due to the need to compensate.

Maslow's need hierarchy model is probably the best known motivation theory. Due to its simplicity it is used in industrial, organisational and social sciences texts regularly. Maslow has proposed a hierarchical arrangements of individuals needs. He argued that of none of the needs in the hierarchy was satisfied, then the lowest needs, the physiological one would dominate individuals behaviour. If these were satisfied individual would be motivated by next level in hierarchy.

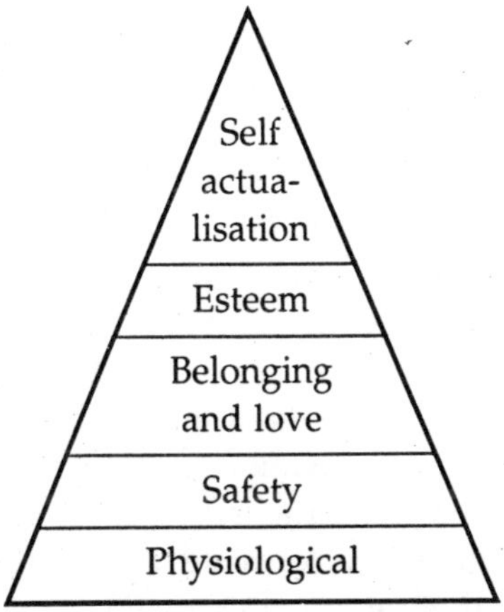


Maslow identified two types of sequence mechanisms in motivation, i.e., (a) tension-reducing motives (b) arousal seeking motives. His theory is holistic and is applicable to both work and non-work spheres of life. If we carefully analyse we see that this theory is very much applicable to tourism and its scope also extends to decision making in tourism.

(C) The image of a destination created through induced or organic communication channels will influence motivation and subsequently affect the type of travel undertaken.

These basic behaviour indicators show that motivation is an essential concept behind the different patterns of tourism demand. However, we should remember that although motivation can be stimulated and activated in relation to want for a product, needs themselves cannot be created. These needs are dependent on human element through the psychology and circumstances relating to the individual. This analysis also raises a question on what type of motivation is inherent in all of us (e.g., curiosity, need to meet people, etc.) and what types are learnt (e.g., status, prestige, achievement) because they are evaluated as valuable or positive.

Various theories who have identified tourist roles have concentrated upon assessment of socio-cultural and environmental impact of tourism or the nature of tourist experiences but none has provided an in-depth understanding of process of holiday purchase behaviour. In other words, for consumer behaviour study in tourism it is most pertinent to study accepted notions of tourist roles. Goffman (1958), a sociologist initially suggested that individuals behave differently in different situation in order to sustain impression associated with those situations. As actors have different stage and backstage performances, participants in any activity vary their behaviour according to the nature and context of that activity consequently individual roles can be identified and managed according to social circumstances.

Whereas tourists can be characterised into different typologies or roles which exercise motivations as an energizing force linked to personal needs or goal oriented forms of behaviour/holiday choice activity. On the other hand Cohen (1972) proposed a typology of tourists based upon element of tourist experiences in particular related to similarities/novelties between tourist's home environment and that of destination. But in spite of destination being novel, as Cohen suggests, most people prefer to explore it from a familiar base. Underlining this degree of familiarity, Cohen identifies four tourists role:

(a) Organised mass tourist
(b) Individual mass tourist
(c) Explorer
(d) Drifter

When we talk about organized mass tourist we refer to large number of families undertaking holidays. Family being a fundamental social unit of group formation and calling for supplying the needs of perhaps two or more generations which socializes children to adopt particular form of purchasing and act as a wider reference group. Given the importance of family behaviour in the purchase of leisure product we may highlight the fact that family decision-making assigns role to specific members of the family. One family member may be the facilitator, while information may be gathered by another and decision taken by head of family. Thus, the family acts as a composite buying unit with the different role patterns leading to a particular form of tourism product purchase. All research in this direction herald an inevitable increase in joint decision making in the family. It is more pertinent where risk involved is high or where purchasing decision making is important to the family as a whole or where there is high involvement in the purchase and where there is no time pressure (Sheth, 1974).

**Common Features of Consumer Behaviour**

These and many more researchers have developed grand models of consumer behaviour. These models share several common points :

(a) They all exhibit consumer behaviour as a decision process.
(b) They share that behaviour is rational and can be explained.
(c) They all provide a comprehensive model focussing mainly on behaviour of individual consumer.
(d) They view buying behaviour is purposive with consumer being an active information seeker from both internal and external channel (sources).
(e) They believe search and evaluation of information is a key component of decision making. Through this tourist move from general ideas to specific criteria and preferences for alternatives is fixed.
(f) All theorist include in their grand model a concept of feedback, i.e., outcomes experiences from purchases, that will affect future purchases.

**Consumer Behaviour Models in Tourism**

Some of the examples of models of consumer behaviour related to tourism can be summarised as :

*Earliest Consumer Behaviour Model*

Wahab, Crompton and Rothfield (1976)

Mode of Wahab *et al.*, is influenced by uniqueness of tourism product buying decision, i.e., it does not provide any tangible return on investment (or no physical transaction or change in ownership). It involves considerable expenditure in relation to earned income because expenditure involves savings and this purchase is not spontaneous but a result of pre-planned exercise as shown in model:

Initial framework
↓
Conceptual gathering
↓
Fact assumptions
↓
Definition of alternatives
↓
Design of Stimulis
↓
Forecast of consequences
↓
Cost benefit of alternatives
↓
Decision
↓
Outcome.

In 1977, Schmoll developed a consumer behaviour model based on the model of Howard Sheth and Nicosia. His model is built upon motivations, desires, needs and expectations as personal and social factors affecting tourists behaviour. Schmoll believes that the eventual holiday decision is in fact result of a distinct process involving a successive fields, viz :

Field I : Travel Stimulus
Field II : Personal and Social eterminants of travel behaviour.
Field III : Internal Variables
Field IV : Characteristics of Service Destination

Schmoll's field model of travel decision behaviour is developed by succeeding researchers for instance Mathieson and Wall (1982) offered a five stage process of Travel buying behaviour:

Felt need/Travel desire
↓
Information Collection and Evaluation by Image
↓
Travel decision
↓
Travel Preparation and Travel experience
↓
Travel satisfaction outcome and evaluation.

An insight study of work of Mathieson and Wall reveals that there 5 stage model is influenced by 4 interrelated factors :

(a) Tourist profile—age, income, motivation and previous experience.

(b) Travel awareness (Image of destination and its services).

(c) Destination resources and characteristics (attractions).

(d) Trip features (distance, duration, perceived risk).

Moutinho (1987) provided a model consisting of three individual parts related to specific tourist purchase behaviour, viz:

Part I : Pre decision and decision process

Part II : Post purchase evaluation

Part III : Future Decision making

To conclude much has been written by researchers on consumer behaviour and factors affecting it through models and ground models but much of it is general in nature and not substantiated by empirical studies. For instance while travel is a special form of consumption behaviour involving an intangible, heterogeneous purchase of an experimental product, yet they fail to develop an activity based theory.

*Twenty Three*

# Sustainable Tourism Development

The stock of natural and man-made resources for tourism and recreation are unspoilt countrysides, coastlines, lakes, rivers, island, mountain regions, forests, wildlife area, and historical cities and monuments. Till recently, it was assumed that tourism industry would not adversely affect these resources. However, the upsurge of world tourism in the seventies and in India during the eighties has shown in an unrestricted use of these resources for tourism purposes can bring to its wake unforeseen adverse effects. Modern tourism demands vast infrastructure. Development takes many spatial forms — roads, hotels, restaurants, etc. which has the effect of altering the environment. In the process, the major tourist sites are inevitably transformed. At best their natural attraction or primeval innocence is impaired, and at worst irreversible environmental damage is caused by a rush to build tourist facilities on the most attractive sites, by speculative land and building booms (recreational urbanization), and by major inroads into the local ecology through the development of tourist infrastructure and services.

There are four major kinds of places where ecological damage by tourists takes place: (a) sites of historical interest like Taj Mahal in Agra; (b) coastal areas like Goa; (c) mountain resorts like Srinagar and (d) forest and wildlife areas including national parks and sanctuaries. These are dealt with briefly below.

**Tourism Development at Historical Sites**

In the case of historical cities and old villages developed as tourists resorts, their native inhabitants are often distressed to find their narrow streets choked with tourist traffic and their market places turned into car parks. Worst such towns are cluttered with souvenir stands and the bazars packed with roadside *dhabawallas* and fastfood restaurants. St Pauls' in London, for instance, has become more like a department store than a church. In Vienna's Schonbrunn Palace, the priceless inlaid floors that survived centuries of duchesse's slippers are now tattooed by the spike heels of thousands passing through every day. Similar damage to our monuments like Taj Mahal, Fatehpur Sikri, Budhhist temples in Gaya and Varanasi, is becoming apparent though our level of international tourist traffic is as yet very low, barely 0.3 per cent of global arrivals. It will certainly become pronounced as the tourist traffic to India increases. It is, therefore, important to ensure that the exposure of our historical monuments and sites be carried out with sufficient care to avoid the damage observed in Western Europe due to the rapid growth of tourism.

Unfortunately, all such damage is not inadvertent. More of it is caused by petty vandalism of the "new barbarians", the tourist hordes. They furtively chip away pieces of marble to take home as scouvenirs. They steal artifacts from village Churches in Goa, gouge out mosaics from walls and floors, cut noses off statues, often carving their initials into ancient walls to add insult to injury. Those charged with looking after our historic sites like the staff of the Archaeological Survey of India, are hopelessly outnumbered and helpless. So tourists continue to threaten our cultural heritage.

**Tourist Development in Coastal and Marine Areas**

In the case of coastal and marine areas, massive and packaged tourist development has often destroyed their natural charm and even eroded their stability. The beach resort facilities of Goa are a case in point. They are spread thinly all along the coastline undermining the natural sand dunes ecosystem of the locality. This ecosystem is nature's defence line against tidal waves and land erosion by sea.

The sand dunes system with the dune vegetation plays a major role in protecting the coastline. But the uncontrolled spurt in construction activity provoked by tourist influx in Goa, particularly the extraction of sand from sand dunes for development works, has led to a continual erosion of coastal areas by the relentless sea.

The degradation of coastal beaches under pressure of development of tourism and other economic, industrial, transportation and recreational needs is not peculiar to beaches on Goa coastline only. It occurs all along our extensive coastline. The primary problem in its management arises from the fact that beach resources, unless wisely managed are liable to get dissipated even to the point of extinction. For example, the construction of a protecting wall for the shore temple at Mamallapuram, resulted in erosion of a large chunk of beach, north of the shore temple, wiping out a fishing village and seven cottages built for tourists in a nearby complex. The straight shoreline also changed to a curved bay thereby altering the topography of the coastline at Mamallapuram.

Apart from beaches, other coastal ecosystems severely affected are mangrove forests, coral reefs, and marine waters. Mangrove forests are one of our most unique and rich ecosystems, a product of a complex interplay of sea, coastal land, and river deposition. Apart from harbouring varied wildlife, mangroves also protect our coastline from erosion by the sea. But this vital significance has been often ignored. One instance of such damage is the denudation of mangrove forests along the Digha coast in West Bengal resulting in extensive erosion of beaches.

Similarly, coral reefs and marine waters have been destroyed by tourist activities like coral and shell collection, pollution and littering. Such damage in the Gulf of Kutch and parts of the Andaman Islands around Port Blair is very glaring.

It is, therefore, important to undertake an exhaustive environmental assessment study of all beach development projects before actually carrying them out. The environmental assessment study has to specify the nature and degree of interaction between (proposed) economic activities and their ambient physical environment. These interactions occur between two or more of the following major areas of concern in beach development and management.

- The sea,
- Human settlements and habitat,
- Natural resources and ecosystems,
- Level of economic development and socio-cultural environment,

- Environmental health,
- Industry and technology,
- Natural/aesthetic potential,
- Energy, and
- Type of tourism

They are inter-related to each other in a delicate and intricate manner.

While measures for the environmental protection of tourist beaches have to be devised having regard to the specific situation of the beach site concerned, the problem of tourist development in Andaman, Nicobar and Lakshadweep Islands is peculiar. These islands are ecologically far more fragile than Goa coast or any other coastline of the Indian subcontinent. In the case of Andamans, the tropical climate, the long rainy season and high average relative humidity have nurtured a magnificent rainforest cover practically all over the islands. These forests are a vital part of the worldwide tropical vegetation so crucial for the preservation of global climate and survival of living system. The Andaman forest cover is probably the most efficient bio-converter of solar energy. Its metabolic processes help maintain atmospheric balance, control run-offs, conserve surface water and prevent soil erosion. The forests, by control of situation, also protect the fragile coral beds. The organic nutrients leached into the surrounding sea sustain both Mangrove and Marine ecosystems. The denudation of forests and of the coral reefs and beaches of the Andaman and Nicobar, by laissez faire tourist development (or any development for that matter) must be completely stopped.

Tourism in these Islands can destroy the very natural resources that make them an attractive tourist resort. The "unspoilt" coastal lagoons and seascape can be 'spoilt' by the uncontrolled construction of large hotels and accessory facilities, as has already happened around Port Blair.

**Tourist Development in Mountain Areas**

The environmental problems connected with tourism and recreation development in mountain areas like Srinagar, Gulmarg, Nainital, Darjeeling, etc. are equally onerous as in coastal areas. The physical impact of tourism en masse consists of serious detrimental effects to the mountain system—soil, vegetation, wildlife, water balance, break-down of accessibility by landslides on mountain roads, etc.

One of the major problems is the growing incidence of landslides on hill roads like the Rishikesh-Badrinath road constructed to provide access to tourist resorts. In many cases, landslides cause flash floods. Landslide disasters in the Himalayan region have become endemic due to reckless construction and maintenance of roads to provide access to new tourist resorts and towns without due regard to ecological considerations either in their design, construction or maintenance. The result is that road construction in the ecologically frail hilly regions has often cased more problems than solving them. Hindsight has now taught us some of these new ecological problems we have to face. These are: (a) loss of forests and vegetation, (b) geological disturbance, (c) soil erosion and loss of hillside stability, (d) interruption/disruption of natural drainage pattern, and (e) siltation of water reservoirs, etc. These problems are inter-related in a complex way.

Other manifestations of environmental degradation in hilly regions are decay of lakes like Dal lake in Srinagar or Naini lake at Nainital in Uttar Pradesh littering and deforestation by huge trekking parties along the popular trekking routes, overcrowding. Commercialisation and pollution in major hill resorts and so on. Ironically, all of these impair the future of tourism itself by reducing the tourist potential of these places. Widely appreciated and important values of these areas for tourism and recreation, especially natural scenic grandeur and relatively low population densities are quickly being eroded.

**Tourism Development in Forest and Wildlife Areas**

A good number of tourist, both international and domestic, visit the forest and wildlife-rich areas—national parks and sanctuaries which are spread all over the country. The major impact of tourism in the wildlife areas is habitat destruction due to construction of facilities like roads, buildings, transmission lines, etc. pollution from vehicles; disturbance to wild animals by uncaring tourists and so on.

Among the affected areas are the 10-15 national parks and

sanctuaries which have become popular and famous such as Kanha, Bharatpur, Corbett, Bandipur, etc. These reserves are now criss-crossed by roads, dotted with tourist complexes, and in many other ways severely disturbed by tourism. The biggest problem is that most of the people who visit these places, are not genuine wildlife enthusiasts. They are out just to have a boisterous picnic, regardless of the harm this may cause to the ecosystem. They leave behind litter and a legacy of disturbance which continues to affect the wild animals. To give one typical example, it was recently reported that elephants in Corbett National Park have become increasingly sensitive and irritable due to constant tourist disturbance.

**Root Causes of Environmental Damage by Tourism**

The environmental damage described above stems from the fact that the type and scale of tourist development often exceeds the carrying capacity of the natural and human-made resources available. This in turn is because :

(a) No effort is made to assess the carrying capacity of the area concerned, i.e., the extent of tourist activity the area can absorb without degradation of its ecological or aesthetic value.

(b) There is no effort to assess the adverse ecological and social impact of the tourism in an area, and thus no knowledge on how to avoid or minimise this trend.

(c) Tourism is promoted with little or no regard for the ecological and social characteristics of the area. Short-term gains become the over-riding factor at the long-term cost of the local environment and the local people.

(d) Tourists are usually ignorant or uncaring about the ecological and social significance of the areas they are visiting and of the fragile nature of these areas. This is not entirely their fault, since there is very little effort to make the whole exercise more educative and informative.

(e) Those responsible for the conservation and protection of the historic sites or natural ecosystems like the Archaeological Survey of India, or the Wildlife Wing in National Parks and Sanctuaries, are not equipped to deal with the hordes of tourists who descend on them. They, thus, get bullied by the tourists, who demand all kinds of services and facilities not in harmony with the local environment.

(f) There is little attempt to integrate tourism development into the overall developmental plans of the area, or else minimise the damage already being caused by such activities.

It is well-known that the pilgrim goes to a place with a sense of reverence and respect, and an ecologically harmonious behaviour is usually built into his or her psyche. However, in an effort to provide 'modern' amenities and to cash in on such mass pilgrimages, Govenmental or private agencies have disregarded this factor. The ecological damage being caused in places like Gangotri is typical of the consequences of such short-sighted development.

**Recommendations**

Tourism does have a powerful positive side to it, viz. the inculcation of a sense of pride in the tourist about the place he or she is visiting, and consequently the development of such a person into being a strong supporter of the conservation of this place. Thus, it can be used as a positive force for preservation of ecology and for better maintenance of our monuments and places of tourist interest. However, for this to be so, the various causes of ecologically destructive tourism, mentioned above have to be tackled head-on. Specifically, the following steps are recommended:

1. The first essential step towards harmonising tourist development with local ecological conditions is to assess the carrying capacity of each area in which tourism is sought to be promoted. Such assessment may not be too difficult when the resource exploitation is solely for tourist purposes, as for example, is the case with historic monuments and sites. They, too, share with many natural assets the characteristic of having a limited capacity that cannot be exceeded without destroying their charm which attracts the tourist. But when the natural or man-made resources are exploited not for the sole purpose of tourism but for several others, the assessment of their carrying

capacity for tourism is very difficult to make. Unfortunately many infrastructural facilities like water and electric supply, roads, airline and train services, are not solely built for use by tourists only. They are utilised by other sectors as well. But this difficulty and complexity of carrying capacity assessment is no reason for shirking from such an exercise.

2. Closely connected to the above, it is necessary to assess the anticipated environmental impact of tourist activity in an area. Some of the parameters that must be considered are the focus of tourist activity (i.e., what the tourists are coming for) the number of expected tourists (serious interest groups, picnickers, etc.) the various kinds of activities they will indulge in (driving, trekking, horse riding, shopping, etc.) and the kind of facilities they will need (accommodation, transport, entertainment, commercial services, etc.).
3. For both the above given points it is suggested that assessment techniques based on use of systems analysis be evolved. One such assessment technique is illustrated by the Obergurg case study undertaken by the International Institute for Applied Systems Analysis (IIASA) and the Austrian National MAB Programme (Holling, 1978; IIASA, 1979). The knowledge of businessmen, scientists and government officials was combined to develop a model of human impact on the Alpine ecosystem, and to identify potential areas of conflict. The study predicted a maximum size for the resort, forecast future social problems and indicated solutions. This study is only a forerunner of a new type of multi-disciplinary research. It will, of course, need to be modified to Indian conditions.
4. Based on the above assessments tourism plans will have to be developed for each area. This may include:
   (i) Closing off certain areas completely to tourism if it is established that they are too fragile or important to be exposed to such activity (e.g., most of the Andaman and Nicobar islands);

(ii) Creating specific tourism zones within areas, where the majority of tourist activity can be concentrated (as in some national parks, where the tourist zone diverts pressure from the ecologically more important core zone).

(iii) Rotating areas open to tourists so that an area opened for some time may be closed and allowed to recuperate while another is opened;

(iv) Allowing only a limited number of tourists at any given time;

(v) Allowing only certain kinds of tourism, e.g., only trekking;

(vi) Developing tourist facilities which are in harmony with the local ecosystems. Thus, for instance, alternatives to large-scale road construction in the hills like bridle paths, cycle tracks, ropeways, etc. must be explored.

5. Tourist plans for an area must be integrated into the overall development plans for the area. This would ensure that the demands on local resources are assessed together, and the objectives of tourism do not conflict with those of socio-economic development in the area.
6. It is critical that tourism be made much more of an educative and informative experience than the case at present. For this, inexpensive, well-produced material, both printed and audio-visual, needs to be developed, as also tourist guide services.
7. Non-governmental organizations, especially ecological and adventure groups, have an important role to play in this regard. They often have an intimate understanding of local ecological conditions, and can thus provide the necessary inputs for developing educational tourist literature, guiding tourists, and keeping a vigil over unwanted and illegal tourist activities.
8. It must be ensured that tourism inculcates values respectful to the local cultural traditions, environmental conditions, and economic needs.
9. To ensure implementation of the above

recommendations, it is vital that steps are taken to give them a legal basis. There is some legislation on this, like restrictions on the use of forest areas for non-forest purposes (the Forest Conservation Act 1980), or the restrictions on construction activity close to coastal areas, but these are piecemeal and scattered, and in any case have various loopholes. There are also various guidelines on tourist development which deal with ecological aspects, like the recent guidelines of the Ministry of Environment on tourism in national parks and sanctuaries. These, however, lack legal backing and are, by and large, ineffective. A national level policy, followed by a comprehensive legislation, is imperative.

**Integrated Approach to Preservation of Cultural Heritage**

As is already recommended that tourism be treated as a major plank for economic development and requisite priority be accorded to it in the planning process. This meshing of tourism with national goals, we feel, will give tourism development a planned and concerted thrust. Thus, common policies and perceptions, at the macro-level will naturally guide tourism along the desired path.

Balanced infrastructure development and preservation of our rich cultural heritage is of critical importance. This objective can be realised at three distinct levels: (a) State, (b) The Heritage Centres, and (c) Monuments. At the State level, we recommend formulation of Master Plans, especially for States with a strong tourism potential like Goa, Jammu and Kashmir, Himachal Pradesh, etc. These plans would be a blueprint for tourism development in harmony with the State's total development with due emphasis on environmental protection. Such an approach would ensure that economic activities in these States are so planned that they facilitate tourism development, ensure consistency and avoid overlap.

At the second level are the Heritage Centres, i.e., places rich in culture and steeped in history like Vrindaban, Bodhgaya Varanasi, Fatehpur Sikri, etc. An integrated development is visualized for such centres with due concern for tourism planning, town planning, land-use planning, industrial development, transport planning and leisure service management, etc. In this direction the Ministry of Tourism has identified 14 such centres. However, much more needs to be done at the ground level to complement the conceptual approach. At the same time this approach needs to be adopted for other centres as well.

Finally, at the third level, we have to consider our rich heritage of monuments and architectural wonders. At this level, we recommend a Tourism Complex approach to ensure that all development work is treated in a comprehensive framework encompassing the vital elements of environmental protection, beautification of monuments and building of heritage parks around these monuments, etc.

A related issue is the need to have a single coordinating agency. The multiple agencies at our monuments often function at cross-purposes, leading to overlap and duplication. This is best illustrated by the example of Qutab Minar in New Delhi which was taken up as a case study. It was observed that about six agencies are functioning at this monument, and all in isolation with one another. The study showed that even the basic amenities like drinking water and toilet facilities were lacking. Unauthorised hawkers peddled their wares and trained tourist guides were just not on hand. If such a state of neglect exists in the national capital, the condition of monuments elsewhere can be imagined. This underscores the need to have a single coordinating mechanism for our monuments, as it is at this level where integration of all services/facilities is most needed. We, therefore, recommend that the Ministry of Tourism and the Archaeological Survey of India should treat the monument, the area around it and the infrastructure provided the as a single entity, i.e., as a tourist complex. For such complexes, trained managers should be appointed. They would be responsible for the upkeep of the complex with personnel of different agencies reporting to them. Coupled with this accountability the idea of making these monuments financially self-sufficient should also be explored.

It is equally important to ensure the availability of trained guides proficient in different languages at all monuments. It is vital that professional standards are maintained in this regard. Further, visual-aids, well-produced and documented guide books, maps, etc. should be available in adequate numbers to supplement guide services.

*Part Four*

# Tribes of India: A Rich Tourism Resource

# *Twenty Four*

# Gonds of Andhra Pradesh

**Gonds of the Adilabad District of Andhra Pradesh**

Among the tribal populations of southern India, the group known as the Gonds is by far the largest numerically, there being more than four million members spread over several different regions. Gonds vary in levels of economic development and do not form a culturally homogenous group. Less than half speak their traditional unwritten Dravidian language. Most Gonds were once shifting cultivators—as long as the population was sparse and they had a free run of large stretches of forest, they could periodically abandon their cultivated land and even their settlement, and carve new fields and a new village site from the forest a few miles away. Pressure of population, however, and the invasion of the Gonds' habitat by more advanced populations, have forced many to alter their settlement pattern and to attach themselves more firmly to the land.

One group of Gonds who have retained their tribal language and culture inhabit the Adilabad district of Andhra Pradesh. Although their farming economy is very similar to that of the surrounding Hindu peasants of the Deccan, the basis of their society is completely different. The society is divided into a large number of exogamous clans within which descent is in the male line. The mainspring of clan solidarity lies in rituals performed for deities that are linked with each clan's mythological origins. Each clan has a common cult centre, usually a thatched hut containing ritual objects. It is there that the clan deity is worshipped and members gather here for worship and feasting twice a year. The symbol of ritual unity is the priest, who is responsible for the performance of rites and is supported by a bard, preserving by oral tradition the myths and legends that reflect clan history.

A man's membership of his natal clan is clear and immutable, but a woman's clan status is subject to change. As a girl she is attached to her father's clan, but at her wedding she is transferred to her husband's. After her death she is ritually joined to her husband's clan god and to his ancestors. In the mind of the Gonds, the deceased members of a clan dwell in the company of the clan deities and thereby remain part of their community. The living, through ritual acts such as animal sacrifices, can influence the fate of the departed and the dead are thought capable of aiding their kinsmen in the world of the living. The funerary rites that accompany cremation or burial are the visible expression of this belief.

The Gonds believe in the existence of a multitude of supernatural beings who are not normally visible, though on occasion they appear to seers in dreams or visions, and at certain rites speak through the mouths of oracle priests. Their impact on human life is felt in a number of ways. On a level different from that of clan gods and local deities is Bhagavan, the lord of the gods and supreme deity, who presides over the court of immortals and is the giver of life and death. Although the Gonds consider him superior to all other gods they do not accord him as much worship as they do to many lesser deities, and there is a strong likelihood that the concept of this supreme deity is derived from Hindu ideas. The Gonds also expect gods and spirits to bless their crops, and they relate agricultural work to many activities directed towards these deities. Tillage of the soil with the help of plough and bullock for example, is inextricably caught up with ritual observances.

Unlike neighbouring Hindu peoples, the Gonds believe in equality of sexes, particularly when it comes to taking part of religious rites and choosing a marriage partner. Relations between boys and girls are not hemmed in by many restrictions and no great premium is placed on virginity, but youthful affairs are considered stepping-stones to permanent unions. Marriage, not adventure, is the aim of courtship, and all Gonds expect to be married by the time they reach their mid-twenties. A first marriage can take place by negotiation, by service or by capture. The first type is the most prestigious, but involves heavy expenditure on an elaborate wedding by the groom's family. Men may have two or three wives but this practice is declining in popularity. Divorce is easy, and both men and women can remarry. It is still not unusual for a woman to have a succession of husbands.

Growing contact with politically advanced communities and the opening up of their habitat by newly constructed roads have not proved beneficial to the Gonds of Andhra Pradesh. Much of their ancestral land has been acquired by newcomers, and their economic and social life has been largely disrupted, causing a great deal of unrest in some regions.

*Twenty Five*

# Nishi of Himalayas

**Nishi of the Eastern Himalayas**

The Nishi, or Dafla, are the Mongoloid hill peoples of Arunachal Pradesh in the extreme north-east of India; they speak a Tibeto-Burman language. The total number in the Subansiri district is about 50,000 although a very similar group known as Bangni and numbering 22,000 live in the neighbouring Kameng district.

Arunachal Pradesh, with its luxurious forest growth, subtropical climate and heavy rainfall, provides ideal conditions for shifting cultivation, the traditional basis of the Nishi economy. The Nishi sowing cycle starts in late April, both men and women co-operating in this task. They first sow maize and sorghum in holes dug with crude digging sticks, and then broadcast millet. Women also sow rice and plant taro and sweet potatoes. Most Nishi are self-sufficient in grain, although in bad years they also eat wild tubers.

The Nishi breed mithan (a domesticated form of the gaur) as well as common cattle, goats and pigs. They trade cattle and pigs for rice grown by neighbouring peoples such as the Apa Tani. Mithun are kept principally for their meat and for sacrifice, and they are neither milked nor used for traction. The Nishi are expert hunters, a man seldom leaving his village without carrying a bow and poisoned arrows to kill wild bears and leopards. They are also skilled in setting traps and snares. They catch fish in bamboo traps inserted into dams by stunning them with poison.

Whereas several peoples of Arunachal Pradesh, such as the Apa Tani, live in large compact villages, the Nishi live in small settlements of up to fifty widely dispersed houses. Each longhouse stands on a separate site, preferably on the highest point of a hillock or spur, surrounded by granaries and pigsties. Most of the houses are joint family dwellings in which forty or fifty men, women and children live.

Nishi women enjoy a position of considerable independence within this patrilineal society. Before marriage they can engage in farming and petty trade on their own. Once married they have their own cultivation plot and granary and take charge of their husbands' valuables, which they secretly bury. Marriage ties with other wealthy families greatly strengthen a man's position. Previously a network of alliances gave security from attack, but even though this is no longer needed because of effective government control, it is still not unusual for a Nishi to have six or seven wives.

No one has individual rights to land and the inhabitants of a settlement are free to cultivate wherever they choose. Thus, wealth cannot be invested in land and until recently a Nishi's possessions, consisting of cattle and valuables, could easily be stolen. None were born into a situation of lasting security, and status depended almost entirely on skill, energy and ruthlessness. There was no permanent social stratification and a man born a slave might be given his freedom and rise to the position of a respected householder, while a rich man could be totally ruined by an adversary or captured in a raid and sold as a slave. Slavery was abolished in the 1960s and raiding has now stopped under the effective control of government.

There is no leader among the Nishi, but conventions prescribe the conduct of kinsmen, limit the extent of feuds and provide for the safety of go-betweens engaged in negotiating peace settlements. Sexual offences are unimportant to the Nishi unless they interfere with what is considered a man's property. Thus, a girl's elopement will concern her father only if it deprives him of his brideprice, which may amount to ten or more mithun. A man whose wife leaves him for another man will only be outraged because he may have difficulties in recovering the price he paid to her parents. A husband who learns of the infidelity of his wife will scold and beat her, but will neither kill nor divorce her, as he would lose an economic asset. It is therefore not unusual for the young wife of a rich elderly man to have sexual relations with one of his sons or younger brothers.

**Wives For Prestige**

Most affluent Nishi men have several wives, for this raises their prestige and gains them allies—in the lawless times before government rule, such allies were of assistance in feuds. When a man dies his wives are often inherited by his younger kinsmen.

When hostile parties meet to settle a feud, both keep to details of custom, each trying to prove that their own actions were justified and those of their opponents were a breach of custom. Oaths and ordeals are sometimes used to establish the guilt or innocence of an offender. An appeal to supernatural powers may also be made to strengthen the credibility of an oath, but there is otherwise no suggestion that gods and spirits are concerned with the moral conduct of human beings. Animal sacrifices are tendered in propitiation of deities believed to have afflicted people with illness, but never in atonement of wrongful conduct.

Consistent with this absence of any sense of guilt or sin are Nishi beliefs about the afterlife that the final destination of the departed depends solely on the manner of their death and not on their record in this life. Those who die a violent death are believed to go to a different place from the ordinary Land of Death.

The traditional lifestyle of the Nishi is gradually giving way to modernization. Since the 1960s Nishi country has been opened up by the construction of roads, and cash transactions have replaced much of the barter trade. Many Nishi have attended school and some of them have received higher education in universities outside Arunachal Pradesh. In no other part of India has social change been so rapid as in Arunachal Pradesh, where a small elite of the tribal population has achieved the transition from an archaic way of life to an entirely modern one within the brief span of thirty-five years.

**Nishi Longhouse**

Longhouses are characteristic of the Nishi and several other peoples found in the eastern Himalayas. Each house stands by itself with the granaries of individual families built in groups, some distance away. The interior of a longhouse is not subdivided, even when several related families share it. Fields on which millet and rice are grown occupy nearby slopes, while carefully tended groves provide bamboo.

# Twenty Six

# Bhotia of Central Himalayas

Like the Nishi, the Bhotia are Mongoloid people; their population outside Tibet numbers about 400,000 and they speak various dialect of Tibetan which are not always mutually intelligible. Most Bhotia live in areas of high altitude, and although they share many ecological and cultural features, they are not a homogenous ethnic group but comprise many different populations. Some groups are hardly distinguishable from Tibetans; others, such as the Sherpas of Nepal, have intermarried with neighbouring non-Mongoloid populations. The name Bhotia is derived from "Bhot", the Indian name for Tibet, from where these people are known to originate.

The great majority of Bhotia have long been involved in the caravan trade since they inhabit the gap between two complementary economic zones—the arid Tibetan plateau and the more fertile Himalayan middle-range and foothills. Until the 1960s, they were the main agents of trans-Himalayan commerce in many regions, supplying the Tibetans with grain and many other Nepalese products in exchange for salt, wool and livestock. The pack animals used to carry this trade depended on the nature of the environment—yak were best at high altitudes while mules were more suitable for lower lying routes. On difficult paths only sheep or goats with small bags strapped to their backs could be used.

In addition to trading, many Bhotia communities practised agriculture and animal husbandry, and this they continue to do—the herding of yak, involving frequent movement in search of new pastures, is especially important. Bhotia agriculture may also necessitate a seasonal shifting of labour from one place to another. Barley, buckwheat and potatoes can be grown as high as 4,000 metres (13,000 feet) and these are the main crops. Most agricultural tasks, including reaping are performed by the women, the men being responsible for ploughing and the care and herding of livestock. Ploughs are usually drawn by yak or crossbreeds of yak and cattle, although in a few areas teams of three or four men may do this work.

The Bhotia system of transhumance also determines their settlement pattern. The people of Khumbu as well as the Bhotia of western Nepal own several houses, all solidly built, in widely separated localities at different altitudes. There are three types of permanent settlements, main villages, winter settlements and summer settlements. The main villages are inhabited throughout the year by at least some families and there the people have their principal houses, which contain their valuable possessions and most household goods.

Involvement in long distance trade compels most Bhotia men to be away for much of the year, and in their absence the women are responsible for running the household and farm. As a result there is a high degree of equality between the sexes. Bhotia may marry anyone not closely related to them and the women may take two or three husbands, often brothers. There are no restrictions on the sexual adventures of unmarried boys and girls.

Bhotia society, which is patrilineal, is basically egalitarian. Civic tasks are taken up in rotation and the government of a village community is based on the consensus of all its inhabitants. Authority is delegated to elected village dignitaries whose term of office is strictly limited and whose duties are clearly defined. They have power to impose fines on those whose actions run counter to the interests of the community.

To the outside world a person is identified by the valley he inhabits and the valleys were the main socio-political units of traditional Bhotia society. One of the few large political entities which survived into recent times was the domain of the Raja of Mustang which was, until 1951, virtually an independent state within the Kingdom of Nepal. The Raja still wields great influence, and the ancient walled city of Mustang remains the centre of Bhotia civilization and a focal point of Buddhist culture.

Buddhism is the traditional religion of virtually all Bhotia and the gaining of merit is considered man's most important aim in life. Behaviour believed to result in such gain includes religious and ritual practices, good deeds to other people and kindness to animals. A skilful mediator is more admired than a "strong" man, for the Bhotia ideal is not the heroic personality but the wise, restrained and peaceful man.

## *Twenty Seven*

# The Lamas

At the start of the Christian era, Ladakh was a no man's land. A few nomads spent the following centuries leaving few traces on this windy land. But the Dards of Baltistan, guided by the path of the Indus, decided to lend some touches of green to its banks. The Mons of the Kulu Valley (Himachal Pradesh) came and occupied the southern part of the area. In the 10th century, Skilde Numagan, driven out by his brother, the King of Tibet, invaded Maryul, bringing in the Mongoloid element now predominant in the Ladakhi population. This became the starting point of a dynasty that lasted for 8 centuries. In 1842, Wazir Zorawar Singh invaded Ladakh. Since then it forms part of India.

The recurring theme of the different successions was a definite religious fervour which brought to Ladakh its host of monasteries, *gompas* and chortens. Even though the feudal system was the norm, there was no formal army, and hence the people could easily overthrow a dishonest noble or a tyrannical officer. However, to conquer a new territory or to put up a defence against foreign attacks, some battalions were formed. The fairly numerous lamas have always played an important role in Ladakh. During the eight centuries of independence, the Buddhist spirit dominated the whole of life. It inspired many men and women to give up secular life. It was normal and perfectly accepted by the Ladakhis that a king exchange his crown for a lama's robe.

Family life has its roots deeply embedded in the secular strata. Adapted to the geographical conditions which do not enable any extension of the cultivable area, it has led to a control in births through the rare custom of polyandry.

Indian law forbade this custom 40 years ago, but it requires a longer duration of time than that for such a mode of life to disappear. This system is still predominant in the villages. The eldest son inherits the land and gets married. Unable to become independent, his brothers remain on the land and share the bed of his spouse. Although monogamy was never forbidden, it was subjected to so much economic pressure that it always remained marginal. Polyandry implies a single mistress of the house. Quarrels therefore do not exist with other women, nor with the brothers. Only the daughter-in-law/parents-in-law relationship could be strained as a result of recurrent emotional matters. The social laws of Ladakhis give an effective answer to this scourge. Soon after the birth of the first grand-child, when it is established that the couple is fertile, the young grandfather brings together his family circle for a departure ceremony during which he officially bequeaths his lands to his son. The grandparents then withdraw to another house on the family estate and cultivate their own land as long as they can.

The harmony existing between the brothers and their wife remains a mystery to the external observer. Ladakhi law recognises the husband as the real husband and father. The others are called Little Fathers by the children. Yet there is no tension. The Ladakhis have therefore, out of necessity, developed a great sense of discipline, of civility, perhaps also of restraint....

Before 1974, the only caravans crossing through Ladakh were those travelling along the silk road. Today, other groups are discovering the infinity of these high lands for less commercial reasons. These are the tourists.

Some figures of the Ladakhi pantheon are to be encountered during the Durm Drod (festival) of the *gompas*. The most famous is the one at Hemis. During 2 to 3 days, the monks are transformed into gods and goddesses, wearing the masks which represent these divinities. They teach generations of lamas, and since the last 30 years, every Ladakhi, has the celestial life.

No journey to Ladakh would be complete without a respectful visit to one of these Himalayan cathedrals dedicated to the gods of the upper plateaux. An atmosphere of peace pervades the being, a serene calm invades it. Then the frescos, the tangkas can truly move us, much more intensely than if they were in the midst of other treasures within a museum, or in a city drawing room.

## *Twenty Eight*

# The Dard Tribe

**Dah Hanu: Land of the Dard Survivors**

October the Indus has changed colour. Its brown summer fury has dimmed into an emerald green which, merging into the fiery rainbow hues of the various elements of the Ladakhi east, decorates the sun-drenched slopes and the shady arid mountains, fills the icy air with incense, illumines the Himalayan space. The nearer we approach winter the more Ladakh becomes powerful, entire, disturbing for some, magical for the mountain folk. This is truly the best time to meet the Dard people and to live through a meeting with Time which has taken refuge in the villages still unknown to the foreign gaze.

The road from Leh is simple. All one has to do is to follow the river for 150 kms. On the right bank, some patches of green (children of the Indus?) shelter the Dards. Dah is their best preserved village. Are we still in Ladakh? Tomato fields, a thousand varieties of flowers, apricot trees walnut trees, grape vines climbing over poplar trees, green fields...

Contrary to the Tibeto Mongoloid Ladakhis in the Dards are Aryan. In the 6th Century they were the first to settle down in Ladakh. Archaeological evidence is found of their presence up to Chantang and along the present Srinagar-Leh road. But the major part of this people has been swallowed up in the Tibeto-Buddhist and Islamic waves. It is a miracle of history that about 2,000 to 3,000 Dards still continue their traditions, their customs and their unique religion.

It is the time for harvesting. The dzos and the cows go round in circles over the barley. Their circumambulations crush the harvest. Then the men and women, armed with rakes and the wind, their ally whom they call out to by whistling separate the chaff from the grain while colouring the sky with golden powder.

It is also the moment for gathering the tomatoes, then drying them on the roofs. It will be their main winter vegetable.

The Dard dress is simple but enriched with a strange peculiarity. All the men and women wear a flowery headgear. The alkekengi (a wild strawberry) brings wealth and protection against demons, the others have a more decorative purpose. In the fields, on the roads, bunches of smiling human beings. The Dards are always smiling, conscious of the wealth of their land, proud of their survival, of their liberty between two giants.

Even though officially they are Buddhists, their faith is still directed towards their own gods. Their pantheon which is far less abundant than that of the Hindus, is nevertheless large. Their concept of creation is interesting. Gods and men lived together in the beginning, but there was some lack of harmony between them. Together they decided to put an end to this cohabitation. The gods then took the direction of the skies. To celebrate this separation, they dance, every three years in the square at Dah. And the Gods join them in the dance.

Another valley, flirting with the Pakistani border is also Dard territory. Hanu is much poorer than the Indus villages, the houses seem to form part of the mountain, only the terraced fields indicate some human presence. To reach the villages of Yogma and Gongma, you have to walk a few hours by following the course of a slim river with wooded banks. Still further, around a dozen scattered habitations shelter the shepherds and some permanent residents.

While a family invites us in around their hearth, after having brought in their cattle, after having brought in their cattle, one cannot assert in what century and to which country they belong. Cut off from all points of normal reference, time seems to have stopped. We discover one of the roots of humanity, not aware of the tree it has generated. It is perhaps better thus.

Dah-Hanu is now open to all. It is important that each traveller be made aware of the influence he has over these regions, particularly over their unique people who are in great danger. We know the astronomical speed with which traditions and techniques can disappear when confronted with other modes of life. We tourists have a basic responsibility when we go out to encounter virgin lands. We should not in any event impose on them our world view but try to understand theirs.

# Twenty Nine

# Changpas

## Changpas: Travellers of the Himalayas

A journey in the Indian part of Changtang always begins through a grandiose road. To reach Tsomo Riri and Tazong Tso from Leh, the Highway goes upstream of the Indus for 200 kilometres. The river seems to get younger from one milestone to the next, while becoming at the same time gradually more powerful. At Hemia, the waterway and the road are left behind. A 40 kilometres trail across flowers again leads to the lakes whose salty banks extend around turquoise blue water. This is the summer residence of the Changpas living in the Himalayas at an altitude of 4,600 metres.

They live in around forty tents, made of white cotton. They are bright and chock full of innumerable old things. There are bundles of wool, tools for work, along with a prayer wheel and a water skin in goat leather. An old radio set. A feeding bottle made in China filled with pebbles of different colours....

In the morning the mattresses of straw are rolled up and little carpets put in their place. In a flash, the room becomes on one side a workshop and sitting room for the men; on the other side a kitchen and nursery, the domain of the woman of the house. At the back of the room, carefully arranged on a trunk covered with a fine cotton tablecloth, are photos of the Dalai Lama and other religious personalities, as well as a depiction of the Buddha. Before his relics are arranged a small lamp and some bowls filled with oil: the offerings of a nomadic family to those who guide and protect them.

The Changpas earn their livelihood from their herds of goat, sheep and yaks. These cousins of the cow are very peaceful grass eaters whose primary characteristic is their vital need of altitude.

Below 3,000 metres, the yak wastes away. At Tazong Tso the nomads use them for carrying their goods during their migrations, for fat and meat, and above all for their wool which is incredibly warm and strong. Unfortunately, they do not make yak cheese, which is found in Nepal and Tibet and is delightful to eat.

Around 4 to 5 o'clock in the morning, the shepherds lead their herds of goat fairly far into the mountain. The pasture land is very scanty and full of pebbles, but the Himalayan goat has immense resistance. Some shepherds consider their goats as sisters, and sing songs to them, which does not however prevent them from milking them. And to top it all they are tied up with a rope. Bound in this fashion, they look like just a double coloured mass of wool. One wonders how, after such treatment the herd still has its eyes and heads intact.

Each family has around 200-300 sheep and goats and some yaks. Some have specialized in raising the latter and some herds are found numbering up to 50 head. All this is very little as compared to the nomads of eastern Tibet. It is nevertheless largely sufficient to enable an entire family to live as these goats carry a magic name in this part of Ladakh: Pashmina. The characteristic of this wool lies in the mode of its extraction. While generally the wool is cut by shearing the animal, in this case it is pulled out with the help of a fork or various other substitutes. The cries of the animal, who is more frightened than hurt, are spine chilling. The wool is sold for $ 50 a kilo to Kashmiri traders and subsequently, when sent abroad, takes on the name of the green valley from which it comes and is called: Cashmere.

The animals rejoin the herd for a second grazing which involves a long journey towards the cold of the setting sun in the west, which is the time when the mountain is at its best. Once the tent has been pegged, the nomads continue their wanderings in the Himalayas moving around according to the needs of their animals.

Little Pema has caught up with her father who is teaching her how to manage the animals. There are many dogs, but they are used only to protect the animals at night and incidentally access to the tents is dangerous for an outsider. The herd is therefore led with the help of stones and whistles. Pema fillings a stone with all her might but its only effect is to frighten away two large indignant crows. However, arising from her tiny frame, her whistle, which is already like that of a man's, has a far more authoritative ring.

7 o'clock. Smoke rises out of the now approaching tents. The veteran and his apprentice are on their way back and are discussing the art of the Changpa shepherd. The mother will have taken out her bag of *tsampa* and dried meat; she will have put on the fire the *gurgur* (butter tea), heated the flat bread pancakes (prepared like the Indian *chapati*), which will be soaked in hot milk or in yogurt prepared from goat's milk. Pema and her father return to a room lighted with an oil lamp and more than that, to its stove, the central equipment of the house. Very few words are exchanged as the day, like all summer days, has been difficult for the whole family. Words become softer, sentences slower; sometimes there is a discreet laugh. The last bowlful over, the men pull out their tobacco pouches and make themselves a smoke.

One among the group will not enjoy the warmth of the woollen blankets that have already been spread out, for the presence of a man is required in addition to that of the dogs, to look after the herd. This evening it is the turn of Pema's elder brother, Tsewang. He will take a yak skin and will go out with his back bent to lessen the effect of the piercing gusts of wind. He will sleep out in the open. The lake does not stir; its presence is more important. It is a mute stretch, a reminder of the sea which gave birth to the Himalayas. The daytime landscapes of moving colours now carve out space in a straight line, marking the border between the life of the sky and the night of men. The lake becomes a bit of space run aground on land, and shows simply by existing that everything is intertwined, like a man and a woman in the act of love.

# *Thirty*

# Coorgis of Karnataka

**Coorgis of Karnataka**

The Coorgis are divided into clans and each clan has its ancestral home. Till a few decades ago all members of the clan lived together in a huge house called *ain mane*, for the lands and everything on it were common property. Today, the families and their properties have fragmented. But many *ain mane* still exist and are kept clean and ready for use by any clan member who might wish to stay there. These ancestral homes are interesting four winged structures with impressive main doors.

Though Coorgi families have dispersed, it is during the festivals that they come together to celebrate and rejoice. One of the main festivals of the community is *Huthri* which marks the harvesting of the paddy crop in November/December. The first sheaf of paddy is cut by the male head of the family on a full moon night amidst much dancing and music. The mistress of the house receives it from him and keeps it near a lamp that burns continuously in a Coorgi home. Fire works, dances and a big feat follow.

Another festival during which the martial race worships its arms is the *Keil Poldu*. The Coorgis have contributed more than their fair share of generals and men to the country's armed forces. They are reputed for their valour. On Keil Poldu day, which is in September, the men gather in open spaces to test their marksmanship by shooting the coconuts on the trees.

But it is the *Tula Sankaramana* festival when the Kaveri is worshipped which is of special significance to the Coorgis. On the festival day, usually in October, the water bubbles and gushes out of the little well built around the spring for a few minutes. Thousands gather to witness the event. The time of this significant happening is predicted to the exact minute by the astrologers.

Sumptuous meals form an important part of festival celebrations. But the wedding repast is a treat that should never be missed. Coorg weddings are celebrated with great pomp. The men carrying two knives and wearing flat topped turbans, dress in *kupya*—a long black coat worn over trousers, cut at the elbows to reveal the white shirt underneath and tied at the waist with a gold and red tassled sash. The bridegroom wears a white kupya.

The women wear the Coorgi style sari with the pleats at the back, and the *pallav* draped over their bosom and pinned over one shoulder with an attractive brooch which is either studded with precious stones or made of gold. The bride wears a red and gold sari.

Coorgi weddings are usually solemnised only during the wedding season which is from March to June. The weddings take place in *kalyan mantaps* or weddings halls found all over the district.

The best way for a stranger to see a wedding is just to walk into one of the mantaps. The Coorgis are very hospitable. You will be invited for a wedding lunch. Curried pork is a must on the menu. Little rice dumplings, bamboo shoots, mushrooms and homemade wines at which most Coorgi women excel are much relished items.

The Coorgis have no priests. The weddings are solemnised in the presence of the lamp and the elders who shower the couple with rice grains. *Sanga puja* marks the completion of the wedding rituals. The bride carries a brass pitcher on her head filled with water from the well of the groom's house. She has to go around the house and into the kitchen. But her way is blocked by energetically dancing relatives of the groom's family. The dancing goes on for hours and the bride is allowed to take a few steps at a time. The ceremony tests the stamina of the new member of the family and the mother of the next generation.

Coorg is a place for treks. There are many hills that can be climbed and beautiful spots for picnics. Little shrines dot the landscape. One of the most beautiful temples is a Bhagamandala, the place where the Kaveri after descending the Brahmagiri mountain, meets either the Sujoythi and the Kanike. Built in the multi-roof Kerala style it is a charming place of worship.

The Coorgis were famed as good hunters. Even today they are accurate marksmen and retain their guns. But the shots are fired more to scare away a stray tusker on the estate or to announce the birth of a baby boy. Most of them have turned arden conservationists for they have seen the havoc deforestation has caused the neighbouring districts. So they zealously guard their lands. It is for this reason that they are not keen to throw upon their district for large scale tourism.

But for the visitor who wants to discover the deep silence of the thick forests hear the gurgle of the little brooks, see the gorgeous dance of the peacocks, breathe in the scent of the coffee blossoms, taste the delicious Coorg honey and bamboo shoot curry or climb a blue hill. Coorg holds a welcome.

# Thirty One

# Rabaris' of Kutch

Kachchh has a long seafaring tradition which continues down to the present time. Kachchhi sailors have an image of skill and daring. Mandavi on the Kachachhi coast was an important port. Foreign trade in fact formed the traditional basis of Kachchh's ancient prosperity. Textiles, jewellery, enamel work, embroidery, ivory carving, etc. were exported to Africa and the Persian Gulf.

Much of Gujarati embroidery belongs to Kachchh. Made popular through Bombay films, the colourful embroidery is now famous even in distant shores. The amazing output of intricate works of embroidery, mirror and applique work in the absence of a satisfactory infrastructure is intriguing. After livestock a major share of Kachchh's economy is borne by its handicrafts industry. The most famous area in the Kachchh region for its embroidery is Banni. The area, however, is inaccessible during the monsoon. Repeated draught and famines of the past have compelled the Gujarat Handicrafts industry to take steps to improve conditions of artisans.

Each caste group has a village to itself. Community feeling is dominant in all villages. Marrying outside the *kutumb* (community) is unheard of. During marriages and funerals expenses are shared by the community. Each village consists of a cluster of *bhungas* or *jhumpa* dwellings made of stone, mud and dung. Each bhunga is a rounded structure with conical roof. Bhungas are made to withstand the extreme climate of this place. The thick walls keep the interior cool from the scorching heat of the day and warm during the chilly nights. Each hut is decorated with mud work painted white and inlaid with tiny mirrors. The bhunga is spotlessly clean from inside. A pile of quilts are an essential part of a family's possession. In fact the prosperity of a family is assessed by the amount of quilts it possesses.

Of the various castes in Kachchh the most fascinating are the Rabaris. Their origin is obscure. According to one version they originated from Rajasthan where their descendants lived in Jaisalmer. A Muslim ruler of Jaisalmer fell in love with a Rabari girl. The whole community was against the match and therefore moved out, partly for fear of reprisals from the king, and partly out of a sense of honour. But the king's men gave them pursuit. Many Rabaris were killed but, ultimately, to preserve her honour, the girl was swallowed by the earth. According to another story, a Rajput ruler sacrified his life to save the Rabaris. As a mark of respect and to mourn for the dead, Rabari women always wear black and the men white.

It is customary for a Rabari bride to own three heavily worked bodices and a woollen *bandhni* (tie and dye) shawl. The colour of the shawl is orange for unmarried girls and red for the married. All Rabari girls embroider clothes for their trousseau. Child marriages are common but married girls stay at home with their father's family until they reach maturity. Dowry is exchanged. A Rabari girl receives her mother's jewellery and sheep from the husband's family.

Kachchh wool has long been famous for its quality. The exquisite shawls and blankets woven by the Rabaris command a high price.

Almost all the hills in Kachchh are crowded with buildings shrines or forts. The walled city of Bhuj is overlooked by the citadel of Bhujia, which was built by Rao Godji II. Bhuj was once the capital of the kingdom of Kachch. Kachchh Museum in Bhuj is Gujarat's oldest museum which houses collections of archaeological items and inscriptions.

Little Rann is home to the Indian Wild Ass. The wild ass is a distinctive variety and found nowhere else in the world. The best way to see wild ass is from an open jeep. The Kachchh is also home to a diverse range of fauna. Other forms of wildlife also abound in the region. Visitor species of birds, flamingoes and avocet descend every year to breed.

The best time to visit this region is from November to March. During the nights if you happen to take a stroll, the eerie silence is broken by melodious *Sufi bhajans* (hymns) as men gather around bonifires sing to entertain themselves.

The mystique of Kachch is to be experienced. It is a journey into another world.

# Thirty Two

# Social Groups of Orissa

What these seekers after truth have brought to light is far more fascinating than fiction. No doubt the tribal population of Orissa is primarily concerned with the struggle for survival. It is dogged by drought, near famine conditions, poverty. Yet it has much to teach us. Each tribe is a completely organized society, bound by a common language, religion, cultural background and tradition, all in all a way of life. The better we understand this way of life, the better we understand ourselves for these tribes represent an earlier stage in the development of man.

Of all the states of India, Orissa has the largest number of tribes, as many as 62. Altogether they constitute an impressive 23 per cent of the total population of Orissa. These tribes mainly inhabit the Eastern Ghat hill range which runs in the north south direction. More than half their population is concentrated in three districts—Koraput, Sundergarh and Mayurbhanj.

Tribal economy is subsistence oriented. It is based on food gathering, hunting and fishing and thus revolves around forests. Even the larger tribes like the Santal, Munda, Oraon and Gond who are settled agriculturists, often supplement their economy with hunting and gathering. When farming they make use of a very simple technology and a simple division of labour, often limited to the immediate family. They lose out because their holding are small and unproductive, lacking in irrigation facilities since the terrain is hilly and undertaking. They alos lack funds to buy other inputs and necessarily fall back upon traditional skills and outdated implements.

Many tribes, for instance, the Juang, Bhuiyan, Saora Dharua and Bondo, practise what is called shifting cultivation, also known as slash and burn. They select a plot of land, generally on a mountain slope, slash down all the trees and bushes and burn them to ashes. Spreading the ashes evenly over the land they wait for the rains before planting the crops. Two or three seasons on one plot of land and the soil gets depleted, so the tribals move on. It is a way of life for them but a pernicious practice just the same bringing poor returns and degrading the environment in the bargain.

There are cattle breeders among the tribes, notably the Koya. There are simple artisans too like the Mohali and Loharas who practise crafts of basket weaving and tool making. A sizable part of the tribal population of Orissa has moved to the mining and industrial belts of the State, notably the Santals, Munda, Oron and Ho. This has helped ease the pressure on small holdings but in the process tribal villages have been abandoned. Traditional skills, land and other immovable assets have been lost without always bringing in adequate prosperity via jobs in mines and factories.

But if tribal economy is shaky, tribal culture in its pristine state is rich and distinctive and the Adivasis work hard to preserve it. A tribal village manages its internal affairs very smoothly through two institutions—the village council of elders and the youth dormitory.

The core of tribal culture, the youth dormitory, is the largest hut in the village. It has only three walls profusely decorated with symbols representing animals. The fourth side is open. By night the dormitory is home to the youth of the village. But before and after a hard day's work, people gather here to chat and relax. The council of elders meets here too, to discuss matters relating to the welfare of the village. The open space in front of the dormitory is where youths and maidens dance with abandon every evening for tribal culture allows free mixing of the two sexes. Despite their poverty and the ongoing battle for survival, the tribes of Orissa have retained their rich and colourful heritage of dance and music. Every tribal can sing and dance to the sound of pipe and drum and give tune to impromptu compositions that come to him/her as naturally as breathing.

The tribals of Orissa observe a string of festivals. Some are closed affairs, relating to a birth or death within the family or a daughter attaining puberty. Others relate to sowing or harvest time and thus involve the entire community. Mostly a festival is an occasion for a good swig of *mahua* liquor, a game animal roasted on the spit and a night of song and dance and revelry. But wait, there's an animal sacrifice too, for the deities and spirits must be appeased first, particularly the malevolent ones, so they do not unleash drought or sickness on the land. Tribals are superstitious people and the 'ojha' (witch doctor) occupies a position of honour since he not only prescribes medicines for the sick but is also believed to exercise evil spirits.

The supernatural also figures prominently in tribal folklore which is a body of largely verbal literary tradition. These simple folk tales are linked to occasions in everyday life—sowing, harvesting, birth, marriage and death. Folk tales also teach values dear to the tribal heart. But many of them offer an explanation for natural phenomenon—day and night, thunderstorms, animal behaviour. With the tribals living so close to nature it could not be otherwise.

Christian missionaries have done a lot to remove superstition from tribal society, educating tribals and setting them on the road to economic stability. In the process they have also converted many to Christianity. The OTDC (Orissa Tribal Development Programme) is on, seeking to bring the benefits of development to the area. Much still remains to be done but development must not override the tribal way of life. It would be a great pity to lose something rich and meaningful that has come down to us from antiquity.

**Snippets**

The Saora are one of the most ancient tribes of Orissa mentioned in Hindu myths and classics notably the Puranas. Saora men are marathon walkers. They are also expert climbers and hunters with a habit of carrying an axe on one shoulder. Saora villages are generally inaccessible, hidden in the folds of mountains and reached only by negotiating stony, zigzag paths.

Makers of picturesque houses, the Santals have an eye for beauty. They are also deeply concerned with personal hygiene and the cleanliness of their surroundings. A Santal folk tale says that God placed rice inside a husk so it would remain clean:

Santals adore flowers. They also collect silk cocoons from 'asan' trees in the forest and process them to help make golden hued fabric called tussar.

The Bondo who have lived in near isolation among the higher hills are a fiercely independent, stubborn and aggressive tribe. They still practise the barter systems, exchanging the produce of their fields for articles of daily use. An interesting feature of the Bondo marriage is that Bondo girls prefer to marry younger boys, so they may have someone to earn for them in their old age.

The Bhumias of Korput district have an intriguing custom. Since they wish to avoid paying the bride price, arranged marriges are not welcome. Instead a boy and girl in love are encourged to elope and the marriage is solemnised later.

The Gonds a warrior caste and conquerors of yesteryears are spread out all over the hill tracts of central and south India. Before the Gonds sow a field, some grain fowls and pigs are sacrificed to the presiding deity. Blood from the sacrificed animals is sprinkled on the seeds which are distributed among the villagers, who in turn sow them in their fields for luck.

The Oraon are one of the most progressive tribes. They make use of chemical fertilizers, pesticides, improved varieties of seeds and modern techniques of agriculture. Economically better off than most of the others, they are not shackled by debts and can afford a better quality of life—good approach roads to villages cycles and even motor bikes for transport, transistor sets and wrist watches. Their social life is remarkable in that they accept widow remarriage and permit divorce by either partner on grounds of adultery, bad temper and of all things, laziness!

*Thirty Three*

# Todas of Nilgiri Hills

The chief occupation of the Todays is raising buffalo and it is around this that their entire culture revolves. Compared to that of most Indians, their pantheon is very simple. Although they do believe in ghosts and spirits they worship only one supreme god Unlike most tribal peoples they are for the most part vegetarians and hence do not hunt. They rever the cow, buffalo and her milk, the dairyman is their priest and dairy and milk vessels are regarded as especially sacred. The Todas were in danger of extinction until as recently as a few years ago but of late their population seems to be recovering. This man the dairyman priest of his village is wearing the distinctive striped. Toda Shawl a garment that the tribes people weave themselves

**Todas**

Each state in India contains tribal peoples, descendents of the original pre-Aryan inhabitants of India, who maintain an archaic social and cultural mode of life. The Todas, one of several such tribes living in the west of Tamil Nadu high in the Nilgiri Mountains bordering Kerala, build unusual domed wooden houses that have roofs of grass thatch suspended from central ridgepoles and held in place by bamboo poles and cane. Each house contains one room. When additional space is needed, an unconnected similar structure is built.

## Thirty Four

# Tripuris from Tripura

Despite tremendous modern day provocations, the various tribes of Tripura have pursued with considerable self-restraint their ancient traditions and rites and have thus continued to preserve their cultural identity.

The tribals of Tripura recognize no generic term by which their race may be distinguished as the population consists of various tribes and settlers from surrounding areas.

The Tripuri community constitutes more than 50 per cent of the total population. They are Kshatriyas and have the surname of 'Dev Varma' or 'Deb Burma'. They were sub-divided into groups according to their vocations related to their duties to the throne.

The rulers of Tripura belong to this clan and are descendants of the Chandra Vanshi or Lunar Dynasty—an unbroken line of 179 kings for years of unrecorded history and then beyond that into mists of myths and legends.

They trace their lineage to Duryu, the son of Emperor Yayati of the Mahabharat who was banished from his father's kingdom. He came to the North-East and established another kingdom in a little-known verdant land which came to be called Tripura.

Numerically, the next important tribe is the Reang. They left their original home in the Lushai Hills due to internal strife and settled in the North-Eastern sub-divisions of Tripura. The Reangs call themselves *Rajputras*—sons of the king for they say their forefathers were adopted by Maharani Gunawati Devi. They have preserved to this day a relic of this bond—the *pathor bati*—a stone bowl dating back to the 17th century. The Reangs, at the time, had risen in revolt against the ruler, Govinda Manikya who imprisoned and sentenced the leaders to death. Govinda Manikya's wife, Maharani Gunawati Devi, pleaded for them and set them free. As a guarantee for their loyalty she made them drink milk from a stone bowl and thus made them her sons.

The Jamatiyas, known to be a brave and spirited people, are another clan that had close links with the rulers as many of the rulers married girls from this clan. The Jamatiyas are regarded as a fighting class and they formed the core of the Maharaja's army.

Compared to the other tribals of Tripura, the Kukis or Hre-em as they call themselves are backward. They are divided into 26 classes and are generally settled in the sub-divisions of Dharmanagar, Kailasahar and Amarpur. Originally from the Lushai and Mizo Hills, they emigrated to Tripura in search of new land to cultivate. The Kukis are expert archers and adept in the use of spears.

From the Kukis came the Halams. They are a section of Kukis who pledged allegiance to the Maharaja of Tripura and they adopted the manners and customs of the Tipras and many settled in the towns.

The Mogs and Chakmas are the Buddhists among the tribals. Their orginal home was in the hills of Arakan. They emigrated to the southern parts of Tripura due to political disturbances. The old capital of Tripura, Rangamati, or present day Udaipur, was once within the Mog kingdom which was taken over by King Jugharu Fa of Tripura. The history of Tripura is replete with anecdotes connected with the Mogs. Their dialect is akin to Arakanese which is very much like Burmese. The Chakmas too, are Arakanese immigrants and some still live in the Chittagong hill tracts which is a continuation of the Arakan Yoma.

The Lushais of Tripura are Christians. They live in picturesque villages perched on the Jumpui Hills famous for its groves of small sweet oranges.

The Naotias are the new Tripuris as the very name implies. They are so called as they came to Tripura much after the other tribes.

All the tribes of Tripura live very simple lives. They hunt and cultivate the land following the *jhoom* or shift method of cultivation, weave their own cloth on loin looms and make ingenious bamboo articles and most of the tribes, except the plains dwellers, Mogs and Chakmas, build their houses completely of bamboo. These houses called *tong ghars* are built on platforms raised six or seven feet off the ground. There is one large room divided into sleeping area and hearth with a narrow verandah out front. The family keeps poultry, pigs and other livestock under the house. The tong ghars are clustered around a central courtyard common to all where the women thresh the paddy and the families gather in the evenings.

The Mog houses are somewhat different from the other tribes. Their villages are usually found near rivulets and they dwell in huts built on mud plinths. Every village has a Buddhist temple which is looked after by a priest. A curious feature of Mog village are the long separated dormitories for unmarried men and women.

The Tripuris love to dance, feast and drink. Practically every household brews its own requirements of both distilled and fermented drink—a sort of rice beer. The staple food is rice which is put in a bamboo funnel or wrapped in plantain leaf and cooked over a charcoal fire. This is served with pork or fish. Tender bamboo shoot, herbs and tubers are always accompanied by a chilli paste ground with a special fish spice called *shidol*—a special favourite to which all Tripuris are addicted.

The tribals love bright colours and ornaments. The women wear the *dubra* or *pasra* wrapped around the waist like a sarong with a *ria* or breast piece. The townswomen wear an additional fine veil. Ornaments are of silver, ivory or bone with beads and conch. They love wearing flowers in their hair. The art and culture of Tripura are expressed in their textiles. The range of colourful designs and textures is vast and unmatched for their elegant designs and colour combinations. Each tribe has its own characteristic design, motifs and colour schemes. This variety and creativity is rarely to be found in any other ethnic textiles as weaving is a way of life for the tribals. In fact every young girl has to weave her own trousseau and special attention is given to the design of the ria for it is said "to give a ria is to give one's heart!"

The tribals have a well defined hierarchy. They have their chiefs or *sardars* who are advised by the elders. Though the society is patriarchal, the women play an important role. They are the upholders of tradition. While Dhanya Manikya with a plan to wipe out the enemy. In the invaders' path was the Gumti river.

Balagama had a dam built across its upper reaches making this torrential river look deceptively calm. As Hussain Shah's army began to cross the river, Balagama had the dam opened and the enemy, caught unawares, were washed away.

A special bond has always existed between the simple people of the hills and their rulers. There was the custom of *bainari* which made a princess the kin of a laughing girl from the hills. In a simple ceremony, gifts were exchanged and they became sisters. Henceforth the princess was accepted as one of her *bainari's* clan and she took special interest in their welfare.

Divorce and widow-remarriage among the tribals is accepted and child marriage is rare. There are two types of marriages –by mutual consent or marriage by arrangement. Daughters are precious so prospective grooms are well screened. They have to work in their would-be father-in-law's house for three years! This is called *jamaikhata*. If he proves suitable he is accepted otherwise he is sent packing with compensation for his services!

Although the religion of the majority of the tribals is termed as Hinduism, it is Hinduism with a strong flavour of animism. The old gods have not been ousted but are worshipped along with the Hindu deities. The elements such as water, fire, earth and forests are revered. A trace of the old ways are still to be found in the practice of striking a bamboo in the ground and worshipping it before religious festivals. A dual arrangement is in vogue—the Kshatriya Chantais are the custodians of the old gods and ancient rites and the Brahmins minister to the Hindu gods.

Festivals mark the passage of time. In spring, Holi, the festival of colour is celebrated with much dancing and singing; the new year is welcomed with *Garia Puja* in the month of *Baisakh* (April). It is believed that Garia brings prosperity and happiness. At about the same time is another typically tribal festival—the Gang Puja when the rivers are worshipped. A bamboo temple is built in the middle of a river and puja is performed to ward off epidemics. Come July, people flock to the Chaturdas Devtas temple in old Agartala for the Kharchi Puja. This temple houses the heads of 14 gods. Throughout the year only three are on display and only during Kharchi Puja are all 14 shown to the public. The festivities carry on for a week. Pigeons, goats and clay figures are offered for sacrifice and a colourful fair springs up around the temple grounds. Fifteen days after the Kharchi Puja is the Ker Puja to ward off all evil. During Ker a special boundary is marked within which no one is allowed to come or go for 32 hours. There is a complete curfew. The sick, aged and pregnant women are moved to homes outside the Ker boundary for even births and deaths are considered inauspicious. Those within the limits are house-bound and spend their time making paper lanterns and pastries called *pithas* for evening get-togethers. At sunset a cannon is fired from the palace to relax the curfew for the night. Then there are a few hours of boisterous celebration especially at the 'court' of the Chantai (tribal high priest) for during Ker the Maharaja hands over his powers and the Chantai raja reigns. The Ker boundary was usually marked around the town where the ruler lived but over the years it has shrunk to the area around the Ujjayanta Palace where the erstwhile Maharaja lives.

Harvest is in autumn with *Maikatal,* the festival of the new paddy. It is also the time of Durga Puja and in December, as the winter sets in, the people gather again to celebrate the brewing of new wine made from the winter harvest. They sing, dance and drink the old year out.

*Thirty Five*

# Social Groups of Assam

Assam is a land of myths and mystery. "The land of the Red River and Blue Hills" as it is described has a unique landscape with sprawling tea gardens and unending stretches of paddy fields interspersed with groves of coconut, arecanut and banana trees. Its population is a confluence of streams of different races and tribes like the Austrics, the Aryans, Negroids, Indo-Burmese, Indo-Tibetans and Mongoloid. They have enriched each other and have evolved to give a distinctive identity to the Assamese people.

A vast majority of people in the State, as in most other States in the country, are closely associated with agriculture. It is therefore natural that almost all the important festivals and dances are rooted in agricultural activities and the changing moods of nature.

The festivals of Assam are a synthesis of diverse cultures which have blended to become a common heritage of the people of the State.

The *bihus* are the most important festivals of Assam. Basically non-religious, these festivals have an agricultural and seasonal background. The most important and also the most loved festival is called *Rongalior Bohag bihu*. It coincides with the Assamese New Year in April and corresponds to the month of *Chaitra* in the lunar calendar. People welcome the spring season and pray for a bountiful and rich harvest.

The week long festival of Bohag bihu starts from the *Vishuva Sankrant* day. It comes when the first shower of the year, the blossoming of varieties of colourful flowers, the sweet voice of the cuckoo and the fragrant breeze kinds of leaves.

The rest of the week long celebrations are known as *Manuh bihu*. A mood of festivity and gaiety is seen throughout Assam during the seven days of Rongali bihu. Some people celebrate it for almost a month. Hundreds of *bihutolis* or groups of young men and women perform bihu dances and sing to the accompaniment of drums and *pepa*, a flute made of buffalo horns. The sensuous and brisk bihu dance is performed in the fields, at roadsides and over specially erected stages. They also sing couplets expressing love for sweethearts. The *bihugeets* as they are called are tuned to rhythmic beats to which the bihutolis dance.

During the bihu days everyone transform the environment into an earthly paradise. Rongali bihu inspires unbounded joy and enthusiasm expressed through dances, songs and other festivities.

The first day of the week is called *Garu bihu* and is dedicated to the cattle and livestock. In the morning the cattle are taken to nearby ponds or river banks for a ceremonial bath. The horns and heads of the animals are rubbed with the paste of newly harvested turmeric and black gram. Pieces of aubergine, turmeric and sweet gourd are thrown on the cattle and are also fed to them. The animals are tethered with new ropes and garlanded with vegetables. In the evening a small fire is lit in front of the cow shed with a collection of different wears new clothes. Cakes are baked. People invite each other for feasts. Fairs are organized at several places and the mood of festivity is palpable everywhere. Each day different programmes are organized.

Rongali bihu is associated with two types of folk dances—*Husari*—is carol singing and dancing in a group consisting of only men led by the elderly ones. The group starts visiting the houses in the village before noon. Husari songs are more religious than festive. The residents honour the group by offering betel leaf and arecanut, sweets and money in a brass dish. The funds collected are spent on repairing the village community prayer hall and on community feasting.

The bihu dance is performed in open fields or groves or even in jungles by young unmarried men and women dancing and singing sometimes throughout the night. The girls dress in their best traditional clothes—a red floral mekhala with a red border, a shawl woven out of golden silk fibres and a red blouse. Their feet and palms are painted with the red pigments made of myrtle leaves. The brisk and sensuous bihu dance with the various movements of hips, arms and the upper parts of the body suggests that it is a fertility dance.

Besides the Rongali bihu, the people of Assam celebrate two other bihu festivals. The *Kati bihu* or *Kangali bihu,* falling during the last day of the Hindu month of *Ashwin,* is generally a solemn affair. However, there are no festivities on that day and the people spend it in solemn prayers.

The third bihu is called the Magha or Bhogali bihu. This is a harvest time celebration falling in January (the day corresponding to Makar Sankranti). The people light fires and distribute sweets and cakes. Young boys visit houses in their neighbourhood and sing *huchari* to collect donations. A interesting aspect of the celebrations is the practise of constructing small straw huts which are burnt later at night.

The Rongali bihu in particular reflects the primeval urge for fertility, survival and growth. Interestingly, similar festivals are observed not only by the different tribes of Assam but also by tribes in several neighbouring countries like Tibet, China, Thailand and Burma.

The bihu festivals of the Brahmaputra Valley not only remind her people of the traditions of Assam but also tell the story of man built on the edifice of agricultural and pastoral life.

# Thirty Six

# Khasis

Anyone who comes to the Khasi Hills expecting a backward tribal people is in for many surprises. This region has been a crucial crossroad in the history of North-East India through which immigrants from Assam, Bengal, Burma, Tibet, Nepal, China and British India have passed creating a very mixed and sophisticated genetic group. But the original Khasis are the only Mon-Khymer people in the entire area. Their legends say that they were orginally seafaring people from the coastal areas of Thailand and Cambodia who moved into Khasi Hills via Burma after being defeated in war and driven out by the more aggressive Chinese. In fact, most of the old surviving thatch-roofed houses in the Khasi-Jaintia Hills resemble upturned boats with crossed oar beams. Cowrie shells are still used in their socio-religious ceremonies and sewn onto ceremonial shawls, sashes and bags besides being used as ornaments.

Khasi facial features and costumes are very similar to those of Thailand, Cambodia and Laos and their language also belongs to the Mon-Khymer group of dialects. Another interesting legend says that these highlands were part of Khublai Khan's domains and the traditional Khasi greeting *Khublai* was a password throughout the Mongol kingdom. The Ahom and Jaintia Burunjis say that the Khasis moved here in the late thirteenth century, remaining independent until the British established an Agent to the Governor General at Cherrapunji in 1822. After leasing Shillong from the Syiem or Raja of Mylliem in 1874, the British turned this beautiful place into a European haven quite distinct from any other Indian hill station or city. The quaint admixture of tribal culture and colonial customs has given the Khasis an enviably liberated lifestyle.

All Khasis claim descent from Ki Hynniew Trep or the Seven Huts of the original sea men and two divine mermaids. Archaeological finds at Jaintiapur indicate a fairly advanced material civilization as do their jewellery, costumes, agricultural implements, metalwork, pottery and social structure. There are geographical clan subdivisions among them and Khasis in the Jaintia Hills are called Jaintias or Phars. Those in the southern highlands—Wars, and the lowland and foothill people—Bhois.

The original Khasi religion is pantheistic nature worship with belief in a universal Creator U-Blei Nongthaw and the Great Mother Goddess, Ka-Mai-Khya. Even today, all the Khasi Syiems send annual tribute to Guwahati's famous Kamakhya shrine. Ancestor worship is another strong element in Khasi belief, even though 60 per cent of the people profess Christianity, taking full advantage of the splendid schools, colleges, hospitals and churches run by various Christian missions. Mysterious Khasi monoliths remind one of the Stone Henge and the Druid Circles found in the British Isles and France. Another persisting belief involves snake or U-Thlein worship as a sure way to acquire wealth. Reading omens from raw broken eggs and cockentrails, casting out evil spirits and faith healing by wise women are also important to Seng Khasis. Sacred groves, grottos, caves and burial sites of clan elders are preserved throughout the Khasi and Jaintia Hills and the taboos connected with each of them religiously observed and enforced by local chiefs and priests.

Clan solidarity is an important facet of Khasi society. The Syiem is considered to be the clan's chief cum high priest through nature deities and ancestral spirits communicate their wishes. Khasi society is matrilineal, nor matriarchal. Among them, the husband moves into his wife's home, children carry the mother's clan name and daughter's inherit ancestral property. Every child is perfectly legitimate with or without the mother being married because Khasi society is based on this tenet. Maternity is a certainty while paternity only a myth. Female babies are actually more welcome and marriage is a two way partnership with the husband having full right over his salary or business earnings. Divorce is easy, remarriage frequent. The youngest daughter or *khaddu* becomes custodian of the family property in order to fulfill all social obligations and perform essential religious ceremonies. But under the guidance of her maternal uncle. Traditionally, Khasi males were preoccupied with war, hunting and trading with the plainsmen of neighbouring Assam and Bengal leaving their wives at home to tackle everything from spring planting to community affairs. This, plus real economic freedom, social equality and sheer efficiency give Khasi women an edge over their menfolk.

But modernization has changed many things in Khasi society. Private ownership now outweighs community ownership of land and other resources like forests, coal mines and limestone quarries. Bureaucracy now takes precedence over village durbars. Only the matriarchies remain enthroned, still controlling vital family and clan decisions, but wisely leaving political games and elections to their menfolk.

The only women who do not weave their traditional clothes are the Khasis. Relatively more affluent and gainfully employed, they are a well dressed lot. But the two piece jaynsem worn over a long-sleeved blouse and a calf-length skirt gives them a shapeless cylindrical look. Checked cotton or plain silk is preferred. Old fashioned Khasi men still wear round turbans, white handloom *dhotis*, high-necked sleeveless jackets over long shirts and Scottish tartan-like plaid shawls to keep out the sharp winter winds or monsoon chill of their land. Most of them also carry hand-woven shoulder bags for their pipe, tobacco, *kwai* (betel nut) and personal effects. The younger generation today sport denims, combat jackets and latest fashions.

Dangling gold earrings set with single coloured stones are the signature jewellery of every Khasi woman. Their heirloom gold and silver filigreed ornaments are very elaborate and attractive. Jewellery worn for weddings, festivals and special occasions includes huge coral and gold beads, long, pure gold necklaces, amulets, cuff bracelets, rings and circular silver or gold coronets. Men don feathered turbans, beads, silver embossed daggers, quivers, sword belts and cowrie shells or silk embroidered sashes and jackets for ceremonial occasions.

Being hospitable and fun-loving like all the North-Eastern tribals, the Khasis enjoy entertaining with live music and dancing. It is a pleasure to visit even the smallest of tribal homes with their scrupulously clean rooms and compounds, highly polished wooden floors, white-washed walls and sloping red or green CI sheet roofs. Every room has an open fireplace where Cherrapunji coal fires are lit every winter evening but families still gather in the scrubbed and shining kitchen for most meals.

Born agriculturists, all Khasis love gardening and every home has its vegetable plot, plotted geraniums, begonias fuchsias, ferns, orchids, fruit trees, bamboo grove, pines and ornamental azaleas, camellias and climbing roses. The frequent year round rain and high altitude are also very conducive to horticulture, floriculture beekeeping, paddy and potato farming. This is an affluent society that works hard, lives well, often combining private enterprise with government jobs, teaching, transport or construction work and intensive farming. Poultry and pig keeping are also popular but dairy farming remains a Nepali-Bihari monopoly because the Khasis never were a milk or dairy produce consuming society.

Every Khasi offers visitors tea and *kwai*, the raw betel nut they all chew almost constantly, wrapped in betel leaf touched with lime. This keeps them warm in the coldest weather and stimulates them when engaged in hard labour. Rice and millet beer, Indian whisky and other alcohol is freely consumed in most Khasi homes. Their staple food is rice, usually eaten with boiled vegetables, dal, pork, chicken, fish, beef, salads and spicy Khasi chutney called *tukrimbai* consisting of fermented soyabeans, green chillies, bamboo shoots and onions. They also make a flat rice pancake called *putharo*. This and pounded maize porridge, eggs in any form, Chinese noodles. English roasts, cutlets, puddings and paranthas are popular in all Khasi homes. Good quality bread, cakes, buns, meat, patties and biscuits are made in local bakeries throughout Meghalaya, providing tasty treats and tea time snacks for residents and visitors.

Apart from Christmas which they celebrate wholeheartedly with the entire Meghalaya government machinery coming to a halt, the Khasis honour four festivals connected with spring. crop sowing, fertility and harvest time. The *laho* dance of the Jaintias is purely for community entertainment. Held after the spring sowing it involves only youngsters. Led by the Jainti chief's sister, daughter or niece, each girl pairs up with two boys. The local poet cum wit recites ribald verses as these dancers in festive attire keep step to the single deerskin drum. A jolly atmosphere prevails and new liasions launched.

Shad Sukh Mensium is a fertility rite celebrating the coming of spring after the severe highland winter. Tribals in colourful clothes gather in an open field or ground which can accommodate the whole village. After the ritual sowing dance which is performed by young boys and girls in two concentric circles, the fields are blessed by the clan priest or Lyndoh, and the community feast begins. This is followed by an archery contest at which bets are laid. Like the Bhutiya Lepchas of nearby Sikkim and Bhutan, the Khasis are marvellous archers. There are fruit, tea and food stalls for the general public and a fairytale-like atmosphere prevails.

Dancing forms a vital part of all religious ceremonies and social occasions in all tribal societies. The Nongkrim Dance Festival was originally just a part of the Pom-Blang or ceremonial goat sacrifice performed by the Syiem of Khyrim-Nongkriym to Ka Blei Synsar or Great Earth Mother for clan prosperity and good harvest. Firmly excluded from other Khasi socio-religious functions outsiders are permitted to attend this open air festival. Now thousands flock to Smit for this celebrations and Shillong observes a holiday. The Nongkrim dancers wear handwoven silk Jaynsems with contrasting borders and all the traditional jewellery, adding spikes of fresh or artificial flowers to their coronets. The Shad Khyntlei is danced with great decorum by virgins shuffling their feet. If there's rain during the five day Nongkrim festival, the Khasis believe that one of the dancers has committed sacrilege by pretending to be a virgin. The Shad Mastieh which follows is a warrior dance. Pipes shrill, drum beats quicken and after gyrating for a while, khyrim clansmen in pairs carrying swords and shields engage, each other in mock combat, other clansmen whisk silver handled yak tails keeping time with the *dholiyas*.

Baden–Khlam is held at Jowai at the beginning of the monsoon season after the paddy sowing. Locals believe that it originated at a chiefs' meeting where colourful festivals held by their neighbours were enviously discussed so they took something from every religion around—tazias from the Muslim Muhurram, music and dancing from the Assamese Bihu, feasting and immersing the pagodas in water from the Bengali Durga Puja. Baden-Khlam is essentially a rowdy occasion when people pelt each other with water, slush and grass very much like the Holi celebrations in north India. After the beautifully painted tazia like pagodas are smashed and tossed into water, a great community feast is held. This is followed by a unique football game played on Jowai's main road with wooden ball. Each team tries to kick the ball towards their own locality believing that this enhance their harvest prospects.

## Thirty Seven

# Nagas (Nagaland)

Fifteen Naga tribes and sub-tribes inhabit the seven districts of this State. In addition there are some Naga tribes in Manipur, Assam and across the border in Myanmar.

Each tribe speaks a different dialect of Tibeto-Burmese language (the official language is English and the commonly spoken language is Nāgamese or pidgin Assamese). The names of the tribes such as Angami, Lotha, Ao and Konyak help the Nagas to distinguish themselves from the other hill tribes living in the surrounding regions. Despite the differences in local customs and practises, some features are common to the majority of Nagas. Except for the Angami and Chakhsang tribes, who primarily cultivate rice in terraced fields, all the other Naga tribes practise *jhum* or slash and burn cultivation. Invariably all the Naga villages are built on the highest points of the hill ranges or spurs—a practise being carried on from earlier days which provided them with a good view of any advancing threat from the valleys down below. Each village is a congregation of units known as *khel*—each khel having been traditionally occupied by a single clan.

The Nagas are patrilineal and patriarchal. Marriages as a rule, take place outside the clan, though this norm has been often violated.

The traditional political set up of the different Naga tribes ranged from a form of democracy ruled by a council of elders close to the chieftains. Even today, the Konyak chiefs have a hold over their village as well as the satellite villages. There was a time when villages of the same tribe were at war with each other. Trophies of both human and animal heads were much sought after during times of war as well as during peacetime rituals. It is for this reason that the Nagas were known as head-hunters and were feared by the people of the plains.

Nowadays a glimpse of the traditional lifestyle, albeit with some obvious outside influences, can still be seen in the villages. Nagaland is a good example of the cliche 'continuity in change'. Pristine methods of cultivation, traditional houses and artefacts of bamboo and cane, the well known Naga cloth and the myriad festivals defy the overtly Westernized image which the Nagas are associated with. Villages have more or less retained their traditional features despite the fact that most of the thatched roofs of the village houses have been replaced by corrugated iron sheets. Among the Nagas, the Angami villages stand apart because of their highly stylized houses and clan gates which are hewn out of a single wooden pole. The village paths are lined with memorial stones of various sizes which were installed at the great feasts given by the ancestors.

Westernization and modernization came to Nagaland with the conversion of the populace to Christianity and forthcoming education. Like in other spheres, some of the old institutions such as the youth dormitories have crumbled though youth clubs and age-grade systems in the villages are still present.

Although Naga society has rocketed its way to a modern present, the best of the old has not disappeared with the zest for the new. The loin loom remains steadfast and today weaving is the only cottage industry extant.

Today Naga youths have gone in a big way for ultra-modern garments. Latest trends reach these remote hills long before the cities even awake to them. But the hand-woven cloth is still favoured. Old designs have preserved but many new designs have been inspired by inter-tribe marriages resulting in a fusion of various tribal designs.

Gone are the days when tribes eyed each other with suspicion from their hilltop eyries. There is now a new-found feeling of oneness with the various tribes uniting under the common banner of Nagas. The ring of church bells have replaced the resonance of the village drums and ballads by pop music. Music and dancing in the old Naga style is reserved for special occasions and visiting VIPs. Where earlier each tribe had its own dialect, English and Nagamese is now the language of the people.

However, the best of the old has not disappeared with the zest for the new—a balance has been struck. They are infused with a long-standing sense of pride in the creative talents of their people and this spirit is the greatest incentive to the Nagas to keep alive the beauty and vitality of their craftsmanship—a living tradition for all time.

# Thirty Eight

## Mizos (Mizoram)

Once known as Lushai, Mizoram, according to local lore, has a fairly recent history. It is said that the Mizos, who are of Mongolion origin, passed through China and Burma while migrating to Lushai some 200 years ago. The British arrived in the Lushai hills later—in 1891 and by 1898 Lushai was firmly under their administrative control. After independence of India in 1847, it was only in 1971-1972 that Mizoram acquired a territorial status of its own.

The development of Mizoram dates from roughly this period. With vast tracts of forest and a sparse population scattered over the largely mountainous terrain, Mizoram and its people had remained remote, relatively inaccessible and largely undiscovered. The building of roads after Mizoram was declared a Union Territory in 1972, in addition to providing benefits for the local population, opened up some truly splendid areas for casual visitors and a glimpse into the life of the Mizos.

The people who inhabit this finger shaped protrusion of mountainous terrain known as *Mizoram* (the Hill People's Land: *Mizo* means inhabitant of the hills, and *ram* means land) are predominantly Christian.

The Mizos warmth and zest for life is reflected in their dress, their songs, their soul-stirring music and unusual musical instruments such as the *ting-tong*, and their beautiful crafts. Using traditional looms, Mizo women weave shawls, *puans* (long loin cloths worn by Mizo women) in a whole range of designs and colours. Though every woman in Mizoram learns to weave at an early age, the main handloom centres which have sprung up in recent years to cater to a growing demand outside their territory are situated at Aizwal, Chite Veng, Bethlehem Young, Saiha, Serchhip, Lunglei, Champahai, Luangmual and Bikhawthir.

Curiously, it is unusual to see Mizo girls wearing jewellery. Traditional ornaments which consist mainly of the *dar-thi* (a necklace of glass beads), *thi-thus* (a necklace with large amber beads) and the *thi-fen* (a necklace of small beads) are generally confined to a few older women.

Mizo men are as skillful in crafting cane and bamboo as Mizo women are at weaving. Baskets occupy an important part in the lives of the Mizos: they are used to carry or store virtually everything and anything—rice (the staple food of Mizoram), vegetables, pineapples (which grow in abundance in Mizoram), firewood, clothes, and even water. Mizo men weave exquisite baskets, combining cane, bamboo, leaves and grass. The charming Mizo homesteads, with bamboo floors and walls and thatched roofs, are also the handicraft of Mizo men, as are cane hats and screens.

Cane and bamboo products displaying a high degree of craftsmanship and ingenuity can be seen at the handicrafts centres at Aizwal, Bethlehem Veng and Luangmual.

Both Mizo men and women love a good smoke from pipes crafted locally. While the women smoke from wooden pipe's shaped like a miniature *hukkah* (bubble-pipe), Mizo men use a pipe made from bamboo and weed.

Music is as dear to the Mizos heart as a good smoke. The *ting-tong* (a one-stringed musical instrument) is as popular as the guitar. Sadly, however, the passage of time has taken it toll. The traditional gongs and drums and musical horns, the *benz bung* (a telephone-like wooden instrument) and the rewchhem (a long pipe) are now heard and seen only rarely—chiefly on festive occasions. Similarly, the *vakiria* (beautiful headgear consisting of a bamboo band with a parrot's feather decorated with colourful beetles) worn by Mizo women on festive occasions is less in fashion today.

Fortunately, the Tribal Research Institute at Aizwal has embarked on the task of augmenting its already impressive collection of tribal crafts, especially those that are on the verge of becoming extinct.

Aizwal, with its attractive houses and a profusion of eye-arresting orchids, is a lively place, always humming with activity.

It is a hill-station in the true sense of the word—clean, pure and invigorating with lovely walks and views in and around it. Out of a doorway comes the strumming of a guitar and in Bara Bazaar you can hear the distinctive sound of handlooms emanating from the weaving centre. The Mizoram Museum takes you on a rewarding round of discovery.